PLEASE RETURN THIS ITEM
BY THE DUE DATE TO ANY
TULSA CITY-COUNTY LIBRARY.

FINES ARE 5¢ PER DAY; A
MAXIMUM OF $1.00 PER ITEM.

T4-ABN-464

DUE DATE			
APR 18 1994			
FEB 20 1997			
DEC 18 1997			
OCT 17 1998			
MAR 11 1999			
MAR 27 199			

Printed in USA

Drumright II

Out door Toilet - 133
mike Maars - 198

Drumright II
(And Shamrock, Pemeta, Oilton, and Olive)
A Thousand Memories

By D. Earl Newsom

Evans Publications, Inc.
Box 520
Perkins, Oklahoma 74059

Copyright © 1987 Evans Publications, Inc., Perkins, Oklahoma 74059
All rights reserved. No part of this book may be reproduced in any form
without the permission of Evans Publications.
Printed in the United States of America
Library of Congress Catalog Card Number 86-83299
ISBN: 0-934188-25-4

Young and Old

When all the world is young, lad,
   And all the trees are green;
And every goose a swan, lad,
   And every lass a queen;
Then hey for boot and horse, lad,
   And round the world away;
Young blood must have its course, lad
   And every dog his day.

When all the world is old, lad,
   And all the trees are brown;
And all the sports is stale, lad,
   And all the wheels run down;
Creep home, and take your place there,
   The spent and maimed among:
God grant you find one face there,
   You loved when all was young.

                      Charles Kingsley
                          1819-1875

CONTENTS

Foreword		ix
Acknowledgements		xi

Chapter		Page
1.	In the Beginning	1
2.	Memories—Shamrock	21

    Shamrock—How and Why It Happened
    Erin Go Bragh! (Ireland Forever!)
    Schools and Happy Days

3.	Memories—Pemeta	51

    Pemeta—A Dream That Died
    The Turkey Track Ranch

4.	Memories—Oilton	63

    Oilton—Toughest Town of All
    Main Street Grows in a Hurry
    Scottie Enters the Sin Dens
    Oilton's First Schools
    What It's Like Today

5.	Memories—Olive	103

    Olive—First on the Scene

6.	Memories—Drumright	111

    Very Special Moments
    Historic Homes and Buildings
    Babe Ruth & Sports Memories
    Those Very First School Days
    U. G. 5, Vida Way, and Markham

7.	Memories—The Founding Fathers	195

    Aaron Drumright - by Everett F. and Florence Drumright
    J. W. Fulkerson - by Carrie Fulkerson McLain
    Harley Fulkerson - by Clarence G. Fulkerson
    W. E. Nicodemus - by Edgar Nicodemus
    P. J. Stephenson - by Charles E. Stephenson

8.	Days When Talking Ended and Shooting Started	221

    The Day Sam Cook Went Hunting
    The Day Officer Bice Shot Jeff Curlee
    The Day Willie Glimp Was Kidnapped

9.	Memories—Ben Russell and His Camera	243
10.	Epilogue	265
	Appendix	267
	Sources and Documentation	268
	Index	271

FOREWORD

In a letter written in 1914, Phyllis Andrean described the Drumright oil field as "one big scattered-out town with Drumright as its center." Her description meant that while many communities existed throughout the field, they were all a part of a great unit with Drumright as the hub. The first book, *"Drumright! The Glory Days of a Boom Town,"* emphasized Drumright and gave a detailed history of how the field and the towns came into existence.

This book expands on Drumright history and adds several new dimensions. It tells the stories of other towns and villages of the oil field — Shamrock, Oilton, Olive, and Pemeta — how they lived and eventually declined. It brings back memories of communities such as Frey, Crow, Markham, Villa, and Shafter that were once part of daily conversations in the field but which have for the most part been forgotten. Maps have been drawn to show locations of these places and in even layouts of Shamrock, Pemeta, and Oilton in the boom days. The book is a history of most of western Creek County.

The reader will find considerable sentiment along with historical facts including a few poems. But even the poems tell a great deal about the people and the times. So do the 200 or so pictures, many of them very rare that descendants of pioneers have provided from their private collections. Pictures are different from those in the first book, except for the map of the Drumright oil field shown in Chapter 1. This has been revised to show the important smaller communities.

This volume, like the first, reflects a tremendous amount of community spirit, of people joining together to help record a memorable story on the 75th anniversary of the great oil field.

D. Earl Newsom

ACKNOWLEDGEMENTS

Only those who have been involved in historical research can appreciate the tremendous amount of time, effort, and expense involved in producing a book of this type. In some ways, the stories of the oil field towns and their people are the equivalent of several books. Thanks to the help and encouragement of scores of individuals, the project was completed. Usually three to five individuals were interviewed to verify information. Credit lines under pictures are one means of expressing appreciation. Giving recognition in the text is another. But a number of individuals have provided special help. These deserve mention here.

I am most appreciative of the help of Mrs. A. B. (Sandra) Still of Still Wel-Service, Jayne Russell Agnew, Billie Linduff, and Jackie Cook Drew. They not only provided information for both books, but helped greatly in marketing the first volume. Mrs. Still's familiarity with the oil field communities led to many sources of information. Jayne is administrative aide to the Superintendent of Schools and located many old school records.

The Drumright Historical Society is one of the finest in the state and its Oil Field Museum is evidence of that. My thanks to Robert W. Smith, its president, and its directors for their tremendous support. The Society has made available the museum's resources to help compile the oil field history.

Special thanks are due Charles and Betty Stephenson. They are largely responsible for reorganizing the museum and making it so useable. Charles also contributed some of his own pictures and wrote an interesting profile of his father, P. J. Stephenson, Sr., one of Drumright's earliest leaders and business men. Similar profiles of their fathers were written by Everett F. Drumright, C. G. (Tex) Fulkerson, Mrs. Carrie Fulkerson McLain, and Edgar Nicodemus. Jacqualine (Jody) White, museum hostess, helped located material.

Eileene Russell Coffield has graciously permitted the use of unpublished pictures taken by her father, Ben Russell, Drumright's first photographer, who began recording oil field history in 1912. Eileene is a well-known free lance writer and has done considerable research on the oil field area. She also shared that information to help make complete the Drumright story. Wilma Mills, director of the Drumright Housing Authority, helped arrange the Community Center facilities for the 1985 autograph party and also provided pictures from the family collection for this book.

We appreciate the pictorial material from Evelyn Daly and the sharing of her early-day memories. Experiences of Chester Ferguson and Roy Townsley are related in the text. Tom J. Caldwell, Melvin Cook, Mrs. Louise Kane, Jack and Katharine Schickram, Mrs. Mary Scheer, Wilma Allard, William E. Scribner, Otis Stump, Roland Cook, and Mrs. Mildred Jarvis were among other Drumrighters called upon for information.

Digging up the story of old Pemeta was difficult, but through memories of Homer Wilson, Claude Hicks, Maggie Jones McClary, Ruth Salisbury Ruyle, and Wesley Bingamon, and through research by Roy Keith Shoemaker, the story has been pieced together. Our barber, Abe Nasalroad, once a resident of the Pemeta area, led us to some of these sources. And what a pleasure it was to interview Winifred Stayton, who taught at Pemeta, Silverdale, and Third Ward in the early '20's.

Although former Shamrock residents are scattered far and wide, they are still fiercely proud of their town and schools. They contributed generously and eagerly to help reconstruct the town's past. Ben Ferren, son of Eric Ferren, and Lillian Ferren Beavers, Eric's sister, made their pictures and memorabilia available. Don and Cecil McKnight Corbin, both descendants of Shamrock pioneers, shared their excellent picture collection. Mary Hubert Lesco, whose father worked on the Wheeler well, and David White, who still lives in Shamrock, helped us find old sites and identify sources of information. Phoebe Shaffer Hurst, who came to the oil field in 1913, Alma P. Friend, who taught at Shamrock and later at Drumright, D. C. Sellers III, and Kenneth Sullivan helped us with information and pictures. Darla Glimp Graves, whose family was among the first on the Shamrock scene, provided material not only on Shamrock, but on the shooting of Ben Clark and the kidnapping of her father, Bill Glimp.

The task of putting together Oilton's story was difficult and time-consuming, but it resulted in a thorough account of the town's beginning. Fortunately our research started with Dr. Dan Parker, superintendent of schools. He directed us to very valuable sources. These included the Riley Harris family, Frankie Jo Posey, Mrs. Mary Ramsey, and Ada Jackson. Our friends, James and Pearl Todd, former Oilton residents, sent us to Burnie Mann and Paul Peck, who in turn sent us to Tom Spradlin, Jr. and Lewis Lindsay.

You will find special references to the Harris family. Riley Harris came to Oilton in 1914. His children were among the first to enroll in Oilton's schools in 1915. They were also active in the business district from the beginning. In 1986, four of the Harris family were still living. Their memories of early Oilton were vivid and each wrote memories of those days. Marie Harris Howe, one of them, is the last surviving graduate of Oilton High School's first graduating class in 1919. The information and pictures of the Harris family were very important to this effort. The Harrises also led us to Lora Davis Dentler, another pioneer, who sent her memoirs.

Frankie Jo Posey not only permitted use of her Oilton picture collection, but provided much information about Vida Way School and Markham. She showed us the Vida Way area, and Lewis Lindsay took us on a tour of old Markham and pointed out the location of early business establishments.

Tom Spradlin, Jr., who has practically an Oilton museum in his backyard, provided interesting pictures and information on Crow. Paul Peck and his wife, Fern Doolin Peck, both from pioneer families, shared their early-day memories. The author is especially grateful to June Taylor, granddaughter of Rev. Laurence L. Scott for background information and pictures on the colorful "Scottie."

Several individuals helped greatly in compiling the school history. Ada Jackson, showed us sites of Oilton's old schools. Mary Ramsey, secretary of the Alumni Association, let us borrow old yearbooks and provided other information. Mary Lou Wood, Patsy Schrick, and Judy Browning, aides to the superintendent and principal at Oilton High, found data in old school files. Jim Todd, Burnie Mann, and Virgil Anderson, recalled star athletes. Among others called upon for information about early Oilton were J. D. Tyree, Mrs. Ben (Myrtle) Clark, R. E. Pope, Mrs. Jewel Phillips, and William M. Phillips.

Olive was in direct contrast to the other communities. It existed before many of the others and has always been a stable community. A special thanks is due R. D. (Bucky) Carroll for help on the Olive story. He took us on a tour of the area and led us to several sources, including Susie Lacey, the Whitehead family, and Tom King, school superintendent. King in turn supplied a copy of Olive history done in 1968 by W. R. (Roy) Whitehead. Myra Whitehead, Roy's daughter, permitted use of pictures preserved by this pioneer family.

Mrs. Maxine Barnes Williams is largely responsible for the history of old U. G. 5 School, which was important in the Drumright-Shamrock area. She was a pupil there when the school burned in 1937.

A tedious account herein is the story of Officer Milton Curtis Bice. His daughter, Julia Mae Bice Hoover, lived through these turbulent episodes and has provided information to help record factually and in perspective a part of Drumright history.

Then there are the wonderfully faithful who have helped on each book. Mrs. Thelma Hutchison and Dana Kurena of Helt Photography Studio in Stillwater have become oil field buffs from copying so many old pictures. Rick Bellatti, associate publisher of the *Stillwater Daily News-Press*, is also an expert photographer and keenly interested in preserving the area's history. Except for his help, many of the pictures in this volume would not be there. This is the third cover done for the author by artist Jack Allred. Jack may well be remembered in history more than any of us as his name appears on more covers of southwestern historical books than any other artist. This is manuscript No. 4 typed by Chandra Davis. She was as patient and dedicated as ever. And again Dwight Zimbelman has done an excellent job on maps and drawings. Dwight now has his own drafting firm.

Many days were spent poring over material in the Oklahoma Historical Society. Locating early newspaper files again were Scott Dowell, Mary Moran, and Eleanor Landon. Ellie Hopper and the Drumright *News-Journal* staff were most helpful. Last is a special appreciation for Yvonne and Bob Evans of Evans Publications. Yvonne did much of the layout and production.

Our apologies to those overlooked. The financial rewards are small in an enterprise of this nature, but the author hopes that all who participated share in the satisfaction of having preserved the exciting history of an important era in American and Oklahoma history, and the memories of those do-and-dare hardworking oil field people.

D. Earl Newsom

Chapter I

In the Beginning . . . .

A New World Is Born Around Tiger Creek and the Cimarron

In the Oklahoma oil fields, it is customary to use numbers to describe the location of anything from a persimmon grove to an oil refinery. Thus, oil field people will understand when we say that in 1911, Tiger Creek meandered through the quiet countryside in western Creek County between 32-18-7 and 34-18-7.

While this is awkward, there is no means other than these legal descriptions to pinpoint the location of the small stream that became the center of history in the county between 1911 and 1920. There really wasn't much else around.

Tiger Creek was wider then with a few water holes 50 to 75 feet across. If one could have paddled a canoe or rowboat down the narrow channel, he could as he glided along have thrown stones on the farms of J. W. Fulkerson, Aaron Drumright, Harley Fulkerson, and Frank M. Wheeler. These were some of the men trying to squeeze a living out of the hard clay soil largely by cotton farming.

On the surface, life seemed quiet and uneventful. Farmers sent their children to two small schools, Dry Hill and Tiger. On Sundays, some of them drove in their wagons to a small church called Mount Pleasant, south and east of the Fulkerson farm. Even the section line roads to Cushing and Jennings were scarcely more than dirt trails but passable enough for farmers to get to banks if they ever acquired enough money to need them.

Enter William E. Dunn

In spite of surface appearances, there was tension and air of expectation around Tiger Creek. In 1905, oil had been discovered on the Ida E. Glenn farm 12 miles south of Tulsa. The discovery was the opening of the Glenn Pool, Oklahoma's most exciting oil producing area to that time. The pool extended into eastern Creek County to near Sapulpa and Kiefer.

The important aspect was that the Glenn Pool was a part of the original Creek Nation. So was western Creek County. If oil could be discovered in one part of the nation, why not the other parts? If it could be found at Kiefer, why not at Olive, Tiger Creek, and Cushing? These were the questions asked by many who longed for instant wealth.

Drumright II, A Thousand Memories

Remnants of W. E. (Bill) Dunn's cellar home are still visible near the Cimarron River on the W. C. Bedingfield farm north of Drumright. Dunn lived there during the bitter 1906 winter. It was near Dropright. The boy is Steve Speers, unrelated to Dunn. *Photo courtesy Drumright Oil Field Museum.*

The wise men of the East in the press and oil industry warned them their quests would be futile. Oil would never be discovered west of the Arkansas, they said, and certainly not in Range 7 around Cushing. Some hopefuls heeded this advice, partly because drilling a well could cost as much as $8,000 to $10,000, which made dry holes expensive. Others ignored the eastern prophets, not only because they were willing to take any gamble to be rich, but because they wanted part of the excitement.

Among those who wanted both was William E. Dunn. Towns have different ways of ascertaining their founding fathers, but Drumright might have considered Dunn. Of those who later helped build the new town, he was the first on the scene. He visualized an oil center long before the major oil discovery and leased a large area of land that later became the southwest part of Drumright. His town would have been called Tiger, never Drumright.

Dunn came to Oklahoma as a 17-year old adventurer and soldier of fortune 27 years before it became a state. He explored the Indian Territory as a cowboy and rover until 1889, then made the run into Oklahoma and settled on Council Creek in Payne County. Soon after that, Dunn built a hotel and barn near the old Turkey Track Trail, three and a half miles from Cushing, and traded horses and mules. From there he moved up the Cimarron and acquired 200 acres that later became the site of the oil town of Dropright.

Apparently obsessed with the idea that the future lay to the south and near Tiger Creek, Dunn sold the Dropright land that could have made him wealthy. He bought and fenced land six miles to the south that would later become the west half of Drumright. But here his oil speculations failed and he lost nearly all his holdings. For a time he became a cattle inspector in Cushing for the territorial governor, Tom Ferguson. But by 1908, he was back again in the Tiger Creek area operating a country store and blacksmith shop on an Indian lease. The Drumright *News* said it was Dunn who built the small frame school called Tiger, and who, in 1910, obtained the Tiger post office, which he operated from his store.

Although his business was reasonably successful, Dunn still coveted the land further south and closer to Tiger Creek. When the opportunity arose, he took a three-year lease on the land he had previously owned that would become the western half of Drumright. He moved there and again dreamed of an oil center called Tiger.

By the fall of 1911, Dunn had reasons for optimism. Drilling rigs had been set up throughout the Tiger Creek area, even to the west. A few minor discoveries had been made. Shacks and tents, and even a few small stores had cropped up in the area. On a visit to Bristow, Dunn told the *Record*, "Tiger Creek is up and coming. Watch us grow. Already our population is equal to that of Olive and we comprise less than a third of what was then the Olive township." And Dunn prophesied with remarkable accuracy, "Before the robins come again, we'll be in the middle of a tank farm."

What About Exeter?

While Dunn was promoting Tiger, others also had dreams and were rapidly bringing them to reality. The most important of these came from Bristow, which had become headquarters for many oil speculators. Among them were Charles Wrightsman, Bernard B. Jones, and Thomas B. Slick.

Wrightsman was a lawyer who started in Bristow as a partner with C. J. Benson, a banker. He later moved to Tulsa and branched out into the oil business. He had already acquired modest wealth when exploration started in western Creek County. Jones arrived in Bristow in about 1905 from Kosciusko, Miss., to join his brother, Montfort, in the Bank of Bristow. Jones was an adventurer, promoter, and speculator, and it may have been the hope of oil wealth that brought him to Oklahoma. The third of the trio, Tom Slick, was sent to Creek County to seek leases by Charles B. Shaffer, who had amassed a fortune estimated at $20 million in Pennsylvania oil fields. Shaffer had employed young

Slick in the past to explore in Canada and in several midwestern states. Both men believed Creek County held great promise for oil.

Wrightsman and Jones had done some exploration before Slick's arrival. Most of Wrightsman's drilling had been near 34-18-7 about two miles east of Tiger Creek. His crew settled in tents wherever Wrightsman chose to drill. The lawyer called his settlement "Exeter Camp," named for Exeter Academy in Massachusetts where one of his sons was attending school.

Like Dunn, Wrightsman had concluded a new oil town would soon spring up in the vicinity of Tiger Creek. He wanted it named Exeter. Slick and Jones gave their approval, and Wrightsman sought the support of a delegation of Cushing businessmen. They, too, solemnly agreed, and Wrightsman announced in the Bristow *Record*, the naming of the new oil town. Unfortunately, the *Record* reported, no one could locate Exeter on the map. As Wrightsman moved around, so did the camp. One permanent site was purchased as an Exeter townsite, but when it showed promise of oil it was abandoned. When the great oil field opened the following spring, all of Exeter Camp's settlers packed up their tents and belongings and moved overnight to a new camp called Fulkerson. That was how Drumright escaped being named Exeter.

Jones started exploring shortly after he arrived in Bristow. In 1907 he purchased a farm on the edge of Tiger Creek. Its legal description was 32-18-7. After several fruitless efforts to find oil, he sold the farm in May 1910, to young William F. (Billy) Roberts, who had come down from the Illinois oil fields hoping to do better in Oklahoma. The price was $1,500.

After two months Roberts began to wonder about his decision. Jones had made no major discovery on the farm in three years and the eastern experts were saying there would be no great oil field in the area. Roberts was also short of money. He decided to unload his property.

He was overjoyed in mid-July when someone sent him a prospect named Frank M. Wheeler, a cotton farmer and stone mason from Lincoln County. Wheeler was selling his farm there for $11,000. He wanted something in western Creek County. Wheeler was not a talkative man. He looked over the land and asked Roberts to set a price. "I'd have to have $2,500," Roberts said, and held his breath. Wheeler accepted and the deal was closed on Aug. 10. Roberts wondered how a 53-year old man with nine children could eke out a living on the hilly, rocky cotton farm, but he decided that was Wheeler's problem.

The Excitement Grows

It was the arrival of Tom Slick that stirred excitement around Tiger Creek and in Cushing. It was not so much the young leasing specialist that caused the stir, but the man who sent him. Charles B.

In the Beginning

Shaffer's name was already a legend in the oil industry. A native of Franklin, Pa., Shaffer was sent to live with his grandparents in Clarion when his parents separated. He lived in poverty during his childhood but began oil field work as a youth and became rich in the Pennsylvania fields. Shaffer was 46 when he sent Slick to Oklahoma and had amassed a fortune. He had moved his office from Pittsburg to Chicago. People speculated that if Charles B. Shaffer was exploring in Creek County, it meant something big was about to happen. Tom Slick spent most of his boyhood and youth in Clarion and his father, John, was a drilling contractor. The Shaffer-Slick association undoubtedly began there. After Slick arrived in Oklahoma, the Cushing *Democrat,* which often had trouble spelling names, reported:

> That the Cushing oil field will be speedily developed is now practically assured . . . . Messrs. Schaefer and Sleek . . . . assure the people that they mean business and they evidently do. The prospects are very bright and at least we may see some results.

The newspaper's optimism was premature. As Slick roamed the area seeking leases for Shaffer, a desire grew to acquire some for himself. He, Bernard Jones, and Charles Wrightsman, saw each other frequently in Bristow as well as in the field. The three formed a loosely-organized leasing company. Each could pick up leases on his own and they might do drilling jointly. Slick resigned his job with Shaffer. Shaffer's friends said Slick held back choice leases for himself and let Shaffer have the rest he had gathered, but others said Slick let Shaffer have his choice of leases as they parted company.

The three-man company lasted only a few months. Slick picked the drilling sites and Jones and Wrightsman apparently were supplying the money. Slick hit so many dry holes, mostly around the Olive area, that he acquired the nickname, "Dry Hole" Slick. By late 1911, he was very discouraged and was quietly seeking steady employment. He later told friends he would have taken a job at $150 a month. Jones and Wrightsman were also discouraged at the turn of events. The new firm disbanded, although Slick and Jones continued as partners at several drilling sites, and Jones and Wrightsman were partners at other locations.

The Grand Opening

Slick became convinced that his last hope lay in extreme western Creek County. He was seen often in his buckboard pulled by two ponies crisscrossing the area. His son, Tom, Jr., told how Slick managed to acquire leases from farmers:

> He would move out into the selected area, spending time with the farmers so they could get well enough acquainted with him to have . . . confidence in him . . . . He would call

together the landowners of the community to a meeting where he would tell them of his proposal . . . if they would give him the leases on their land, he guaranteed to have a test well drilled for them on their block of acreage, which, if successful could greatly increase the value of their royalty.

Even though he admitted to the farmers that he had no money for drilling, Slick talked them into giving him leases. After that, he went to people with capital and offered them a half interest in all production from the first well if they would provide him financial backing. This strategy worked well for many months, but after nine dry holes and whispers among oil people about "Dry Hole" Slick, confidence waned among both farmers and capitalists.

As he studied the formations in 32-18-7e, Tom Slick was sure the evidence pointed to a major find. As he explored north and east of there, he believed a vast oil pool lay underneath. The most promising drilling site appeared to be on the farm now owned by Frank M. Wheeler. He was especially heartened by the fact that Bernard B. Jones held drilling rights on the land through a lease signed in December 1910.

Slick's next move was to visit Frank Wheeler, who was living in the neat frame farmhouse with his wife and five of his nine children. Wheeler was keenly interested in Slick's desire to drill on his land. Jones had done little since he had leased the property. Wheeler invited Slick to spend the night, and the next day the two looked over the farm. Although much of the farm was in use for cotton crops, Slick chose as a possible drilling site the bottom of a deep ravine where the brush was so thick it was barely accessible even on foot. It was about a quarter mile from the Wheeler home which was on the edge of Tiger Creek.

When Slick approached Bernard Jones, the latter was ready and willing for a partnership deal for Slick to drill on the Wheeler farm, but after helping finance three of Slick's previous dry holes, he was not ready to invest again. One can imagine his saying, "Thanks, but no thanks." Jones' own resources may have been exhausted, although he had been joined in his oil ventures by Montfort Jones and four other brothers.

Slick jumped into his buckboard and headed for Cushing. There he pleaded with a group of businessmen to invest $8,000 to cover drilling costs. In spite of great returns he pictured for them, they, too, remembered the dry holes and rejected his plea.

It is possible that Slick was reluctant to take the next step, but it was his last hope. He borrowed $100 and went to Charles B. Shaffer in Chicago. He told Shaffer he believed he had found a large oil structure—one so vast he had not been able to ascertain its full dimensions. Shaffer apparently had no ill feelings about young Slick having left his employment. He gave him a check for $8,000. Shaffer was not being entirely magnanimous. He obtained in exchange for his money some oil

In the Beginning

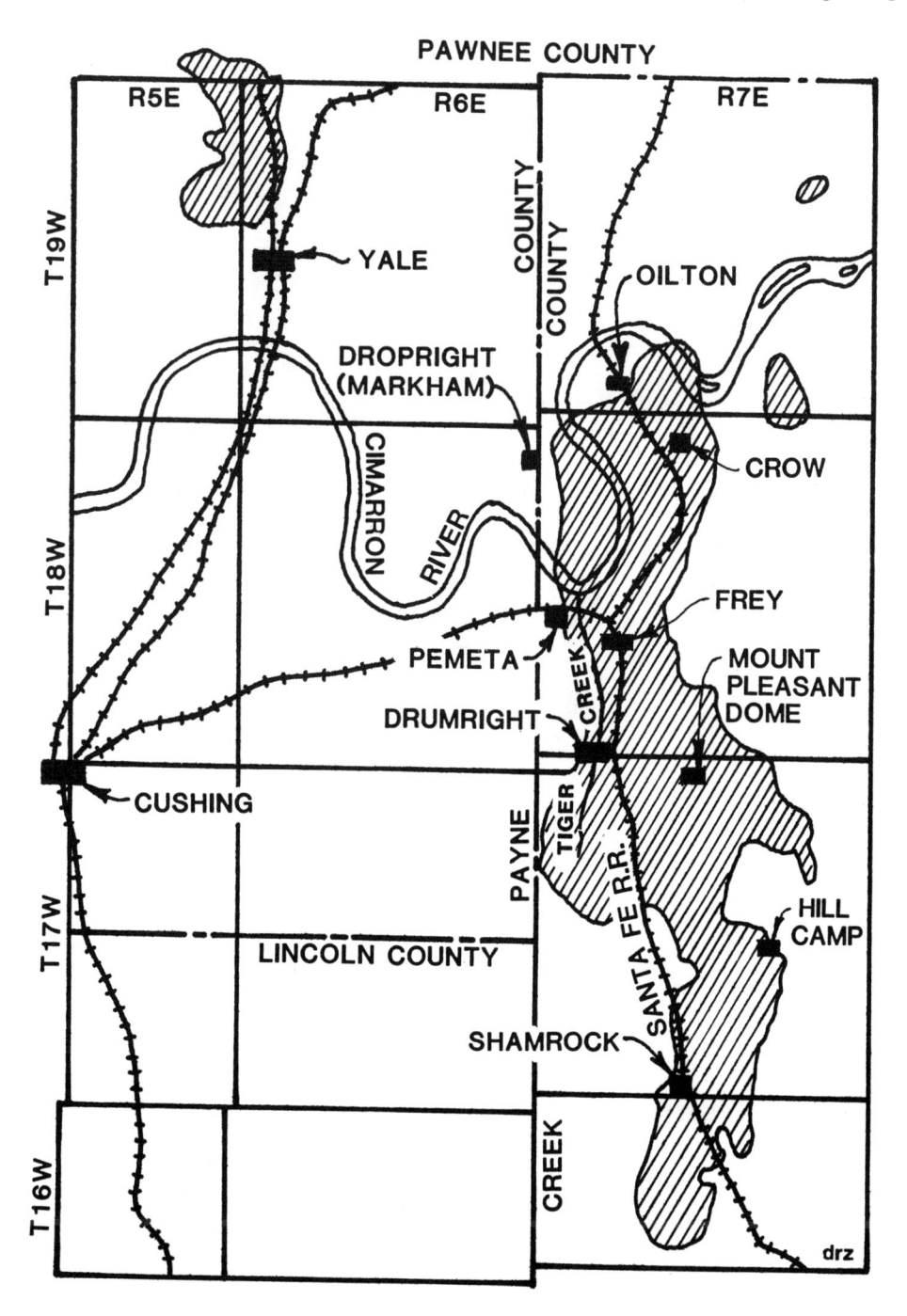

Hill Camp, Frey, Crow, and Mount Pleasant have been added to this map of the great Drumright oil field since the first Drumright book. Maps of Markham, Pemeta, Shamrock, and Oilton are in other chapters. Drawing by Dwight Zimbelman Sources: Luther C. Snider, *Oil and Gas in the Mid-Continent Fields,* Harlow Publishing Co., Oklahoma City, 1920, and interviews.

Drumright II, A Thousand Memories

This 1912 picture may be the earliest ever taken of Broadway in Drumright. The "x" barely visible on the roof to the right marks O'Dell & Stephenson's "Store for Gents," the first retail establishment. The two-story building back from the street is L. E. (Shorty) Gibson's rooming house, possibly the first building on Broadway. *Photo courtesy Charles E. Stephenson.*

In the Beginning

leases in the heart of the pool, and before the excitement was over, he had a lease from Jones for rights on the entire Wheeler farm. And Shaffer knew, as did his leasing expert, L. K. Gano, that in spite of the dry holes, Slick was a competent geologist. It was not a big gamble for a man with $20 million.

What happened after Slick's return is history, told in the first volume, *Drumright! The Glory Days of a Boom Town*. Those interested in a detailed history of the oil field and its production, should read that account. On February 29, 1912, the Slick-Jones well struck oil at 1,400 feet on the Wheeler farm. On March 17, it became a gusher.

While this was happening, another major event was brewing just two miles east in 34-18-7. Within a few days after the Wheeler gusher, Bernard Jones and Charles Wrightsman brought in a 5,000,000 cubic feet per day gas well. This was near where Wrightsman had hoped for a town named Exeter.

Word of the two wells brought an avalanche of humanity to the Tiger Creek area. Oil speculators, drillers, pumpers, roustabouts, tank builders, and retailers came in hopes of sharing the wealth of a new oil field. As a new town arose, the names of Exeter and Tiger were cast aside. J. W. Fulkerson owned the farm that made up the south side of the town and for a time people called Fulkerson Camp their home. In December 1912, a committee of citizens, including Fulkerson, decided to name the town Drumright, for Aaron Drumright, whose 120-acre farm covered most of the north half of the community.

The Glory Days of the Cimarron

For the first year and a half after the Wheeler well discovery, the excitement of the new oil field centered around Tiger Creek between the Wheeler well in 32-18-7 and the Jones-Wrightsman well in 34-18-7. After that, it followed another stream to even greater discoveries and the creation of new oil field towns. Names such as Frey, Pemeta, Dropright, Markham, Crow, Oilton and Shamrock were to become a part of history. About two miles northwest of Drumright, Tiger Creek empties into the Cimarron River. In 1914, the oil field seemed to follow Tiger Creek to the river. From there the Cimarron was like a magical spring. As it flowed northward, oil derricks sprung up like a forest along its banks.

The first wells on the Cimarron were drilled at Pemeta, sometime in early 1914. Pemeta, once called Wilson's Bend, was a small settlement on the edge of Euchee Creek, about two miles northwest of Drumright. Cutting through the farms there on the way to the Cimarron river just north of Euchee Creek, was Tiger Creek. Pemeta had once enjoyed some fame as the headquarters of the Turkey Track Ranch, but in 1914, it

Drumright II, A Thousand Memories

The town was called Fulkerson in late 1912 when this scene was photographed on the south side of Broadway. In the center is Smith & Gooch, the first dry cleaning shop. The drug store sign at the top of the hill may be that of Ed Thomas' City Drug Store. *Photo courtesy Tom J. Caldwell.*

had faded into obscurity. When oil was discovered there in 1914, all that changed. Another boom town was born.

Oil speculators rushed frantically to the river. A short time later a major discovery was made on the farm of John H. Markham, Jr., five miles to the north. A native of Pennsylvania, Markham had engaged in oil exploration there before coming to Oklahoma to participate in the Bartlesville boom of 1903. His farm near the Cimarron encompassed much of the land to the southwest and to the north of present day Oilton. The discovery on his farm caused a virtual stampede to what became known as the north pool. Almost overnight, oil derricks lined the banks of the Cimarron from Pemeta to the site of the new discovery.

The first town in the north pool was called Dropright, a small settlement at the west end of the present Cimarron River bridge on the road that leads to Markham from Highway 99. John Markham became worried the oil derricks and concentration of natural gas might be hazardous to Dropright's residents so he obtained a court order forcing them to move. They transferred immediately to the Frank Marrs farm two miles west and set up a new town called Markham, which had a post office until July 31, 1930.

In the Beginning

An oil field worker in 1915 puffs on a cigar as he looks down from a high Cimarron bluff on a part of Dropright. *Photo by Ben Russell, courtesy Eilene Russell Coffield.*

11

Drumright II, A Thousand Memories

Soon came other communities that have long since disappeared from the vocabularies of oil field residents. Villa was built on a square south and west of Markham on what is now the W. C. Bedingfield farm. In the center was a water pump built on a concrete block which is still visible in the pasture. Villa once boasted a population of 500, but never had a post office. North and west of Markham was Shafter, best known for Tom Scribner's grocery store and trading post. In addition to these were clusters of homes at oil camps and scattered along dirt trails. (See map of Markham area in chapter on early schools.)

The rush along the Cimarron created a rare phenomenon. Caravans a mile long of mules pulling wagons loaded with casing, pipe, and boilers to the wells along the river were a common sight. From the high bluffs of the Cimarron, hundreds of men along the river bank below appeared as busy ants parading back and forth to drilling sites. Winding steps helped men get from the bluffs to the banks below. Swinging bridges, some 600 feet long, carried foot traffic across the river. Within a short time, two companies, McMan and C. B. Shaffer, had ferries carrying heavy equipment from one side to the other.

Long before the discovery on the Markham farm, major companies had gobbled up all the leases on the river banks. A 1914 map shows leaseholders included C. B. Shaffer, B. B. Jones, Thomas B. Slick, McMan Oil Co., Prairie Oil and Gas, Gypsy, Producers Oil Co., and Bermont Oil Co. Smaller operators, desperate for a share of the wealth, claimed a right to drill in the riverbed. Often they were denied access to their rigs and had difficulty getting from one drilling site to another. Soon quarrels and fist fights in the riverbed became common.

As exploration spread northward, business speculators were right behind them. For a time it appeared that a thriving oil town might develop at Markham but as drilling moved another mile and a half up the river, it also spread eastward. A new townsite began to take form and it was attracting attention. It was a mile and a half northeast of Markham and it had been named Oilton.

The story of Oilton, its history, and memories are told in another chapter of this book. By the time its Main Street took form in mid-1915, oil derricks, foot bridges and even a ferry brought the river alive less than a mile from town. And to the southeast, the village of Crow came into existence. In June 1915, the Santa Fe railroad linked Drumright with Frey, Pemeta, and Cushing to the west. As the road forked at Frey, it reached into Crow, Oilton, and Jennings to the north and east. Markham never had a rail stop.

The Drumright oil field was described as a series of domes. The Drumright dome was in the center. To the north was the Dropright dome, which included Oilton, and east of Drumright was the Mount Pleasant

In the Beginning

Oil derricks arise in the middle of the Cimarron River as the field moves northward. Foot bridges provide access to the wells. Barricades on the sides of the river prevent debris from wrecking well housing after heavy rains. *Photo courtesy Drumright Oil Field Museum.*

dome, named for a church. Six miles south of Drumright was the Shamrock dome.

Scarcely had success been achieved at Oilton than speculators moved into the Mount Pleasant and Shamrock domes. A gusher on the Jackson Barnett lease and a big strike on the Fred Tucker farm kicked off activity in Mount Pleasant. A major strike by Hill Oil and Gas Co. of Tulsa started the wild rush into Shamrock. Shamrock once claimed a population of 25,000 within a several mile radius and the town itself was said to have reached 10,000. Its story is also told in a special chapter as it has probably been publicized more than any town in the field.

The great oil field began to fade not long after Shamrock came into existence. So eager were oil speculators for wealth that they wasted billions of cubic feet of natural gas needed to force oil to the surface. They drilled wells within a few feet of one another, each seeking a different sand. The great field reached its peak in 1915 with 73 million barrels. By the end of 1916, production had decreased by more than 30 million barrels. The boom was ending. Additional figures are given in the first Drumright volume.

Drumright II, A Thousand Memories

No bridges existed across the Cimarron in the north pool area in 1914. Major operators such as McMan and Charles B. Shaffer quickly installed ferries to transport oil equipment across the river. *Photo courtesy Frankie Jo Posey.*

The Magic of Black Gold

Drumright is remembered as the field that made at least a hundred millionaires and launched 100 oil companies. Oil was known as black gold and it quickly turned into gold for many who came seeking wealth. Tom Slick stayed about a year and a half and sold his holdings for $2,500,000. Before he left, he performed a last kind deed. After the Wheeler oil strike, Slick boarded and roomed for awhile at the Blue Goose, Drumright's first hotel built near No. 1 well. A young woman who also stayed there owned a piano. She played at all hours and also rendered vocal numbers. Slick was a nervous, easily irritated man, and the music kept him awake nights. Her voice reminded him of a cat wailing on a back fence. Slick solved the problem by purchasing the piano and having it moved to his room, even though he had to pay four times its worth. He put a lock on the piano to make sure no one would use it. When he moved from the Blue Goose, he handed the keys to the young woman and gave her back the piano. When Slick died in 1930, his holdings were estimated at more than $75 million.

In the Beginning

On the edge of the Susie Crow lease southeast of Oilton nestled the village of Crow, which had a rail stop, a one-room school, and several small stores. It was about five miles north of Drumright. Crow was convenient for families who lacked transportation to Oilton or Drumright. *Photo courtesy Drumright Oil Field Museum.*

Charles B. Shaffer started with $20 million and easily netted that much more at Drumright. He organized the Deep Rock Oil Company, became its first president, and sold his holdings to the new corporation. Shaffer bought a choice farm in Kentucky and spent much of his time there raising thoroughbred horses.

Bernard B. Jones and his brother, Montfort, had similar ambitions. They moved to Virginia and also raised horses. When Montfort died in 1927, he left an estate of $4,800,000. Charles Wrightsman sold his interests in the Drumright field at the end of one year for $1 million. John H. Markham, Jr., sold his holdings in the north pool to Carter Oil Co. for a reported $7 million in early 1915. R. M. McFarlin and P. A. Chapman, who operated as the McMan Oil Company, sold out to Magnolia Petroleum Co. in 1917 for $35 million. Harry F. Sinclair and Joshua Cosden were among the many others who profited handsomely from the great field.

Frank M. Wheeler's income from oil on his farm in 32-18-7 started almost immediately. He bought an attractive home in Stillwater so his children could attend Oklahoma A. and M. College, and later a farm in the Rio Grande Valley. After he became wealthy, he loved to sit in the lobby of the Cushing Hotel and visit with oil field friends.

Drumright II, A Thousand Memories

Behind this early version of a portable rod-pulling machine is a rare view of the impressive Mid-Continent Refinery and later gasoline plant on the edge of Crow. *Photo courtesy Tom Spradlin, Jr.*

    Not everyone did well. Billy Roberts, who sold his farm to Wheeler, wound up first as a barber and then part owner of the New Smoke House, a pool hall, with Bob Achterman. The two men were among the promoters of the Roberts Hotel in 1916, but Roberts died while the hotel was being built. It was named for him. William E. Dunn never became wealthy. He built rental property in Tiger Town, which he called his property on the southwest corner of Drumright, but he lost his bid to have the town named Tiger. J. W. Fulkerson became moderately wealthy, but his descendants say he was bilked out of much of his money when he returned to Kentucky for three years and left his holdings in care of a local investor.

The Forgotten Men and Women

    Names and pictures of those who made millions in the Drumright field appear in many books and newspapers, but those who did the back-breaking work in the field largely remained in anonymity and poor. Most of the workers were on tour (pronounced tower), which meant a 12-hour shift. Some went to work at noon and worked until midnight. Others started at 3 p. m. or 4 p. m.

In the Beginning

The terrain and picture may both be on a slant as Frank Marrs with his wife, Flossie, drives his Model-T along the bank of the Cimarron in 1914 near Markham. Ferry is at left. Markham's business district was built on Marrs' farm. *Photo courtesy Mrs. M. L. (Clara) Marrs.*

As the field opened, men slept on creek banks around the Wheeler camp. Soon rooming and boarding houses opened and those who could afford it rented rooms. Others slept on the boarding house tables. Many of the workers were accustomed to spartan living as they moved from one field to another to keep employed.

A worker was fortunate if his pay covered expenses. At the bottom of the pay scale were roustabouts, utility men performing a variety of duties around the drilling sites. A payroll sheet of 1917 shows Prairie Oil and Gas paying roustabouts $85.50 a month. Just above that were pumpers at $100 a month. It was their job to keep oil production from the wells at a steady pace and to keep the wells operating properly.

On a higher level were the rig builders, drillers, and tool dressers, whose pay ranged from $12 to $14 for a 12-hour tour. For the most part, the workers seemed grateful to have employment, although they never had fringe benefits, vacations, and rarely even Sundays off, and they never shared in the wealth as did Tom Slick and the Joneses.

Oil field life may have been harder for women than for men. Homes were usually tents or shotgun houses with outside privies. Many shacks had no running water. Sometimes a man, his wife, and small

Drumright II, A Thousand Memories

Frank M. Wheeler was struggling to eke out a living from his 160-acre cotton farm when oil was discovered on his place in 1912. Here, in back seat on left, he is enjoying a cigar and being chauffered around as his income neared $10,000 per month. *Photo courtesy Drumright Oil Field Museum.*

children lived in one or two rooms of a rooming house. Women washed clothes in a tub and scrubbed them on a washboard. Flatirons heated on an open fire were used for ironing. Women who lived on leases thought nothing of walking one to three miles over rough terrain to town. More often than not they carried a small child. The mortality rate was high among children during the cold winters.

A Wealth of Memories

Few oil workers ever acquired enough money to leave an estate, but they left something precious to their descendants—a treasure of memories. Their children, grandchildren, and even great-grandchildren can tell the stories and legends of pioneer days. These are passed from generation to generation along with pictures and other artifacts.

Even school children know about the Blarney Stone in Shamrock, and the time when Tipperary Avenue was painted green, or about the days when students struggled up long Depot Hill.

In Oilton, nearly everybody still knows about Scottie and how he built the Baptist Church, of the big gambling den called the Oil Exchange, and how kids had fun riding the train for a nickel to the village of Crow, or to Player across the river north. And only a new youngster on the block in Drumright would not have heard of The Hump, of

In the Beginning

Broadway, when horses fell dead trying to pull heavy oil equipment up the muddy hill, and the legends of Tiger Creek.

And of course, there are still a surprising number of old timers left in the oil field who lived through the oil boom days. Some would like to turn back the clock. "I was so happy," said Mrs. Bess Alexander Harrington, now in her 90's, whose husband was a driller on the Wheeler No. 1 well. "I enjoyed the hills, the hollows, and the people of Drumright. Just a half block away from our house was the Blue Goose Hotel, painted a bright blue, where everybody gathered to eat. I'd love to live those days again, and I love the memories of that day."

Olive Clark Whitehead came to the Oilton area long before the town started, and she has a different view. "The memories are fun, but for heaven's sake, don't take me back there. I wouldn't relive those times again for anything."

In 1914, Albert E. Peck took his store apart at Avant and moved even the walls to Oilton, where he established the first funeral home. His son, Paul, operates that business today. Paul, too, prefers the memories to a real return to the past. "Everything seems better to you when you are a youth. As a kid, I thought I was happy during the wild days. I wouldn't particularly want to go back, but the memories are wonderful."

And that's what this book is about — not only the history but the memories of the world's greatest oil field to that time, the ordinary people who were there, and of the towns that were so primitive, yet so full of life. Of Frey, Pemeta, Crow, and Markham that no longer exist, and of Drumright, Oilton, and Shamrock, where there are still reminders of a great era. There are at least a million such memories, but this book will cover no more than a thousand of them, starting with colorful Shamrock, then winding back through Pemeta, once tough Oilton, Olive, and to Drumright, the heart of the great field where many remnants of the wild days still exist.

Memories — Shamrock

How and Why It Happened,
Erin Go Bragh! (Ireland Forever),
Schools and Happy Days

This once bustling Shamrock intersection is quiet now but the green and white markers still remind people of the great days when nearly everything was painted green.

Shamrock
By Roy Smith

Shamrock was crowded with Irish men
Some, I guess, with fame.
Anyway, the rumor is
That's how it go its name.
Streets named Tipperary, Cork and Bantry
These are just a few
But you can see that they are Irish
Just as Irish Stew.
The oil patch brought on a boom
And you couldn't find a room
Some slept in tents, shacks and cars
While others slept beneath the stars.
Oil wells were being drilled every day
All the men got good pay.

When they stopped work
They had to play.
So they came to town every night
And usually wound up in a fight.
For there were dance halls, gambling, Blind Tiger bars
Now some old timers still have scars
From those houses of ill repute
But some of those dancing girls were real cute.
Now, of the old timers there are few
And all they want to do
Is talk of the good old days.
That when you came to town at dark
You couldn't find a place to park
And such a crowd upon the walk
You couldn't even stop to talk.

As you read this
You will think it's untrue
And the one who wrote it was full of brew.
I admit I took a nip of brew
If you'd been there, you would have, too.
When the old town finally settled down
With churches and schools it did abound
Also sewing circles and other clubs, you bet
An Irish mayor, named Ferren, we'll never forget.
For he's the one who got the old town out of debt
In its early days it was a merry-go-round
But now you'll find it a mighty quiet town.

This poem by Roy Smith remained on the wall of a Shamrock cafe for several years. Many thought it summarized the Shamrock story. Smith came to the oil field as a Magnolia Petroleum Company employee during the boom days and spent most of his life in Shamrock. He wrote the poem in 1968 while a member of the Shamrock city council.

Chapter II

Shamrock —
Why and How It Happened

The Roaring Gas Wells
Silenced the Medicine Shows

Of all the towns that emerged during the 1912-1917 Drumright oil boom, Shamrock is probably remembered most. Long after the boom subsided and the town faded, newspapers and magazines sent reporters and photographers to recall the story of the town that took such pride in being Irish. The Blarney Stone, Irish street names, a Main Street once painted all green, and colorful St. Patrick's Day celebrations still hold a fascination for media and tourists.

This once teeming community that boasted a population of 10,000 and another 15,000 in the surrounding area from 1916-1920 is quiet now, but among its 200 or so inhabitants in 1985 were still a few pioneers who were a part of Shamrock's exciting glory days. Family names such as Cargill, Stevens, Ferren, Pittser, Glimp, Gemmel, Bearden, Shaw and Rodebush were still around at this writing to tell of the exciting bygone days. Scores of former Shamrock residents return each year to the high school reunion and as late as 1986, many former residents and visitors came from afar for the annual St. Patrick's Day Parade.

Drumright has good reason to feel kinship to Shamrock. As the oil boom declined, many businessmen moved from Shamrock to Drumright. The Sellers brothers, D. C. (Coin), and R. A. (Dick), once operated the Citizens Bank in Shamrock. When the Drumright State Bank folded in 1932, the Sellers moved to Drumright and operated the Citzens Bank for many years.

Claude P. Hall's hardware was one of the first businesses in Shamrock as the oil boom began there in 1915. He moved to Drumright in the mid-1930's and became the partner of Everett C. Smith in a hardware store and funeral parlor. Fay Facker moved his Central Chevrolet Co. to Drumright when dealer Fred Way died. Denny and Pat Cawley, who operated a men's clothing store for years in Drumright, also had a store on Shamrock's Main Street in 1916. L. R. (Louie) Geiser and his brother, Chris, brought the Geiser general merchandise store to Drumright after operating for years in Shamrock. Jim Winterringer operated a variety store and later a dry goods store in Shamrock. He moved his store to Drumright as Shamrock began to fade.

Drumright II, A Thousand Memories

Tipperary Road, Shamrock's Main Street, was rather barren in late 1915 before oil exploration shifted to that area, but wagons were coming in from other parts of the field to get material from the F.D. Misener Lumber Co., probably the town's first retail business. *Photo courtesy Mrs. Lillian Beavers.*

When Shamrock High closed in 1961, many students and some teachers became a part of Drumright High School. Although the two towns were only six miles apart, a friendly spirit always existed between the communities, perhaps because so many worked closely together throughout the oil field.

The Beginning of Shamrock

The community had its beginning in about 1909, about a mile west of present Shamrock, across the road from where the cemetery is located. J. B. Ownesby set up a small grocery store on the south edge of his farm to serve farmers scattered throughout the area. A post office was established in the store on July 9, 1910, with J. M. Thomas as postmaster. But the town had its real beginning in 1915 as oil exploration in the Drumright field switched from the Markham and Oilton areas southward to the Shamrock dome.

The speculators who led the Shamrock exploration would make a Who's Who in the petroleum industry. Among these were Charles B. Shaffer, Thomas B. Slick, Bernard and Montfort Jones, Gypsy Oil Co., Prairie Oil and Gas, Cosden, McMan, and Carter. But more important to Shamrock was the Hill Oil and Gas Co. of Tulsa. Hill made the first major strike in the area in late 1915, about three miles northeast of the

Shamrock—How and Why It Happened

Early in 1916, Tipperary Road had concrete sidewalks but it was never paved. Cars seem to outnumber wagons on the Main Street. *Photo courtesy Mrs. Lillian Beavers.*

townsite. Eventually the company leased more than 5,000 acres. The Hill Camp became a community in itself with a nearby store and a one-room frame schoolhouse, also named Hill Camp. The Sapulpa and Oil Field Railroad built a spur into the camp.

"Why Is Shamrock?"

From the beginning, almost everything in Shamrock had an Irish name, including its newspaper, the Shamrock *Blarney*. On March 23, 1916, the *Blarney*, in a front page article, told "Why Is Shamrock".

> Shamrock was necessary. Right here in the center of the biggest oil field in the state are at the present time, with a radius of three miles . . . . from six to eight thousand men employed with a daily payroll of more than fifty thousand dollars.
> This area now has about three hundred producing wells, and this is only the beginning. In all probability there will be five thousand wells put down in this field next year.
> This field with Shamrock as the center of a circle six miles in diameter, is now producing about 35,000 barrels of oil daily and more than 100,000,000 cubic feet of gas with millions of feet shut in. There is one well, the Nora Williams, that

Drumright II, A Thousand Memories

Judge Ben F. Berkey
The "sage of Shamrock" was known as Colonel Berkey when he arrived in late 1915. He was the first editor of the Shamrock *Brogue*, and after that dealt in oil leases and real estate. For a time he was a justice of the peace and known as a counsel and story-teller. His small dog went with him everywhere. *Photo courtesy Mrs. Eric E. Ferren.*

produces 100,000,000 cubic feet daily. This well is almost uncontrollable but is now shut in.

There are four big oil supply houses here, and four big lumber yards, and the field is using all supplies as fast as these big concerns can get them on the ground.

Shamrock is the commercial center of this vast business, and this is, Why is Shamrock.

At first oil production was from the Layton sand about 1,400 to 1,500 feet deep, but soon drillers began to reach the Bartlesville sand about 2,800 feet below the surface. This was a highly productive sand and derricks sprouted up all over the area almost as by magic. Sometimes wells were drilled within a few feet of one another, each reaching for a different sand.

The most astonishing production, however, was from gas wells. Within a few months the total daily output reached a half billion cubic

Shamrock—How and Why It Happened

feet daily. Medicine shows, with comics hawking all kinds of cure-alls, were a favorite entertainment in the oil field, but at Shamrock, the performers complained they could not be heard because of the loud roar of the gas wells. McMan Oil Co. brought in a gas well from the Bartlesville sand on the Nora Williams lease two miles south of Shamrock that blew the drilling tools out of the hole and splintered the oak walking beam 12 by 18 inches in size. The *Blarney* reported other gas discoveries:

> McMan Oil brought in a 30,000,000 cubic foot gasser on top of the Bartlesville sand . . . and a 25,000,000 gasser on top of the same sand on the Mickey farm . . . . The total daily production of the Williams well is fully 46,000,000 from the various sands, while that from the Mickey well is 60,000,000 cubic feet . . . .The second well on the Mickey farm is also a 20,000,000 gasser in the Lawton sand, while C. B. Shaffer has a 30,000,000 gasser in his first well on the Chastain farm . . . . The Hill Oil & Gas Co., which has 5,400 acres under lease just east of Shamrock, has 100,000,000 cubic feet of gas shut in on its properties and is also furnishing 100,000,000 cubic feet daily to the Oklahoma Natural Gas Co. which has one of its main pumping or compressing stations at Shamrock.

The *Blarney* estimated that the Hill Oil & Gas Company would, within the next twelve months, have a daily output of 500 million feet daily.

Erin Go Bragh!*

The Town Is Painted Green
And Everybody is Irish

On January 1, 1916, the *Brogue* said Shamrock was named by a farmer eight years previously who set up a post office in his small store west of the new townsite. This was probably J. B. Ownesby. Old timers of the boom era say people considered three names: Shannon, the name of the township, Art Moore, an early-day citizen, and Shamrock. Many were of Irish descent so without much debate, they chose Shamrock. Homer Breeding was the first mayor.

Irish names also prevailed in the platting of the town. The section line on the west edge, running north and south, was named Ireland. It is now State Highway 16. In the beginning, only the area east of Ireland was officially a part of Shamrock. Intersecting Ireland and extending mostly eastward, was the Main Street where most businesses clustered. It was named Tipperary Road. Other streets running north and south had Irish names such as Cork, Bantry, Killarney and Dublin. Streets running east and west were given numbers, such as First, Second, etc.

Shamrock never ceased to be proud of its Irish heritage. It held a wild St. Patrick's Day parade and celebration on March 17, 1916, with most of Tipperary painted green. These celebrations continued annually for many years.

The *Brogue* said Shamrock was the only town in the United States with green postage stamps. This started as a joke, but soon people came from miles around to buy the green stamps. The postmaster, Virgil Morgan, had a stock of regular reddish colored stamps, but no one would buy them. And, said the *Brogue*:

> In truth, green is everywhere . . . . The post office is housed in a green building, the stores of the merchants are of that color, the lumber yard offices are emerald, the big station of the electric railway company has a tint that rivals the shamrock itself, and residences scattered throughout the forest that covers the town have a color like unto the leaves of springtime.

*Ireland Forever

Erin Go Bragh! (Ireland Forever!)

A half-mile long parade follows the first Blarney Stone into Shamrock in early 1916. The stone was placed in a tent at the intersection of Tipperary and Dublin. For 25 cents one could come in and kiss the Blarney Stone. Those who declined the opportunity were asked to tip their hats as they walked by. *Photo courtesy Don and Cecil McKnight Corbin.*

Many business houses also had Irish names. Some were the two newspapers, the *Brogue* and the *Blarney*, the Irish Stew, the Erin and Shamrock hotels, and the Killarney theatre. The city park was named the Emerald Isle. The small bridge across a brook on Tipperary, was called O'Connor, and the east residential district was called Parnell heights. The *Brogue* made it clear that people of Irish descent were everywhere:

> John Murphy has located a bank at Dublin and Tipperary, Lantry has the contract to build the railroad into town. Ryan is the leading painting contractor, Casey is in the lumber business, Sullivan oversees the gas meters, Ed Dunn looks after the welfare of the town, McFarlin is drilling for oil, McBride is a merchant, Mrs. Casey has a rooming house, Mulligan is a sign painter, Quimby a carpenter contractor, Mrs. Finney has a hotel, Patrick is a banker, O'Neill is a drilling contractor, Flannigan is a driller, McCall the town clerk, Riley a plumber, and Jerry Hastings is in charge of the big gas compressing station.

The new railroad joined in the Irish theme. The first line into Shamrock was the Sapulpa & Oil Field Railroad which came from Sapulpa and connected with the Frisco line at Depew. J. A. Frates, C. F. Hopkins,

Drumright II, A Thousand Memories

Hill Camp, the first oil camp in the Shamrock dome, is in the background behind two of its residents, Minnie Ezell and Goldie Gleason Corbin. It was about three miles northeast of Shamrock. Hill Camp had two stores, a power plant, and a barber shop. Homes and tents clustered along a gas main to get free heating fuel. *Photo courtesy Don and Cecil McKnight Corbin.*

Barely visible on the right is the frame of the Shamrock depot being constructed in 1915. This may be the earliest picture of the steep incline that became known as Depot Hill. Children trudged a half mile up the hill to school. *Photo courtesy Don and Cecil McKnight Corbin.*

and Frank Brown financed the road, which was later taken over by Frisco. Frates, the father-in-law of Thomas B. Slick, was also president of the Frisco line. The line to Shamrock was named "the Tipperary Route," and the trains were known as the Irish Mail, the Dublin Express, and the Killarney Special. The depot was painted green. At first the heavy volume of business required five passenger trains daily, but by 1920 only two passenger trains and one freight train were operating. The first passenger train came to Shamrock on January 13, 1916. J. J. Goggins was agent for Shamrock.

Dying was Awkward

While most conveniences quickly became available to people of Shamrock, one service was lacking. The town had no cemetery and in the beginning, no mortuary. The problem, said the *Brogue*, was partially solved by the Model-T Ford:

> Perhaps nowhere else in the southwest, if in the nation, has the automobile been used to such a great extent as a carrier of coffins and corpses in the oil field. It is necessary, frequently, to have a coffin and box hauled from one of the towns to an oil lease or camp somewhere in the field, and always is this service performed by a Ford car. It is nothing unusual to see a car with a coffin box occupying the back seat and after the corpse is placed in the box, it is again put across the back seat and taken in the car to the railroad for shipment or to one of the few burying grounds in the oil field district.

In July, 1916, the *Blarney* said the population within the 160-acre townsite was 1,800 with about 10,000 people within a three-mile radius. And the *Blarney* added:

> There are within the town 107 business houses, 76 hotels and restaurants, and 17 supply houses that handle oil field supplies. This makes in all 200 business places of all kinds.

Scores of businesses have come and gone since those early days, and a map of Tipperary Street in this chapter shows names and locations of some who made lasting impressions. Among those remembered most are John Haught's Millinery Store at Tipperary and Ireland, Eric Ferren, and the Sellers Brothers. Haught's store is closed now, but it is still highly visible to anyone approaching Shamrock. It is painted a bright green. Along with the green Blarney Stone in an open field just north of Shamrock, remind passers-by of Shamrock's Irish heritage.

The Sellers Brothers

Two Shamrock pioneers whose influence is still felt in Creek County 70 years later were the Sellers Brothers, D. C. (Coin) and R. A. (Dick). From the time they arrived in early 1916 until the World War

Drumright II, A Thousand Memories

The Sellers Brothers
R. A. (Dick) Sellers, left, and D. C. (Coin) Sellers played a prominent role in early Shamrock. They operated the Citizens Bank, which they moved to Drumright in 1932, an elaborate clothing store, and a horse and mule farm on the edge of Pemeta. *Photo courtesy Janice Sellers Crouch.*

II era, they were active in business, banking, farming, oil, and even politics. They acquired several thousand acres of land, mostly in the Shamrock-Drumright area. Coin left more than 5,000 acres in his estate when he died in 1955, and it was said he owned land he had never set foot on.

The two were sons of Hugh A. Sellers, who owned a farm near Grove. Here the brothers learned a great deal about farming and cattle and their first business was dealing in cattle in the Grove vicinity. They spent a great deal of time on horseback tending the cattle. Shamrock and Drumright citizens in later days remember Coin in his broad-brimmed hat and cowboy boots riding his horse in the Drumright area. Dick was impeccably dressed and was rarely seen on horseback, but he, also, was an expert horseman.

The Sellers brothers were known best for their operation of the Citizens Bank, first at Shamrock and later at Drumright, but they were not the bank's original owners. Two banks staged a race to see which could open first in Shamrock. Both were moved from other towns. J. B. Charles transferred his Citizens Bank from Avery in Lincoln County. The American National Bank of Sapulpa owned the First State Bank and moved it from Markham.

Erin Go Bragh! (Ireland Forever!)

Gypsy Oil and then Gulf owned this gasoline plant three miles southeast of Shamrock. Harry McKnight, a Shamrock pioneer who helped bring the second Blarney Stone to Shamrock, walked to Liberty Ward school from here. *Photo courtesy Don and Cecil McKnight Corbin.*

The most visible and best known oil camp near Shamrock was probably Sinclair Gasoline plant No. 3 on the northeast edge of town. Residents of the homes in background were the E. M. Caspers, the Russell Vannattas, the Charles Adcocks, and the Bill Dolans. The latter was superintendent. *Photo courtesy Don and Cecil McKnight Corbin.*

Drumright II, A Thousand Memories

A construction crew worked all night, partially by moonlight and partially by lantern to make sure this bank was the first to open in Shamrock. On the left is the town's first water tower. *Photo courtesy Kenneth Anderson.*

Erin Go Bragh! (Ireland Forever!)

The depot, completed in January 1916, was painted green and all the trains had Irish names such as "Dublin Express" and "Irish Mail." *Photo courtesy Drumright Oil Field Museum.*

    A. J. (Andy) Reid, a Drumright contractor, ran a construction crew all night to get the Citizens Bank tent ready for opening. The men worked by moonlight until after midnight and then lighted lanterns as they placed rock cornerstones, laid the foundation and floor, and put up stringers to hold the tent roof. During the night, another crew hauled a big safe from Avery to Shamrock. The *Brogue* called the race a draw as both banks were open for business by the morning of January 1, 1916. John Murphy was president of the Citizens Bank and John E. Moore came from Markham to be president of First State.

    The Sellers took over the Citizens Bank soon after that, probably in March. They began construction on a new brick building immediately. They operated the bank in Shamrock until August 13, 1932, when they moved it overnight to Drumright to replace the Drumright State Bank, which had been forced to close. The brothers owned a large horse farm near Pemeta and a horse and mule barn in Drumright on South Ohio Street, south of the *Derrick* office. Their horse and mule business was for a time one of the largest in Oklahoma. In Shamrock, they also operated a clothing store on Tipperary Road.

Eric Ferren—'Mr. Shamrock'

    The name that personified Shamrock for nearly forty years was that of Eric Edward Ferren. Even years after his death, when people speak

Drumright II, A Thousand Memories

This big engine was named "the Casey Jones Express." It brought the first trains into Shamrock from Sapulpa and Depew. The railroad wanted it to have an Irish name. *Photo courtesy Don and Cecil McKnight Corbin.*

This post office on the corner of Tipperary and Bantry is the one remembered by many early residents. *Photo courtesy Ben Ferren.*

Erin Go Bragh! (Ireland Forever!)

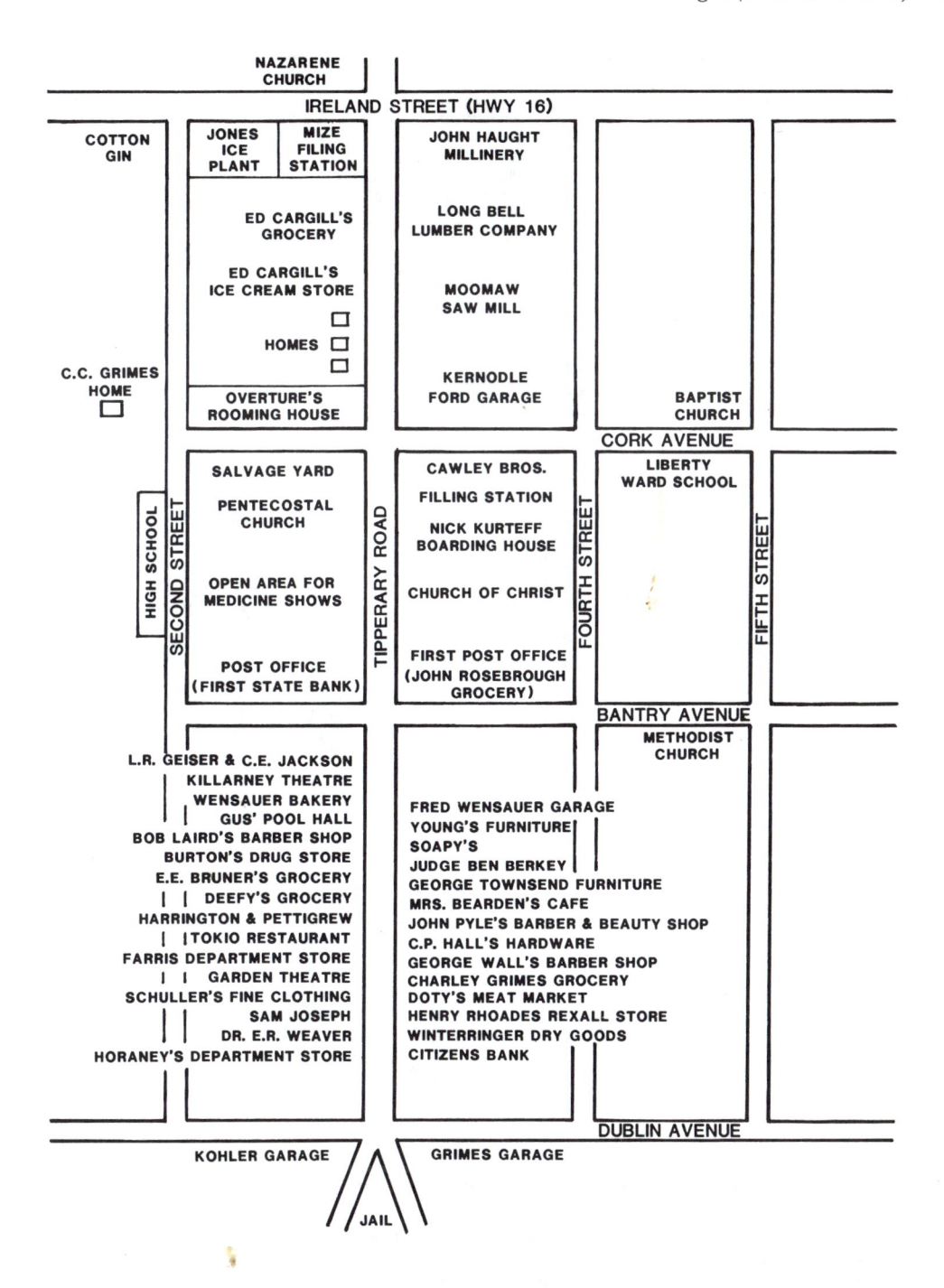

```
                    NAZARENE
                    CHURCH
              IRELAND STREET (HWY 16)
  COTTON    JONES   MIZE    JOHN HAUGHT
   GIN       ICE   FILING    MILLINERY
           PLANT  STATION
           ED CARGILL'S     LONG BELL
             GROCERY      LUMBER COMPANY
           ED CARGILL'S
          ICE CREAM STORE    MOOMAW
                            SAW MILL
               HOMES
 C.C. GRIMES
    HOME      OVERTURE'S     KERNODLE
            ROOMING HOUSE   FORD GARAGE     BAPTIST
                                            CHURCH
                                          CORK AVENUE
           SALVAGE YARD    CAWLEY BROS.    LIBERTY
                          FILING STATION  WARD SCHOOL
           PENTECOSTAL
             CHURCH        NICK KURTEFF
                          BOARDING HOUSE
          OPEN AREA FOR
         MEDICINE SHOWS   CHURCH OF CHRIST

           POST OFFICE     FIRST POST OFFICE
         (FIRST STATE BANK) (JOHN ROSEBROUGH
                              GROCERY)
                                          BANTRY AVENUE
                                          METHODIST
                                           CHURCH
   L.R. GEISER & C.E. JACKSON
        KILLARNEY THEATRE
         WENSAUER BAKERY   FRED WENSAUER GARAGE
           GUS' POOL HALL  YOUNG'S FURNITURE
   BOB LAIRD'S BARBER SHOP  SOAPY'S
     BURTON'S DRUG STORE   JUDGE BEN BERKEY
    E.E. BRUNER'S GROCERY  GEORGE TOWNSEND FURNITURE
          DEEFY'S GROCERY  MRS. BEARDEN'S CAFE
   HARRINGTON & PETTIGREW  JOHN PYLE'S BARBER & BEAUTY SHOP
         TOKIO RESTAURANT  C.P. HALL'S HARDWARE
    FARRIS DEPARTMENT STORE GEORGE WALL'S BARBER SHOP
           GARDEN THEATRE  CHARLEY GRIMES GROCERY
   SCHULLER'S FINE CLOTHING DOTY'S MEAT MARKET
               SAM JOSEPH  HENRY RHOADES REXALL STORE
            DR. E.R. WEAVER WINTERRINGER DRY GOODS
  HORANEY'S DEPARTMENT STORE CITIZENS BANK
                                          DUBLIN AVENUE
         KOHLER GARAGE   GRIMES GARAGE
                         JAIL
```

Tipperary Road, Shamrock's Main Street, was about a mile long. This shows the section from Ireland Ave. (Hwy. 16) to Dublin Street, where most businesses were located. Early day stores and their approximate locations are shown on the map. The other section of Tipperary is on another page. *Drawing by Dwight Zimbelman.*

Drumright II, A Thousand Memories

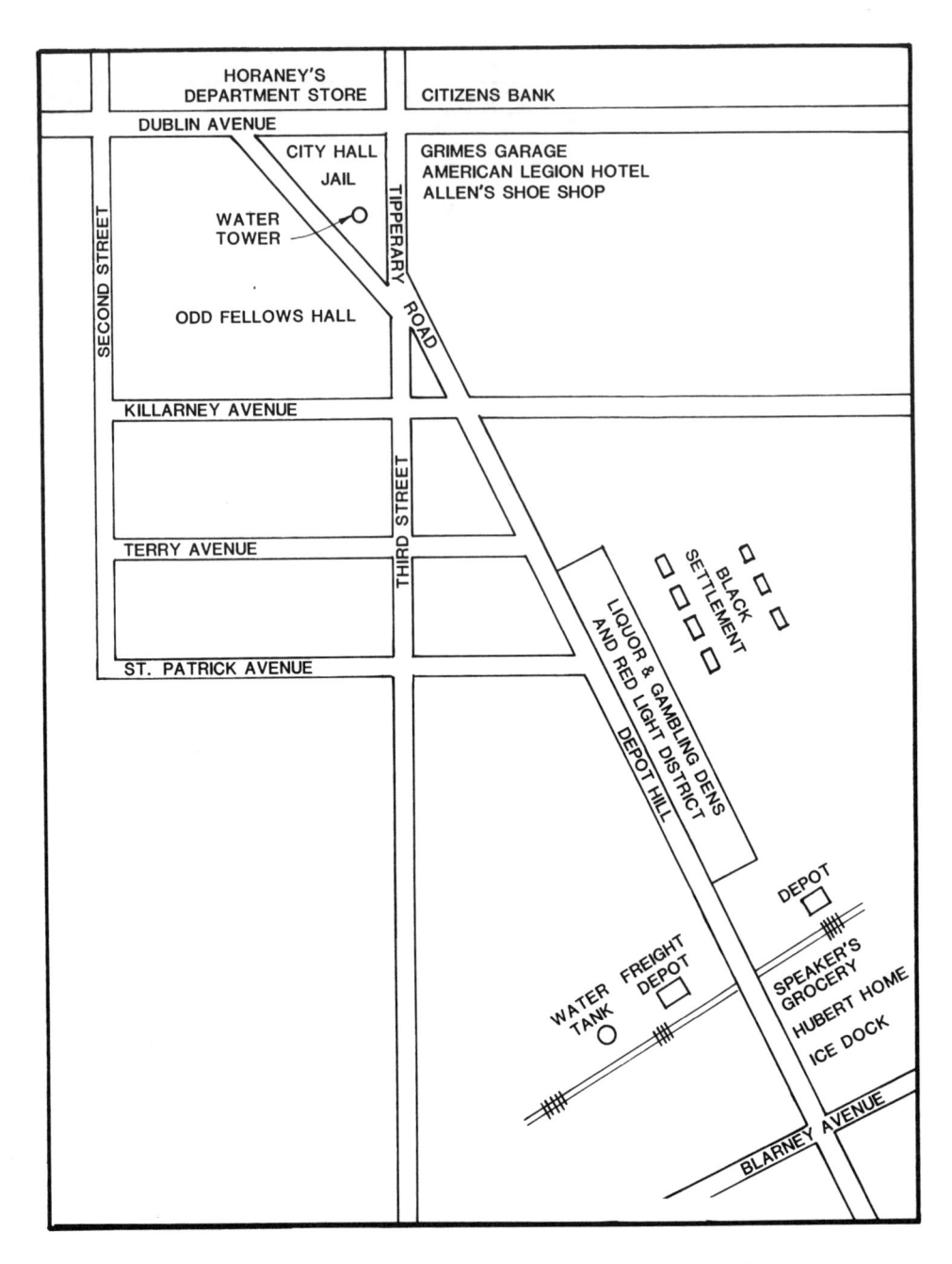

The city hall, jail, and gambling and liquor dens were on this section of Tipperary Road. At the bottom of the long hill was the Santa Fe Depot, established in 1916. The depot and stores were painted green for Irish accent. *Drawing by Dwight Zimbelman.*

Erin Go Bragh! (Ireland Forever!)

Eric E. Ferren, "Mr. Shamrock," stands beside the second Blarney Stone brought to Shamrock. He and Harry McKnight painted it green. The stone at bottom is still visible in a field on the east side of the highway north of Shamrock. *Photo courtesy of Ben Ferren.*

ERIC FERREN
"MR. SHAMROCK"
1904 — 1971
MEMORIAL PARK

Shamrock citizens planned a city park to honor Eric E. Ferren and this marker was to be at the entrance. The plans never materialized but the marker is now on a pedestal at Tipperary and Dublin Streets. *Photo courtesy Ben Ferren.*

Drumright II, A Thousand Memories

Oil field relics surround the old fire bell on Tipperary Road. The relics and the bell have disappeared and the once elegant theatre next door is in ruins. The Masonic Lodge met upstairs. *Photo courtesy Don and Cecil McKnight Corbin.*

of Shamrock, they recall Eric Ferren, and when they speak of Eric Ferren, they immediately think of Shamrock. For more than 30 years, starting in 1933, he was mayor of the town, and for a decade after that he was a peace officer. But to most people, he was Shamrock's heart and soul.

Eric's father, S. T. Ferren, came to the oil field from Norfolk in 1913 and helped build the large tank farm southeast of Cushing. As the boom spread to Shamrock, he brought his family there and operated as a teamster. Eric was 12 at the time. His imaginative mind conceived ways to make money. Drinking water was scarce at first and Eric sold water for five cents a bucket.

Mothers sometimes fed their sick babies goat milk in the early days, but in Shamrock there were no goats. The mothers tried mare's milk. Eric supplemented his income by milking mares and selling the milk to mothers. In summers he delivered ice in Bristow. He was captain of the high school football team in 1923. He helped bring the second Blarney Stone to Shamrock, and he and Harry McKnight painted it green.

In the years that followed, Ferren operated a general store, hardware, feed store, grocery store, restaurant, and a green house. In 1933, at age 29, he was elected mayor and held the office for 30 years. Starting in 1963, he was Creek County Deputy sheriff for 8 years, first for Dee Ausmus and later for Brice Coleman. For many years, Ferren had hoped and believed that Shamrock would rise again and become a thriving community. He backed his belief by buying up several business buildings as they became vacant. His dream had faded during his last few years, but he was still Shamrock's most enthusiastic booster when he died on January 29, 1971.

Schools and Happy Days

The Old Town and S. H. S. Still Live in Memories

Shamrock's school system was organized in May 1909. The first school was a one-room log house near the Lincoln County line. Another room was added in 1913. But the real beginning of Shamrock schools came with the oil boom.

A census taken in February 1916, showed there were 849 school children in the district. The school board met hastily and employed nine teachers for the term opening September 4, 1916. Already the new $15,000 all-grade school building was under construction and would be ready by fall. Ray Powers was the first principal at the school. It was to be called Liberty Ward school. Two of the first teachers were Hazel Woods and Nell Bland.

The town was very excited when the three-story brick building was completed. It had three stories with nine rooms, offices and a basement. The exterior through the first floor was of beautifully chiseled stone. Drinking fountains with ornamental faucets were in the school yard, as were toilet facilities. These facilities were moved inside in 1919.

In one large room, which served as an auditorium, was a piano. The school also boasted a "graphaphone" with a horn, which was used for teaching folk dancing. In the basement was a boiler room that provided steam heat. A wide sidewalk surrounded the building and led to entrances on the north and west. Lower grades were taught on the first two floors and some classes were held in the basement.

While the building seemed elaborate for 1916, it could not handle the avalanche of children who reported in September. Few high school students enrolled as most of the oil workers were young parents, but the lower grades attracted hundreds. As more pupils arrived, more seats were added to the rooms and finally the school board had to provide school in shifts with children attending only half-days. Most of the children lived in shotgun houses in and near Shamrock and brought sack lunches to school.

The High School

The pressure for school facilities caused Shamrock to move quickly. By the fall of 1917, a new $40,000 red brick high school building was completed for students in grades 9-12. The one-story structure

Drumright II, A Thousand Memories

Shamrock's first school after the oil boom was called Liberty Ward, although in the beginning it was for all 12 grades. The school was torn down in the 1930's. It is now remembered as "old ward school." *Photo courtesy Alma P. Friend.*

provided an auditorium that also served as a study hall. On the front was a large area for home economics training, several classrooms and school offices. A manual training or woodworking shop and other classrooms were on the south. Even in 1916 Shamrock High boasted an orchestra with several violins. While the school had steam heat, its toilet facilities were outside.

This was Shamrock's only high school, and in 1985 the building was still standing and being used as a grade school. For the nearly 800 who graduated there from 1918 to 1961, the school symbolizes home. It is the home of Shamrock's Fighting Irish and the Irish Peppers in their green and white uniforms. It brings back memories of state baseball championships in 1923 and 1938, of football teams that challenged large towns such as Bristow, Drumright, Cushing and Chandler, and high academic achievement.

Shamrock High's first graduate in 1918 was Fay Facker, who later operated the Central Chevrolet Co. in Drumright. Its first superintendent was E. P. Baldwin, who arrived in March 1916 and remained through the exciting years until 1925. Other early superintendents included Leo Bowers, E. C. Bray, C. W. Guisinger, and Gordon T. Mills, who served

Schools and Happy Days

Three old grads, David White, Mary Hubert Lesco, and Billie Smith O'Kelley reminisce in front of Shamrock's first and only high school, which opened in September 1917. It is still used as a grade school. *Photo by author.*

from 1929 until 1945. James D. Grubbs was superintendent from 1954-1961.

Declining population in the area forced the school to end its colorful era in 1961. Since then, most of its young people attended high school in Drumright, and some of its teachers also made the switch. Among teachers in the Drumright system who started in Shamrock were Alma P. Friend, Opal Clifton, Ronald E. Gerard, and Mabel Grimes Miles.

Shamrock's last graduating class in 1961 consisted of Johnny E. Campbell, Larry D. Slane, Jerry L. Slane, Gary Max Cackler, Edna Mae Brown, Larry Endicott, Judy Kay Shelton, Ruby Pearl Wiseman and Lovella Sue Duke. Ellen Sherill was class sponsor.

The Lasting Memories

Every community has its memories and some were special in early Shamrock. Elbert J. Stevens came to Shamrock when the community

Drumright II, A Thousand Memories

A remnant of Liberty Ward school days is this carousel behind the high school building. Lillian Ferren Beavers, who attended Liberty, takes her first ride in more than 65 years. With her are two present-day pupils, Lori Roberts and Tricia Brady. *Photo by author.*

centered around the Ownesby farm west of the present townsite. For the past forty years he had lived in the same house a block off Tipperary Road. In 1985 he still missed the hurly-burly of the boom days and often walked down Tipperary reminiscing. He remembered the fights, the saloons, and red light district on the east side. His most vivid memory was of being held up on his way home in 1916. "Almost everybody got robbed," he said. "You couldn't even walk between two stores without being held up." He remembered when Isham Ownesby was shot and killed near the Ownesby farm. "They tracked the killer back to a 'choc house' on the east side," he said, "but they never caught him." Elbert Stevens died in March 1986.

Lillian Ferren Beavers liked to recall school days. "The first school had a fire escape running all the way from the third floor to the ground," she said. "It seemed so high to the top." Children swarmed into the school yard in the mornings and each day one pupil was the envy of others when he or she was chosen to bang the triangle as a signal to march in.

Women teachers wore skirts almost to their ankles and they had to shuffle to class. Later, when skirts were shortened, the wind would sometimes blow the skirts so high it would expose the teachers'

Schools and Happy Days

FACULTY

Mrs. Waas — English
Miss Friend — Science
Miss Savoy — Home Economics
Mr. Boatmun — History & Coach
Miss Norris — Commerce
Mr. Paulding — High School Principal
Mr. McKeown — Grade Principal
Gordon T. Mills — Superintendent of Schools
Miss Morgan — 7th Grade
Miss V. Butler — 8th Grade
Miss E. Butler — Primary
Miss Hudson — 2nd Grade
Miss N. Dressler — 3rd Grade
Miss O. Dressler — 4th Grade
Miss Haught — 6th Grade
Miss Ewing — 5th Grade

These are familiar faces to hundreds of former Shamrock students. Gordon T. Mills was Shamrock superintendent for 16 years. Left of Mills is Haskell Paulding, whose basketball teams competed against Drumright and other area schools for many years. Top center is Alma P. Friend, who taught at Drumright after leaving Shamrock. Lyndall Hudson and Elsie Haught, in bottom half of picture, were two long-time faculty members. *Photo courtesy Don and Cecil McKnight Corbin.*

45

Drumright II, A Thousand Memories

Shamrock High was proud of these bandsmen in their green and white uniforms. Seated are Paul Price and Director Ronald E. Gerard. Second row: 2. Harold Baker, 3. Desmond Gerard, 5. Goleman Mize, 6. Howard Payne, and 7. Curtiss Palmer. Back row: (l. to r.) George Ford, Harold Keller, Ty Williams, Cleo Wilkes, John Sullivan, Dickey Haught, Warren Wall, Earl Sanders, Floyd Speaker, Harry McKnight, Bill Cason, Percy White, and Whitey McCutcheon. Picture taken in about 1925-26. Identifications by Darwin Kirkman, Lillian Beavers, and Mary Hubert Lesco. *Photo courtesy Don and Cecil McKnight Corbin.*

undergarments. "The girls would get to see the fancy bloomers they wore," Mrs. Beavers recalled. "They were satin-like and so pretty. All of us girls were envious and looked forward to the day when we could have something that nice."

One incident has always remained in the memory of Mabel Grimes, who graduated from Shamrock High and later taught in the Drumright system. One day as a small girl, she visited the office of her father, C. C. Grimes, who was a judge for a time. In his office sat a young man with a pink shirt and a straw hat cocked to one side of his head. "Young man, if you don't straighten up and change your ways, you're headed for real trouble," her father was saying. Shortly after that, the youth strolled cockily out the door. Her father muttered, "That Matthew Kimes . . ." and shook his head in consternation. Kimes later became one of Oklahoma's most notorious bank robbers.

Kenneth Sullivan, a 1925 Shamrock High School graduate, recalled how Hallowe'en was next to St. Patrick's Day importance in

Schools and Happy Days

These old store buildings are remnants of Tipperary Road's business district. Once the block boasted such names as Citizens Bank, Henry Rhoades Rexall Store, James Winterringer's Dry Goods, Charley Grimes Grocery, Judge Berkey, and Fred Wensauer Garage. *Photo by author.*

Shamrock. "Every Hallowe'en, pranksters would take trucks and gather up all the outhouses and bring them to Tipperary Road. They would be lined up all through the main business street. The next morning, people came and got them and took them home."

    Mary Hubert Lesco's father, Frank, was a driller for Tom Slick and Charles B. Shaffer. For a time the Huberts lived in a tent high above the Cimarron River. The tent leaked so much that often her parents sat up in bed at night holding umbrellas. Each day her father walked down 100 steps to reach the river and then crossed it on a narrow swinging bridge.

    A more vivid memory was of the Ku Klux Klan in Shamrock and the time it came to get her father, who was a Catholic. A friend brought word to him in time for them to find a hiding place. The Klan was strong in Shamrock and usually met in the old Odd Fellow building near the first water tower. In 1922, after a Cushing attorney had been abducted and flogged for making speeches against the Klan, 12 prominent Shamrock men were arrested and charged.

    And there are other memories old-timers tell about: Judge Ben Berkey, the notary public, judge, and counselor, walking down Tipperary

Drumright II, A Thousand Memories

This vault is all that is left of the First State Bank that opened in 1916. The post office once shared the building with the bank. *Photo courtesy Larry Mashburn.*

Road, his snow-white hair rippling in the breeze. He lived to be 99 .... Dr. John Erve Cargill, one of the first doctors, making the rounds .... Saturday nights when the entire population congregated on Tipperary.... Youngsters gathering at Soapy's, (also called Soapsuds Susies's), Candy and Novelty store to buy licorice and valentines. When they tormented her or put soap on her windows, she chased them with a bucket of hot water usually mixed with soap or lye.

Life was hard and survival difficult in Oklahoma's boom towns, and some people were happy to see the era give way to more civilized

Schools and Happy Days

St. Patrick's Day is always homecoming in Shamrock. This 1981 parade is one of many that for a brief moment rekindled the spirit of the old days. Former residents return and relive memories. *Photo courtesy Ben Ferren.*

times and an easier way of life. The old-timers of Shamrock look back longingly on the exciting days. Recalling such memories restores a twinkle and sometimes a tear to Irish eyes. Almost any of them will tell you, "Those were the days, my friend!"

Memories — Pemeta & Frey

A Dream That Died, Skimming for Oil, Picking Berries, and the Turkey Track Ranch

For years, oil field people converged on Pemeta to pick berries at the James and Maude Salisbury farm. From left, Ruth, James, Sr., James, Jr., and Maude.

Chapter III

Pemeta — A Dream That Died

Even the Marshal Left
When His Store Was Robbed

Pemeta (pronounced PEM-uh-TAH) was once a town of 3,000 only two miles from Drumright, but many present-day citizens never heard of it. It once had visions of becoming a thriving agricultural and oil center of 10,000 population. It had reasons for such dreams. In 1914, oil exploration by Thomas B. Slick, C. B. Shaffer, B. B. Jones and others, shifted from Drumright to the northwest. Derricks sprung up all along the Cimarron River on the north edge of Pemeta.

The Oklahoma Pipeline Co. and the North American Refinery set up operations on the banks of Tiger Creek. Pierce Oil Company, Conley-Riter and other smaller companies were nearby. In 1915, the Santa Fe Railroad connected Drumright with Frey, Pemeta and Cushing. Oil workers set up homemaking in shotgun houses and a few tents. The future seemed assured.

Pemeta made big plans — for parks, churches, and tree-lined boulevards. The one-room school perched atop a hill on the west side of Tiger Creek was replaced with a bigger building that once offered a high school diploma. Most of the plans, however, never got off the drawing board. The town once boasted a population of 3,000 with another 2,000 in nearby camps, but these seemed to fade away as oil production fell below expectations and the boom fizzled.

Pemeta survived until the mid-1920's, but its Main Street, instead of becoming a wide, paved, well-lighted thoroughfare, remained a dirt street. Its bank never opened. It never had a church. The post office that opened on August 9, 1915, closed on October 30, 1923. But while it lasted, Pemeta was a thriving oil boom town and it left many memories that are alive today.

Getting to Pemeta Through Frey

In the boom days, there were three routes from Drumright to Pemeta. One was taking the old Oilton highway to a section line about two miles north of Drumright. From there, one could angle northwest to the east edge of Pemeta. One could also go via North Skinner Street past the north cemetery and continue another mile into Pemeta. This route still exists. The third route was via rail, starting in June 1915. A dime would buy a ticket from Drumright to Frey. Another nickel would pay the way to Pemeta.

Pemeta—A Dream That Died

The Oklahoma Pipe Line Co. was Pemeta's most important oil installation. It existed from about 1920 until 1954. Remnants of early-day Pemeta are visible in the background, including the 55,000-barrel tank built by the North American Refinery on the banks of Tiger Creek, and the John Bingamon store on the left. All of this disappeared years ago. *Photo courtesy Marie Jones Story.*

Drumright II, A Thousand Memories

Frey (pronounced Fry) was a small settlement about a mile and three-fourths northwest of Drumright. It had no business district, school or post office, but it boasted a depot, and it was at Frey the rail line forked. From Frey, it veered northwest on into Pemeta three-fourths of a mile away, and northeast toward Oilton and Jennings.

Frey consisted mostly of Elmer High's grocery store, 10 or 12 shotgun houses occupied mostly by Oklahoma Pipeline Co. employees, and a large house where the section crew of the Santa Fe Railroad met regularly. Bill Hatfield was section foreman. Most of the section hands were Mexicans who lived in faded red boxcars beside the tracks.

Since Drumright was little more than a mile away, Frey residents usually went there to shop, spending 20 cents for a round-trip train ride. Frey children walked to the school at Pemeta. Frey's water supply came largely from a well owned by the Santa Fe Railroad or another belonging to the Cade Hicks family. Water in barrels for washing clothes was hauled in by wagon.

Mrs. Maggie Jones McClary lived in Frey as a child. Her father, Charlie Jones, brought his family to Drumright in 1922 and he became a line walker to Sapulpa and Glencoe for the Oklahoma Pipe Line Co. She recalled how children in Frey even in the early days divided into gangs. "There were two persimmon groves along the tracks, one on each side," she said. "Children divided into small gangs, each claiming exclusive rights to their respective persimmon groves. Sometimes they would quarrel and fight when a child wandered across the tracks and got into the wrong grove."

The Mexican families lived so close to the tracks that one of the small children, Juan Valdez, thought it would be a great idea to put his pecans on the railroad track and let the train crack them. He reached out as the next train came by. His idea worked but he lost three fingers as the train mashed the pecans. Juan was apparently an adventuresome child. His disappearance caused great anxiety in Frey one day until he was found on his tricycle approaching the outskirts of Drumright.

Skimming For Oil

Frey's one and only industry was an oil skimming plant operated by Cade and Ottie Hicks. It also had the largest number of employees, all members of the Hicks family. From the earliest days of the oil boom to many years later, oil overflowed from the wells and leaking pipelines into Tiger Creek and the Cimarron River. A number of citizens and even some oil companies found it profitable to skim the oil from the water and sell it. Usually the oil proved to be of very high quality.

Cade Hicks decided that skimming oil was about his only chance of profiting from the oil boom. He and his wife had seven sons, Jim, Ray,

Pemeta—A Dream That Died

Roy, Clyde, Claude, Elvin, and Millard, and two daughters, Mabel and Hazel. This gave him enough personnel to man the skimming plant and even to start three others.

Tiger Creek was about 50 feet wide at Frey then. Cade Hicks put together a skimming apparatus that consisted of two boats with a tipping box in between. The oil would come into the box and float on top. Later, the oil would be put into a pond to settle. Then, the pond gate would be opened and the oil collected and sold.

The Hicks family operated the skimming plant until 1923 when the flow of oil ceased, although one plant on East Fifth Street in Drumright continued until the 1930's. The North American Refinery in Pemeta, using a more sophisticated apparatus, engaged in skimming on the Cimarron River.

Pemeta Was Lively

From late 1914 until 1917, Pemeta was an impressive sight viewed from the east. Wagons carrying pipe, casing and other oil field equipment streamed down the dirt road from the Drumright-Oilton road, crossed the Tiger Creek Bridge and entered Pemeta.

On the left of the section line approaching Pemeta was the Sellers mule farm, owned by D. C. (Coin) Sellers and R. A. (Dick) Sellers. At one time the Sellers brothers had one of the largest mule farms in Oklahoma.

Just before crossing Tiger Creek and on the south side of the road was the Oklahoma Pipe Line Co. with stacks of pipe, casing and scattered buildings. It was one of Pemeta's biggest employers, operating three shifts of pumpers, gaugers and engineers.

An even more imposing sight was the North American Refinery just across the bridge and on the north side of the road from Oklahoma Pipeline Co. Built in 1915, the refinery had a capacity of 2,000 barrels daily. A spur of the Santa Fe Railroad track branched northward into the refinery and ended beside a 55,000-barrel tank on the edge of Tiger Creek. (See map.)

Between the tracks and Tiger Creek were two rows of company homes with four homes in each row. The refinery owned those on the north side of the section line. OPL owned those on the south side. Just past the company homes was the John Bingamon general store, nestled near the railroad track. On the south side of the road perched high on a hill in a pasture was Pemeta's first school, a one-room frame building easily visible because of its yellow color. A winding, well-beaten path led to the school.

Pemeta's business district, just west of all these structures, was crowded together, and sometimes homes were sandwiched between business houses. It was similar to other boom towns in that Model-T Fords,

Drumright II, A Thousand Memories

This dance pavilion was the entertainment center for Pemeta residents for many years, starting during the oil boom. Lanterns lighted up the pavilion at night and string bands provided dance music. *Photo courtesy Don and Cecil McKnight Corbin.*

wagons and buggies crowded into the district, turning it into a thriving thoroughfare. Beyond the main district, Pemeta had few streets. Oil workers set up shotgun houses and tents that were scattered about rather than in rows.

Pemeta's Social Life

Pemeta had few drinking and gambling dens. Those who sought such entertainment slipped across the Payne County line on the west edge of Pemeta to a saloon that fulfilled their needs. This came to an abrupt halt one night when some Pemeta vigilantes slipped over the county line and set fire to the saloon. Between Pemeta and the county line was an unoccupied narrow stretch of land called "The Strip" that served as a divider between the counties.

Adult social life consisted mostly of dancing, baseball, and pitching horseshoes. A large pavilion west of the railroad tracks was the site of many dances. Usually a string band made up of local residents provided the music. Roy Keith Shoemaker, who did a research project on Pemeta in 1985 as a University project, told of community dances also being held in homes:

> . . . usually just whoever wanted to hold a dance at their place. If the weather was bad, they would move all the furniture out

Pemeta—A Dream That Died

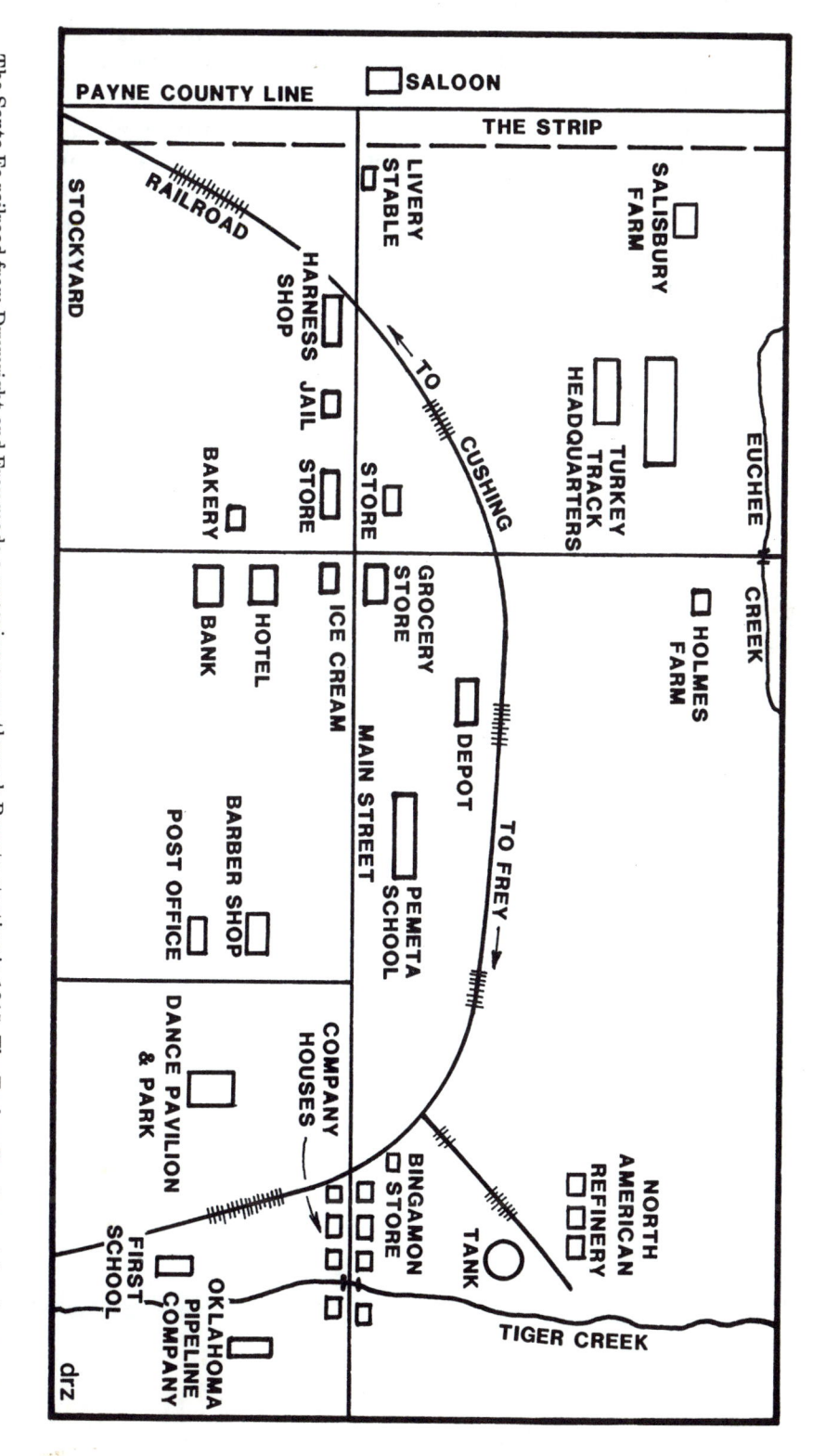

The Santa Fe railroad from Drumright and Frey made a sweeping curve through Pemeta starting in 1915. The Turkey Track ranch headquarters were on the northwest edge of Pemeta near Euchee Creek. Map shows location of oil installations and businesses. (Sources: Homer Wilson, Wesley Bingamon, Maggie Jones McClary, *Abe Nasalroad*, and *James Salisbury Memoirs*.)

of the living room and hold the dance there. If there was nice weather they would hang lights or lanterns and have the dance outdoors.

Pemeta was never incorporated and never officially had a chief of police, but the people banded together informally and gave Horace Cooper the task of keeping law and order. (Cooper was not related to another Horace Cooper who worked for the Pure Oil Co. in Drumright.) Cooper's family operated a grocery store near Pemeta's jail, a small concrete bunker. Cooper was a familiar figure with his wide-brimmed Stetson hat, cowboy boots, and a large shiny star. But one day after his own store was robbed, he put his belongings on a wagon and took off for Texas.

The Turkey Track Ranch

Hide-Out of the Daltons
And a Famed Trading Post

All traces are gone today of Pemeta's most noted historic establishment, the Turkey Track Ranch headquarters. The vast spread, just two miles from Drumright, once consisted of thousands of acres of land extending from the Cimarron River south to the Deep Fork River with the boundaries of the Creek and Sac and Fox Nations as its eastern border. It extended westward through what is now Cushing. The ranch came into existence in the 1880's on Sac and Fox lands, which had not yet been opened to white settlement. Thousands of head of cattle grazed on the open range.

The ranch was a trading post and oasis for Indians, cattlemen, and others who traveled along a trail that extended from Fort Smith, Ark., to Fort Reno, Oklahoma. The trail became known as the Turkey Track Trail. The ranch was also a hangout for the Dalton gang and other fugitives of that day. Harriet Springer, a pioneer teacher wrote of matching pennies with the Dalton brothers when she stopped there in 1888. Others reported how the Daltons, after a robbery, would retreat toward the ranch, sometimes in a hail of gunfire. Boss Neff, a rancher in the Panhandle, reported journeying to the Turkey Track to buy 10,000 pounds of second-hand barbed wire for five cents a pound in 1887. The history of the ranch is sketchy, but in 1891, the owners were reported to be Arthur Hill, James Jerome, and Leslie Combs.

Robert Atkins worked on the ranch for two years starting in 1891. At that time the ranch manager was R. B. Payne and Tom Hobbs was range boss. The owners operated under the name of Saginaw Cattle Company of Michigan. Atkins described the ranch layout:

> The pasture land was 18 miles wide and 25 miles long, and was divided into four pastures by four crossed wire fences: the first pasture for steers alone; the second for cows; the third for beef cattle; and the fourth for "through" cattle, those shipped in each year from Texas.
>
> The round-up grounds were on the exact spot where the city of Cushing now stands. In this pasture, the Company stationed fire-guards about a mile apart to keep fires from burning the grass. The ranch had a hundred and fifty saddle horses and employed thirty men all the time. The ranch held 20,000 head of cattle.

Drumright II, A Thousand Memories

> The old road, later called the Turkey Track trail, was made and used by Indian hunters on their way west to hunt buffalo. . . long before the ranch was started . . . the Indians themselves and neighboring ranchers gave it the name of Turkey Track trail.*

After the Sac and Fox lands were opened to settlement in 1891, the ranch was broken up quickly. By the time of the oil boom in 1912, most of it was gone except for the headquarters at Pemeta, which became a feeding lot for oil field teamsters. Homer Wilson of Drumright, whose family moved to Pemeta area even before the boom, is one of a very few living today who saw the ranch layout. Wilson said the headquarters included a large ranch house, a corral, a stockade surrounded by a picket fence, a large barn and several other lesser outbuildings. The ranch buildings were across the dirt road west of where the Holmes farm was located at this writing. This is near Euchee Creek, just south of the Cimarron River. The ranch headquarters were on the northwest edge of Pemeta during boom days. Entrance to the ranch was from the section line running east and west that was also the Pemeta Main Street. (See map.)

The trail existed even before the ranch. The ranch was said to have been named Turkey Track because its cattle brand resembled a turkey's footprint. As the ranch became well-known, the trail was given the same name.

In 1924, James Salisbury, Sr., purchased a tract of land adjacent to the ranch headquarters which was originally a part of the ranch. By this time all of the ranch buildings were gone and brush had grown up on much of the area. Salisbury and his son, James, Jr., were able to locate the trail where it crossed Euchee Creek "a few hundred feet south of the Delong place," and where it passed through the Salisbury farm. Later Salisbury located a site at Markham where the trail crossed the Cimarron River. Salisbury discovered the ranch well when one of his steers crashed through some timbers and fell 25 feet to the bottom.

The Salisbury Farm

After James and Maude Salisbury established their farm in 1924, it became more familiar to most Drumright people than the old ranch. In 1916, the Salisburys moved their business from Eldon, Mo., to Drumright. They set up the bakery, ice cream plant, and confectionary across the street from Miller Hardware on East Broadway. Later he sold the business and purchased the Wheeler Hotel next door. As the hotel business waned, Salisbury returned to Missouri for six months. He then came back to Drumright, took a job with the Pierce Oil Co. and purchased the farm.

***Indian Pioneer History**, Vol. 12, pp. 496-498, Foreman Collection, Oklahoma Historical Society.

What made the farm so well-known was Salisbury's hobby of raising berries. At one time he grew four acres of strawberries, two of blackberries, and two of dewberries in addition to other areas where he experimented with youngberries and boysenberries. People from surrounding towns were invited to come to the farm and do their own picking. They came year after year from Drumright, Cushing, Oilton and even more distant points. Salisbury once planted seven acres in just dewberries.

Pemeta Today

Roy K. (Keith) Shoemaker of Drumright was particularly interested in choosing Pemeta as a research project since he is related to several pioneer families of Pemeta including the Wilsons and Salisburys. In addition to the paper, he searched through the brush for mementos of the boom days. He found several gates that oil companies had placed along the Cimarron River to prevent trespassing, an Illinios Central Railroad plate fastened to a railroad tie, and some fire bricks that once housed a boiler. Lodged in a tree were a winch and tackle that had been used by the Oklahoma Pipeline Co., probably in the early 1920s. When he retrieved them, the wheels still turned and the winch was in working order.

Beyond these, remnants of Pemeta are few. Railroad tracks are gone, as is the bridge across Tiger Creek. All buildings disappeared long ago except the depot, which now serves as a filling station on Highway 33. A modern brick home has replaced the Salisbury farm house near the old Turkey Track Ranch headquarters. The area that was once Frey is so covered with brush it is inaccessible. Still, memories of the once exciting boom town live on and people speculate on what might have been if Pemeta's dreams of becoming a permanent town of 10,000 had come true.

Memories — Oilton

Oilton—Toughest Town of All, Main Street Grows in a Hurry, Scottie Enters the Sin Dens, the First Schools, Etc.

For 17 years, the U. S. Government and the Ku Klux Klan shared quarters in the KKK building at Broadway and C Streets.

Chapter IV

Oilton — Toughest Town of All

'If Somebody Didn't Kill You, The Osage Moonshine Could'

Oilton was one of more than a half dozen towns created in western Creek County during the frantic search for oil starting in 1912. Its population never equaled that of Drumright, Cushing, or even Shamrock, but Oilton had one distinction: It was the roughest and toughest town in the oil field. Life was hard in the field. It was no place for the timid. But in most areas, hardy, adventurous people could concentrate on going after a share of the wealth that flowed all around. In Oilton, survival was the first concern, and many lacked the tenacity to hang on.

The population turnover in Oilton from 1915 to 1920 was phenomenal. Lora Davis Dentler recalled that in 1916 she was a freshman at Oilton High School with 39 classmates. In 1920 she was a senior and editor of the school yearbook. Only one other member of the freshman class was still around. Parents of the others had decided to move on.

Oilton came into existence in early 1915 with the development of the north pool, known as the Dropright dome. As oil companies moved their drilling rigs up the Cimarron River, business speculators came right behind them. At first it appeared that Dropright, (later Markham) would be the new center for the north pool, but drilling moved quickly to the north and east. Before the end of 1914, a new townsite was laid out a mile and a half north and east of Dropright and it was called Oilton. It appeared to be ideally located to serve as a hub for the north pool.

Even before a townsite had been selected, several families whose names would be a part of Oilton history for years, had picked the area for future homes. J. H. Cacy and Frank Terrill had brought their families from Brookin, an oil ghost town in southern Oklahoma. Albert E. Peck, Robert Keeler, L. P. Gowland, Frank Albert, and Sam Harrah came from Avant. The Clark brothers, Charles, Harvey, George and Steve, all arrived from Nebraska. To the east, Wallace Doolin had built an imposing two-story home on his ranch.

In January 1915, the townsite was only a cotton patch, but as oil strikes occurred along the Cimarron within a stone's throw of the site, things changed in a hurry. People swarmed into the area. By February 20, large wooden buildings were like silhouettes against the skyline. In another month Main Street took form, and by May, Oilton was a thriving oil boom town.

Oilton was fortunate to have rail service almost as quickly as the

Oilton—Toughest Town of All

This cotton patch was all that existed of Oilton in January 1915 when Eaton & Dunn Real Estate Co. set up a table and chair and began selling town lots. *Photo courtesy Frankie Jo Posey.*

town developed. In mid-June 1915, the Oil Belt Terminal railroad reached there from Tulsa through Jennings. Almost simultaneously, the Santa Fe forked at Frey after leaving Drumright and veered into Oilton. As it neared Oilton, it curved eastward to pass through the small oil field community of Crow. The many small canyons in the landscape forced the Santa Fe to make a large loop to get into Crow. Travelers over the Drumright-Oilton dirt road had to cross the railroad track twice as they passed by Crow. The track in Oilton passed through the west end of the business district near the gambling dens and pool halls.

The Santa Fe depot area was always crowded by oil workers boarding the four passenger trains that came through daily. Long lines of wagons came daily to pick up pipe, casing, and other oil field equipment from the freight cars. The townsite office where people purchased lots was just across the street from the depot.

Why Life Was Difficult

As people swarmed into Oilton, they started with bare ground. There were no homes or amenities. Some of the oil workers set up housekeeping in tents, and in a short time a row of tents extended a mile from Main Street all the way to the section line to the south. The heaviest

Drumright II, A Thousand Memories

As building started in Oilton, no water wells or springs were nearby and water was hauled in barrels. This was called the town's first water works. *Photo courtesy Frankie Jo Posey.*

settlement was in the southwest and most of the homes there were shotgun houses or wooden lean-tos thrown together quickly.

Oilton was flat country with virtually no trees and no barrier against the bitter north wind. The tents and wooden shelters had no insulation and most had large cracks in the walls. Small gas heaters warmed most of the homes, but at night and during bitter cold, the gas pressure was low. People were defenseless against the weather.

Most of residents were couples with small children. Young fathers came hopeful of finding prosperity in the new boom town. Parents arose early and tried to find ways to heat their shacks before the children awakened. Often, after school the tents and shotgun houses were so cold the children were put to bed fully clothed to keep them from freezing. In this weather, long underwear was in fashion for men, women and children.

Oilton had no electricity in the early days and at night the streets were pitch dark. Gas torches lighted the oil field southwest and east of town, but the closest torches were a half-mile away. People stumbled down the dark streets, even to church and back. Often they slipped and fell in the mud, fell over oil field equipment, or tripped over a drunk. Children became lost trying to get home from church. Homes and tents usually had gas lights using mantles, which were soft, lacy hoods made of asbestos about an inch and a half in diameter. When placed over a gas light, they provided a clear, bright glow that illuminated a room. Mantles were so fragile they could be destroyed by a puff of wind.

Water from nearby wells was piped into Oilton shortly after the town was established, but some of the faucets were outdoors and pipes froze in cold weather. In 1916, plumbing began to make inroads in the town, but even into the 1920's and early 1930's, outside privies were all most residents could afford.

Gambling and Shooting Begin

Adding to the woes of the law abiding citizens was the heavy influx of bootleggers, gamblers, and houses of sin. As Drumright, Cushing, and Pemeta tried to clamp down on lawlessness, violators found refuge in Oilton. For them, it was a dream situation—a wild town with money flowing everywhere and virtually no law. Dark streets at night aided the lawless.

The Big Six, a Drumright gang that controlled the notorious Hump, set up a den called the Oil Exchange on the corner of Main and C Streets where a city park is now located. Thousands of dollars changed hands at the poker, blackjack, and crap tables of the Oil Exchange, which attracted wealthy oil speculators. Paul Peck saw the interior of the den. "Inside was a steel cage with a slit about 12 inches wide and six inches deep," he said. "A shotgun barrel protruded through the slit and at least one man was shot and killed." Johnny H. Crites, the manager, wore a pearl-handled revolver on his hip. Crites, with two helpers and an armed guard, carried Oil Exchange money to the bank in two No. 3 wash tubs heaping with bills ranging from $1 to $100.

When oil workers tired of the gambling and liquor dens, they roamed the streets firing pistols carelessly in all directions. Ray Harris was one of the first employees of the Santa Fe Depot in 1915 and in 1986, he recalled:

> Children had orders to never leave the house (or shack) after dark. For a time there was at least one person murdered every night, on the average. If you think friends are of value today—then they were priceless. If somebody couldn't kill you with a gun, that awful moonshine from the Osage could do it.

J. D. Tyree's father, Jess, worked for 18 years on the ranch of Dr. J. C. W. Bland northeast of Oilton. Bland was a partner in the first well drilled in the Red Fork field in 1901. Tyree remembers his visits to Oilton with friends who lived in tents:

> The town was wild and through the night there was gunfire over the tents. But there was not as much trouble with

Drumright II, A Thousand Memories

Even before Oilton became a town, Wallace Doolin owned a 180-acre ranch 2½ miles west of the townsite. His two-story ranch home was a landmark for years just off the old highway to Tulsa. *Photo courtesy Mrs. Paul Peck.*

criminals then as there is nowadays. When a crime was committed, a group of 10 or 12 men would form a posse and go after the criminals. I've seen them catch the thugs and bring them in.

Oilton had a few cowboys, too. Tyree watched herds of 1,000 cattle on the road east of Oilton. The cattle extended from fence to fence as they came down the section line herded by a dozen or more cowboys. Most of the cattle were from the Wallace Doolin ranch east of Oilton or from the Bland ranch. The cattle were being changed from one pasture to another.

Oscar Anderson was another who received a dramatic exposure to Oilton's early day life. Anderson was to become one of Oilton's leaders for many years, but in 1914 he was a mechanic in the rail yards at Parsons, Kansas. When the oil boom moved toward Oilton, Anderson and his brother-in-law, Charley Bodwell, decided the new town might be a place to start a new life. they put together a few belongings and headed for Oklahoma.

Parsons was a quiet railroad town, and the two youths were startled when they stepped off the train at Oilton and saw the beehive of activity. They were even more startled as they strolled down the dirt

Oilton—Toughest Town of All

Oil explorers made the same mistake around Oilton as in other parts of the field. They drilled wells very close together, sometimes as many as three in a row searching for different sands. This depleted the field early. These wells are on the George Black lease. *Photo courtesy Frankie Jo Posey.*

street when a man who appeared somewhat inebriated began firing a pistol in several directions.

Alarmed, Anderson told the man, "Be careful, you could hit someone." The gunman reflected for a moment, then with a half-smile, pointed his gun at Anderson and Bodwell and began firing. The bullets whistled around them as they dived into a store.

Oil Leases Were Peaceful

Scattered mostly to the south and east of Oilton were oil company leases where many workers and their families lived. Usually the leases consisted of a frame office building, two or three modern homes for company executives, and a row or two of shotgun houses or lean-tos. By 1915, most leases had two-story frame bunkhouses where unmarried workers could get room and board. A few other houses were scattered randomly on the lease. Few tents were set up on the leases.

Charles W. Davis was a pumper for the Weber Oil Co., which had a lease east of Crow. In 1986, his daughter, Lora Davis Dentler, still had memories of the 1915-1920 era:

> The men worked six days a week or seven if needed as oil wells were everywhere. They were never shut down except

Tents such as these in 1915 were stretched from Main Street all the way south to the intersection of present day Highways 99 and old Highway 33, which once went to Oilton. *Photo courtesy Frankie Jo Posey.*

for repairs and that was considered an emergency. Many wells flowed right over the top of the derrick if anything went wrong with the controls.

My father was a pumper and was responsible for keeping his wells going from noon until midnight, seven days a week, 365 days a year. He was so glad to have the work and steady pay check coming in that he didn't expect time off or paid vacations. He and mother got up early and went to town to pay bills, etc., and got back in time to go to work at 12 noon. We had a Model-T Ford sedan which was used primarily for trips to town. Around the lease, everyone walked and no one seemed to mind. Everyone seemed to have some kind of car or pick-up. I don't recall any wagons.

Most oil lease families purchased their groceries from M. P. Tippin, who set up a store in the south part of Oilton early in 1915. Tippin owned a fleet of five or six spring wagons that circulated through the oil field delivering groceries. Oil workers bought on credit and settled accounts on payday. As a driver left a supply of groceries, the wife placed her order for the next delivery for two weeks later. The Tippin Grocery operated for many years.

Lease people missed the rowdyism that prevailed in town. They were isolated from liquor and gambling dens and even from traffic. Gas torches illuminated most of the field. Even at night children could play their favorite games of follow-the-leader and hide-and-seek. The Black Panther lease even had a tennis court, although it was seldom used. Davis set up a croquet court that attracted many neighbors and friends. A gas torch illuminated both ends.

High Society Comes to Oilton

Social life consisted of simple activities for most families. The few leisure hours that women had were filled with quilting, other needlework, and church activities. Families enjoyed picnics, watermelon parties, or swimming and fishing in Deer Creek or other streams that ran through the dense hickory woods around Oilton.

But it was not long before a higher stratum of social life involved. Lillian Harris Hix, whose father owned a farm north of the Cimarron River recalled in 1986:

> Inevitably a society class evolved . . . businessmen and their wives who had cars and the means to engage in the attractions offered by Tulsa, 40 miles to the east. Here the ladies could shop for latest fashions, and even come home with the newly invented permanent wave and throw away their curling irons! A status symbol for sure. Some members of the elite stratum were college graduates and belonged to some Greek-letter fraternity or sorority . . . and don't you forget it.

In the midst of the Model-T's and wagons in Oilton were fancy cars owned by affluent families. The L. P. Gowlands drove a Stutz, M. L. and Velma Harris a Cadillac, and the Wallace Doolins a J. I. Case. Others who rose above the Model-T class drove Buicks, Overlands, or Dodges.

Main Street Grows in a Hurry

But a Big Fire Destroys
An Entire Block in 1916

In January 1915, Walter Eaton & Ed Dunn, Oilton's first real estate firm, had set up a table and two chairs in the middle of the townsite and had begun selling lots. Louis P. Gowland bought the first lot and immediately began plans for a grocery store. Right behind him was Robert Keeler, one of the early arrivals from Avant. His lot was also on the south side of Main Street, a short distance west of Gowland's.

Albert E. Peck, also from Avant, purchased a lot just west of Keeler. Peck had dismantled his store at Avant and shipped it and all its fixtures to Oilton. Freight cars were overbooked with oil field equipment, and railroads held up all shipments except those with livestock. Peck bought a cow and included it in his shipment. It went through immediately. He established the A. E. Peck Hardware, Furniture, and Undertaking firm with a storehouse on Broadway a block to the south.

Phil Hall established his clothing store east of Peck in a building that was still standing in 1986. Sandwiched between Hall and George's Grocery on the corner was Sam Harrah, also from Avant, who became the town's first barber. Oilton's first well to provide running water for the business district was dug just behind the barber shop in 1915. The water was pumped by electric motor into a storage tank. Other early barbers were Jack Arnold and James King.

E. A. Reap started a drug store in the same block. Other drug stores that followed shortly were M. D. Butler, Palace, and Day's Drug. The First State Bank of Oilton opened in mid-1915 in a brick building on the southwest corner of Main and B. Streets with F. B. Abshire as president and Simpson Hurst, cashier.

The bank building still stands and in 1986 was Oilton's city hall. George's stone building remained a grocery store for half a century. George was succeeded by J. B. Hunt. In later years the Ballard Grocery operated at the location. Another store in the block was Miller Hardware.

This block was important not only because these merchants came early, but because it was the scene of Oilton's greatest fire. On February 17, 1916, two boys, Paul Peck and Lloyd Foster, were walking to town to go to a movie at the Bijou Theatre. About a block away, they saw smoke coming from the theatre's second floor. The film had caught fire. Flames spread quickly through the frame stores and the entire block except

Main Street Grows in a Hurry

A month after lots were sold in January 1915, Oilton's Main Street began to take form. *Photo courtesy Frankie Jo Posey.*

By May 1915, Main Street was thriving and railroad tracks were laid through town. This view is from the far west end of Main. *Photo courtesy Frankie Jo Posey.*

Drumright II, A Thousand Memories

the bank and George's Grocery, was destroyed. Most of the merchants had no insurance but they built again, this time in brick structures.

The north side of Main consisted largely of rooming houses and Syrian-Lebanese merchants seeking their fortune in the new field. These included R. D. Samara, N. Simon, Henry and Frank Barkett, S. H. Bayouth, and Richard Andeel.

Oscar Anderson started his Oilton career in construction, building small frame rental houses, but after a short time he established his Ford Agency that so many remember. At one time his agency boasted the highest volume of any Ford dealer in Oklahoma. In one shipment were 53 Fords, most of which had been sold in advance.

Two other familiar names in the automobile business were Harry Fogle, who operated the Chevrolet agency for years, and S. W. Colvin, who operated the first Studebaker agencies in Markham, Oilton, and Drumright.

Two Fancy Hotels

In 1915, work was underway on a modern two-story brick hotel on East Main, the Royal. Built by N. F. Cheadle, it provided lodgings for as little as $1 a day, or $1.50 a week. The Royal remained until the late 1930's when it was torn down and replaced by a new high school gymnasium. The long, rambling, frame McGeath Hotel, built by Maude McGeath, was completed about the same time as the Royal, just south of Oscar Anderson's Ford Agency on C Street.

Oilton's first newspaper was *The Gusher*, a lively weekly published by Eli Admire. It started June 16, 1915. Admire's paper did well through most of the boom era. One day he stopped for a chat with Albert Peck, the undertaker, about funerals. Admire gave Peck his ideas of what an ideal service should be. The next day he shot himself. In later years, *The Gusher* was published by E. Landingham and his son, Robert.

Everybody recognized Oilton's first transfer van. It was a wagon that resembled a truck bed. This was the Red Ball Transfer and its owner, J. W. (Bill) Goins, kept his team at a gallop as he moved heavy items around the oil field. For lighter hauling, Fred Harris' Santa Fe express was a smaller wagon that somewhat resembled an early-day hearse.

Other early-day businesses included Meacham Furniture, Katz Department Store, Fred Inman's bakery, Parker Jewelry Store, and two lumber yards, Clark-Bates and Long Bell.

Elbert Liked to Run

One young man who attracted attention was Elbert D. Howe. Young Howe had taken a special training course for soldiers at Wesleyan College in Cameron, Mo., during the war. After the Armistice, he looked for a job and Clarke-Bates Lumber Co. in Kansas City said, "Yes, we

Main Street Grows in a Hurry

A constant stream of wagons moved in and out of Oilton's Santa Fe yards carrying pipe, casing, and other oil field equipment. *Photo courtesy Frankie Jo Posey.*

can use a bookkeeper in our yard in the new town of Oilton, Oklahoma." Howe listened to the glowing descriptions of Oilton and excitedly boarded a train for Oklahoma.

He paled as he stepped off the train in Oilton. The muddy streets, the shotgun houses, the crowds of oil workers were not as glamorous as he had been led to believe. While he was debating whether to stay, the train moved on. He took the job with Clarke-Bates and he immediately attracted attention. Howe loved to run, and he ran everywhere. He ran in the sunshine, rain, or snow. He ran to the post office, the bank, the depot, and on errands. He ran until one day while running he looked up and saw Marie Harris. He quit running and started pursuing her. They were married in December, 1921. He became a construction superintendent and later mayor of Aurora, Mo.

The Doctors

Oilton people have fond memories of their doctors. Dr. E. E. White came with the first rush of settlers. Arriving shortly after that were Dr. George Ellis, Dr. J. W. Phillips, and then Dr. D. W. Humphreys. Beyond their medical practice, the physicians lent a hand in community

Drumright II, A Thousand Memories

The freight yard gave Oilton an almost metropolitan appearance from 1915 to 1920. Just beyond the yard are Day's Drug Store and Katz Department store. *Photo courtesy Frankie Jo Posey.*

affairs. Dr. Ellis and Dr. Phillips served terms as mayor. Dr. White was one of the founders of the Methodist Church. Dr. Humphreys was in 1918 elected first post commander of the Oilton American Legion post and later was chairman of the school board. Dr. Humphreys moved to Cushing in 1945. Other physicians who arrived early were E. J. Jones, B. C. Rutherford, and R. M. Cahoun.

Dr. Phillips had the greatest longevity. He began practice in late 1917 and was still practicing on a limited basis when he died in 1958. In July 1956, Oilton turned out en masse for "Appreciation Day for Dr. Phillips." The Drumright *Derrick* reported that several hundred people attended a picnic and evening program.

Dr. Phillips' wife, Jewel, was one of the first teachers and principals in Oilton junior high school, and she said, "It's a good thing I was. He never made any money. He had lots of patients, but he charged very little and if people had no money, he usually charged nothing. He took a personal interest in his patients and made house calls until 1956."

Among Oilton's early dentists was Dr. G. L. Long, a brother to former Louisiana governor and senator, Huey Long. Long was also a part-time police officer and shot an escaping prisoner. The first dentist was Dr. M. Greenberg, whose office was above George's grocery.

Main Street Grows in a Hurry

The Oil Exchange, notorious gambling den, once operated in the building with the awnings at Main and C Streets. West of it were Oilton Real Estate and the stores of A. E. and Richard Andeel. *Photo courtesy Frankie Jo Posey.*

The Lawmen

No sooner had the churches organized and a newspaper begun than demands were made for better law enforcement. It took a long time for the efforts to bear fruit, but people still remember their early-day officers. Among them was Joe Ryan, constable from Markham, who moonlighted as a security officer at the 49'er Club in Oilton; D. H. (Rabbit) Irwin, the first fire chief and also a peace officer who served for many years; Doc Jolliff, a roly-poly deputy sheriff, who carried a gun "about the size of a cannon" on his hip, and who toured the streets in an ominous-looking Model-T touring car with side curtains; and Ben Clark, who served as chief of police in Oilton longer than any other individual.

Clark was first appointed in 1928. The town had no money for a salary and collections were taken from business men to pay his salary. He was still chief of police at the time of his death in 1981. Clark was in several gunfights during his tenure. He was chief of police and Irwin a constable in August 1940, when they faced two escaped armed convicts on the western edge of Oilton. The story is related in another chapter. Clark is remembered by those who were young in the 1930's as "judge, jury, and executioner" of boys who got into mischief. When he caught

Drumright II, A Thousand Memories

	SANTA FE STREET	SANTA FE R.R.	C STREET		B STREET		A STREET	(HIGHWAY 99)	N →
FOURTH				ALBERT PECK HOME					
THIRD					WM MURDOCH HOME · METHODIST CHURCH				
WESTSIDE SCHOOL · MAIN		RED LIGHT DISTRICT · DEPOT · OIL EXCHANGE		POST OFFICE	MEACHAM FURNITURE		JUNIOR HIGH · HIGH SCHOOL		
BROADWAY		FIRST CITY HALL	GEORGE'S GROCERY · KKK BLDG	FIRST BANK · FIRST PHONE OFFICE	SCOTTIE'S CHURCH · BURNIES BARBECUE				
MILL · SECOND			OSCAR ANDERSON · McGEATH HOTEL		FIRST HIGH SCHOOL (STORE ROOM)				
ICE HOUSE · FIRST		RILEY HARRIS HOME					WOODROW WILSON SCHOOL		
drz				CHURCH OF CHRIST		TIPPIN GROCERY			

A number of Oilton's historic buildings are on this map. A post office existed for a time on Broadway but was moved to Main after a short time. Oscar Anderson started operations in a small frame building, but was best known at this location. Royal Hotel was just east of high school. *(Sources: Marie Harris Howe, Ray Harris, Ada Jackson, and Paul Peck.) Drawing by Dwight Zimbelman.*

Main Street Grows in a Hurry

Many of Oilton's first business people started in the 100 block of Main Street on the south side. This 1915 picture shows the Bob George grocery on the right and barely visible on the far end is the First State Bank. In between are Phil Hall's clothing store, A. E. Peck, M. D., Butler Drugs, E. A. Reap Drugs, and Miller Hardware. *Photo courtesy Marie Harris Howe.*

Almost all the stores in the previous picture were destroyed in a great fire on the night of February 17, 1916. The George grocery and the bank, made of stone and brick, survived. *Photo courtesy Frankie Jo Posey.*

Drumright II, A Thousand Memories

Main Street rebuilt in brick and concrete after the fire and Oilton High School students decided to celebrate by blocking traffic for awhile. *Photo courtesy June Taylor.*

a boy, he told him to go home and stay. If he caught the youngster out again, he would yank off his belt and punish him on the spot.

Mail service in Oilton was good from the beginning. At first, wagons brought mail from Jennings to Oilton, but direct service came as the railroad reached Oilton in mid-1915. Oilton's first post office was in a frame building first on Broadway and then on the north side of Main Street across from the bank. A drug store and soda fountain were in the front of the building. It opened for business on May 5, 1915, with Mrs. William Murdoch as postmaster.

The small post office served more than 10,000 patrons, all of whom received mail at the general delivery window or in boxes. Home delivery was impossible because houses had no numbers and some streets had no names. In 1917, the post office moved to the location remembered by most citizens. It set up in the ground floor of the Ku Klux Klan building. It remained there for more than 20 years. The present post office opened in 1961.

Oilton's first city hall still stands in the 300 block of Main on the south side, although it has not been used for that purpose for many years. Main Street was paved in 1924. Phone service came early, but it was unique. Few people had phones and calls were made to the main office. As the calls came in, the company sent Fred Harris out on the streets to locate the person being called. The latter came to the office.

'Scottie' Enters the Sin Dens

A Colorful Preacher Said, 'Roll 'em Once for Christ'

Hundreds of oil men were in and out of Oilton during the big oil production days. They came to make money and many of them departed millionaires. Others seized upon the opportunity to prosper through retail or oil-related businesses. But among those remembered most from Oilton's greatest days was a man who arrived without money, acquired none while he was there, and departed poor. He professed to have something "richer than oil."

Even grandchildren of Oilton's early citizens tell stories of Laurence L. (Scottie) Scott, and tourists visit the structure he built that is listed on the Oklahoma Historical Society's register of Historic Places, the First Baptist Church.

As a young man, Scottie was a highly skilled construction worker whose services were in demand. Of Scotch and Irish descent, he had a penchant for Scotch and Irish whiskey. But he often told of the day when he received the call to preach. He put aside without question worldly temptations and prepared himself for his mission. He studied the Bible late at night and prayed for the talent and wisdom to succeed. His prayers were apparently answered for he became known as a spell-binder pastor with a knack for attracting people. What he enjoyed most was bearding sinners in their dens.

Scottie came to Oilton in 1917 after a revival meeting in Drumright that drew large crowds of oil workers. Many Oilton people attended. They told Scottie, Oilton was wilder even than Drumright and asked him to hold a meeting there. Scottie rallied his brass band, and his song leader, Alba Wiseman. They set up on a Main Street lot Scottie had chosen as his revival site. For the first of many times, oil workers heard Scottie render on the street his favorite hymn, "His Eye is on the Sparrow." He also played the drum. To build his tabernacle, Scottie persuaded one lumber yard to sell half the materials on credit, and another lumber yard to sell him the other half.

His next move was to walk into the notorious 49'er Club, another dancing and liquor den operated by the Big Six, which also owned The Hump in Drumright. Scottie entered during the busy hour. He was greeted cordially by the manager and introduced to a number of "Cowgirls," the name given the 49'er dancing girls. He was told he could dance three minutes for 25 cents but had to buy drinks and pay extra for them. Scottie

Drumright II, A Thousand Memories

Oilton had no mail delivery in 1915 because streets had no names and houses had no numbers. For a time, as many as 10,000 persons came to get mail General Delivery. This is the first post office, located first in the 100 block of West Broadway and then across the street from the First National Bank on Main. *Photo courtesy Don and Cecil McKnight Corbin.*

eyed the steel portholes on the side of the west wall. Behind them were armed guards and he had been told that one man had been shot just because he reached for his handkerchief.

The manager was flabbergasted when Scottie explained he was a minister and had come to the 49'er just to invite everybody to his revival. Joe Ryan, a constable who helped keep order at the 49'er, overheard and said, "Preacher, hell! Let's shake him down and see if he has a gun."

As far as Scottie knew, no one from the 49'er came to his revival, but it was a big success and many oil workers came forward to be baptized. He and his wife were packed and ready to leave town afterwards when Bill Goins of the Red Ball transfer service caught him and told him he'd have to stay over. "One of the 49'er Cowgirls is upstairs in a rooming house with a dead baby. You're a preacher. It's your job to take care of things like that. She has no money or friends," Goins said. "You have to do something." Scottie and his wife agreed to help and the stayover lasted for more than three years. They helped the girl through her tragedy. Afterwards, the girl decided to give up dancing at the 49'er. She and her two sisters promised to lead a Christian life. Scottie called the event one of his greatest days. It influenced him to remain in Oilton.

The Dance Hall Fights Back

After the revival, Scottie held services regularly at the

Mail was at first brought in from Jennings by wagon, but by mid-1915 the trains reached Oilton. *Photo courtesy Frankie Jo Posey.*

tabernacle he built on the corner of the vacant lot. One of his first concerns was the number of young people who patronized a dance hall similar to the 49'er Club. To combat this, he organized a baseball team called the Baptist Batters and set up other youth activities. As more youths were attracted to the church, Scottie had handbills printed urging young people to come to the church instead of the dance hall. Night after night his youth groups passed out the handbills in front of the dance hall.

Angered at Scottie's tactics, the dance hall manager decided that two could play the handbill game. He printed a stack of handbills telling how much more fun young people could have at the dance hall than the church. Each Sunday night he waited outside the tabernacle and passed out the handbills after services. But as he waited at the tabernacle entrance, he could not help but hear Scottie's mesmerizing sermons. He began to show up earlier and earlier. On the sixth Sunday, he tearfully put aside his handbills and joined the church.

Once when he saw a sign "Barkeeper Wanted" in the window of a liquor den, Scottie went in and applied. A patron expressed shock that a minister would take such a job. "A man's got to support his family," Scottie replied. But as customers came in, Scottie told them in a confidential tone he had something much better than they could see on shelves behind the bar, but he would have to take them to the back to

Drumright II, A Thousand Memories

Dr. J. W. Phillips practiced in Oilton from late 1917 until his death in 1958. In 1956, hundreds throughout the oil field attended a "Dr. J. W. Phillips Day" to honor "the good little doctor." Dr. Phillips made house calls for more than 50 years, often without charging. On his lap is his youngest grandchild, Janet. *Photo courtesy W. M. Phillips.*

show it to them. After they passed through the door, Scottie pulled out a New Testament and told the customers of a happier way of life than they sought through liquor. He didn't last long on the job, but he made a few converts.

At other times, he was a familar sight in the Oil Exchange, Oilton's big-time gambling den. As the gamblers put stacks of bills on the dice tables, Scottie would hold up a paper bag and say, "Roll 'em once for Christ. It could bring you luck." Usually the gamblers smiled and dropped a few bills in the sack, especially if they won.

The Great Flu Epidemic

The influenza epidemic that almost devastated the nation in 1918 hit hard in the oil field. It came upon Oilton almost as a giant wave.

Scottie Enters the Sin Dens

Rev. Laurence L. "Scottie" Scott went into the oil fields, gambling dens, and bars seeking converts. Even those he never converted have fond memories of him. *Photo courtesy June Taylor.*

More than 50 died in Drumright. So many died in Oilton that no one kept count. People collapsed in their homes, on the streets, or on their jobs. At times there were so few able-bodied men that Scottie and Albert Peck, the undertaker, had to dig graves and conduct services. In 1956, Bertharee Scott McCourtney, Scottie's daughter, wrote a brief biography on her father entitled "Richer Than Oil." In it, she told the story of the epidemic.

Scottie knew that Oilton needed a building that would serve as a hospital, but none was available. Then one day a girl who worked in the red light district on the northwest corner of Oilton sent for Scottie. She thought she was going to die of influenza. She had heard of Scottie and wanted him to pray for her. People were surprised one afternoon when Scottie knocked on the door of the Queen Bee, one of Oilton's notorious houses. When the madam, who called herself Mrs. Bee, opened the door, she, too, eyed him suspiciously. "What you doin' here, Preacher?" she asked. "You come to close me up?" Scottie explained his mission and was permitted to go upstairs and see the girl. As Mrs. Bee and the other girls watched, Scottie knelt beside the girl and prayed. By morning, her fever had broken and she felt almost well. The girls were very impressed.

Scottie sized up the house and decided it was the nearest he could find to serve as a hospital. "You might as well use it," Mrs. Bee said. "All the men are sick and are spending their money for medicine. Business is awful." The girls agreed to help care for the sick, and Scottie soon had filled the entire first floor with flu victims. Some women who had been brought in unconscious, were aghast when they awakened to find themselves in the Queen Bee. But they mellowed when they observed the girls working day and night caring for the sick.

Near the end of the epidemic, as many recovered, Scottie and his family were stricken. During his stay in Oilton, he lived in several shacks and shotgun houses, always staying close to the center of town so he could be available for service. Oilton had no Salvation Army or other benevolent organization, so he and Mrs. Dollie Peck, Albert's wife, organized a Provident Society to care for the many needy. Sometimes, Scottie would run out of money and food for his family. He would turn his pockets inside out. Within a short time, baskets of groceries and envelopes with money would be left at his door. Often these were left by non-church members.

"He had more friends outside the church than in," Ray B. Harris recalled. "I had no formal religion, but I loved Scottie. He never managed to convert me to his faith." Sometimes Scottie made such friends preaching in the oil field. At other times he played pool with the oil workers, then stood on the pool table or a chair in the corner and talked about Jesus Christ. The workers never seemed offended and bantered with him when he dared them to come to church. When Scottie and his family were stricken, scores of Oiltonians lined up at his home to offer help. It was their expression of love and gratitude.

Building the Church

In early 1920, Scottie decided it was time to build a new church. Attendance had grown, and the people could afford it. It would be on the front of the big lot on which his tabernacle had stood for three years. He was a skilled workman himself and he recruited Tom Spradlin and his crew of rigbuilders to help. He did much of the work himself. At nights he quarried needed stone. The church is still in use, and on Oct. 27, 1985, the congregation observed the 70th anniversary of the building. The church has been certified by the Oklahoma Historical Society for listing on the state register of historic places. It has also been nominated to the National Register of Historic Places.

Scottie left Oilton not long after the church was finished, perhaps feeling his mission was completed. He first went to another oil town, Shidler, where he built a church, and when the Seminole field opened

The Riley Harris family came to Oilton in 1915. The oil field ended just short of his farm but he became a prominent watermelon farmer. His children were active in business and school affairs and four of them in 1986 provided much information for Oilton's history. Front row: Estene, Billie, Ray, and Mr. and Mrs. Harris. Back row: Lillian, Blanche, Lee Etta, Fred, Ollie, and Marie. *Photo courtesy Marie Harris Howe.*

in 1926, he went there and built still another Baptist church. He died in 1956.

The Methodist Church

While the Methodists had no leader as colorful as Laurence L. Scott, they were busily organizing shortly after lots went on sale in early 1915. They started with a Sunday School that grew into a full-fledged church organization by the end of 1915. Rev. M. M. Matthews was the first pastor.

The church met first in the front of a feed store building on Broadway that later became Shadrick's laundry. When Rev. Ralph Hudson succeeded Matthews after two years, he led a movement to get a new Methodist Church building. Eaton & Dunn, Oilton's first real estate firm, donated lots on the northeast corner of Third and B Streets for the church. Hudson and members of the church did most of the work as the church was built. It was believed dedicated in 1918. It is still at the same location nearly 70 years later.

In 1941 while Rev. Coleman Eckles was pastor, the Philathea Sunday School class built a women's parlor which also served as a classroom. The church membership then was 263. L. W. Taylor,

Drumright II, A Thousand Memories

Oilton's jail in 1915 was referred to as "the sheriff's henhouse." It probably seemed like solitary confinement to its inmates, but it was not much darker inside than the streets at night. *Photo courtesy Frankie Jo Posey.*

superintendent of schools, was president of the Men's Brotherhood; and Mrs. C. A. Johnson was president of the Women's Society of Christian Service. Mrs. W. K. Gayman had served as secretary-treasurer for many years.

The Methodists also in 1941 paid tribute to deceased members who had rendered dedicated service in the early days. These included Dr. E. E. White, W. L. Morgan, W. T. Sutton, Mrs. C. A. George, and Mrs. Elizabeth Wagner.

The Church of Christ

The Oilton Church of Christ had its beginning in 1918 when two families moved to the oil field from Cordell. Mr. and Mrs. J. W. Haynie and Mr. and Mrs. W. K. Cunningham had been friends and members of the Church of Christ at Cordell. The two men began work in the oil field and Mrs. Cunningham became a teacher in Oilton schools.

The Haynies and the Cunninghams decided they wanted a place to worship. They found a small frame schoolhouse about a mile west of Oilton and obtained permission to use it for Sunday worship. They felt that an evangelist was needed to stir interest in the church but they had

Elbert D. Howe ran and ran in Oilton until he met Marie Harris. In 1986, she was the only surviving member of O. H. S.'s first graduating class in 1919.
Photo courtesy Marie Harris Howe.

no money. Haynie sold one of his cows for $25 and wrote to Oscar L. Hays. He told him the $25 was all he could promise. Hays came and this became the first meeting by the Church of Christ in the western part of the county. Several were baptized at the meeting and attendance began to grow.

In 1920, the Church moved to a large tent in Oilton and invited W. L. Oliphant to hold a meeting. Oliphant was only 21 at the time but he was regarded as a persuasive evangelist. His song leader was L. F. Marten. Seventy-five were baptized during the meeting and it was like a new beginning.

Almost as soon as the meeting ended, work began on a permanent building. F. E. Pope, a church member, was a building contractor. He was awarded the contract for the church and completed it in a short time. Although the building has been remodeled several times, it still resembles the original structure and is still at the same location of First and B Streets.

Drumright II, A Thousand Memories

Church of God

Oilton's most attractive and modern church today is the Cimarron Valley Church of God, built in 1971 on the south edge of Oilton. It is no longer a part of the official Church of God family, but it is interdenominational. Members come not only from Oilton but from Drumright, Cushing, Yale and other towns throughout the area. Sometimes the pulpit is filled by ministers from other denominations.

This church grew out of the original Church of God that started meeting as early as 1915. Meetings began in an empty store building and then tent meetings were held in Silver City, Lagoon, and other communities. The original board of trustees consisted of George Means, Clint Baker, Kief Walls, J. T. Baker, and W. E. Gilwreath.

Some of the early ministers were W. M. Smith, A. H. Hammond, H. A. Woolman, J. D. Thomason, C. W. Coody, L. D. Hughes, Floyd Beasley, J. J. Coody, Hal Hooker, Russell Robold, and Jacob Wiens.

In 1935, the congregation built a church on A Street between Third and Fourth Streets. This building still stands but is no longer used. In 1969, Rev. Bill Ryan became pastor. Under his leadership, the new church was built in 1971. Reverend Ryan was still pastor at this writing, with Gary Krlin as associate pastor.

Scottie's Baptist Church just after it was built with him in front of it. The church is still in use and is on the Oklahoma Historical Society's Register of Historic Buildings. *Photo courtesy June Taylor.*

Scottie Enters the Sin Dens

The Methodist Church today still appears much as it did in this picture made shortly after it was built. It is still in use. *Photo courtesy June Taylor.*

Oilton's first Armistice Day parade was made up mostly of wagons and Model-T's. The sign reminds that speed limit is 8 miles per hour. It tells drivers to keep right and close their cutouts. Oiltonians turned out en masse at the railroad station to greet every returning World War I soldier. *Photo courtesy June Taylor.*

Oilton's First Schools

A Casket Storeroom Provides Atmosphere for Learning

Oilton's town lots went on sale in January 1915, and a big sale was held on Feb. 15. By May, the Main Street was bustling with activity and by September, something had to be done about the schools. Scores of young children had been brought to the community and there were no school buildings.

The situation was almost chaotic as classes were started in the fall of 1915. George Eastham was employed as superintendent of schools and he in turn found several teachers. Children were herded into several store buildings and shacks and school was underway. Only grades one to eight were taught the first year. There was no high school. If a pupil had already completed the eighth grade and needed to go to school, he was put in the eighth grade again.

But the town got busy immediately and by September 1916, a new school building was ready for use. Oilton named its first school Woodrow Wilson. The red brick two-story structure at the corner of Second and A Streets faced west. It was for students in grades one to eight. Julia Powers was its first principal.

High school classes started in September 1916. Eighteen freshmen and two sophomores made up the student body. Their life started happily in Woodrow Wilson building, but the school became so crowded they were taken out and high school was moved to two wooden store building rooms on the southwest corner of Broadway and A Streets. Ray Harris was elected president of the freshman class and became the first student officer chosen at Oilton High. C. D. Tribbey, a University of Oklahoma graduate from Blackwell, is believed to be the first to hold the title of principal of Oilton High.

The storeroom was equipped with a blackboard, a teacher's desk and desks for students. Tribbey taught a wide range of subjects, including history, plane geometry, bookkeeping, and general science. Tribbey is remembered as "handsome, very smart, and dignified," but one day, irritated as a student kept tapping an ink bottle on a desk, he grabbed the bottle and threw it down Broadway. All of the students watched intently as the bottle arched and landed about 40 yards away. Then came the day that Alta Mauzey, a sophomore, became bored with the lecture and peeped through a knothole in the back of the room. As she gave

Oilton's First Schools

The first school was Woodrow Wilson for elementary students. The two ruts in front of it have since become Highway 99. The school faced west at the intersection of Second Street. *Photo courtesy June Taylor.*

a loud gasp, Tribbey hurried to the back to see why. As he looked through the knothole into the adjoining room, he saw caskets piled from floor to ceiling. It was Albert E. Peck's storeroom.

High school students were overjoyed in April, 1917 when a second school building was completed. This was a junior high school between Main and Third Streets on the east side of A Street. This was immediately behind the present high school building. Although only a month of the term was left, the high school students left the storeroom and moved to new quarters.

An Unusual High School

In the fall of 1917, high school and junior high were held in the new building, but a new high school was on the drawing board. Educators and observers came from afar to see and talk about Oilton's unusual plan for a one-story high school building. It is believed to to be the first in Oklahoma. The structure was completed in time for high school students to move there in February 1919 and in time for a big moment in Oilton history, the first graduating class of O.H.S. in May 1919. Six students, five girls and one boy were in the class. One of them, Marie Harris Howe, still survived in 1986. By 1919 Oilton had 1,600 school children.

By the fall of 1920, Oilton had completed its town school system as West Ward School was opened. Located on the northeast corner of

Drumright II, A Thousand Memories

The junior high school, left, later called Roosevelt, was completed in 1917, and Oilton rejoiced when its high school building, right, was completed in time for the first graduating class in 1919. *Photo courtesy Frankie Jo Posey.*

Oilton's First Schools

Oilton High's first basketball team in 1918 had a winning season, losing only one home game. It was made up mostly of Terrills. L. to r., Ray Harris, Ralph Pulliam, LeRoy Stover, Omer Terrill, Valus Terrill, Jessie Terrill, and Paul Young. *Photo courtesy Fred Harris.*

Second and Westside Streets, the red brick school was also known as Eugene Field. It faced east. A school for blacks was started near the Santa Fe Depot. The Odd Fellows lodge used the first floor of the building and the school was held on the second floor. The few blacks who came to Oilton settled on the northwest edge of town.

Also in the Oilton school was a small school named Emerson at Crow, about a mile and a half south and slight east of Oilton on the Susie Crow oil lease. Many oil field children could walk to the two-room frame building that taught grades one to eight. Crow as a community could boast a general merchandise store operated by H. W. Straw, the Blue Front Pop Stand owned by F. E. Pope, and more important, a flag stop of the Santa Fe railroad. In bad weather, high school students could hop on the train, ride into Oilton and return in the evening. A concrete tornado shelter is the only remnant of early life at Crow today. The school building was moved to Oilton in the late 1930s and became Burnie Mann's Barbecue.

West Ward school completed the school system in about 1920. It had four rooms and a basement. It was also known as Eugene Field. *Photo courtesy Mary Ramsey.*

In spite of the rough life at Oilton, the schools offered comparatively high salaries and attracted outstanding talent from both Oklahoma A & M College and Oklahoma University. They were also well-equipped. When Woodrow Wilson opened in 1916, it had an outstanding domestic science department directed by Norma Hewitt of Oklahoma A & M. The labs had hot plates, high quality cookware, dishes, silver, and utensils. The department also had latest model White and Singer sewing machines.

Elementary pupils were taught music by means of a portable phonograph. Marguerite Blake, music supervisor, had studied in Europe and she brought Victor records that exposed them to renditions by Caruso, Galli-Curci, Madame Schumann-Heink, and many others. Singing patriotic songs and ballads was part of the curriculum. Mrs. Paris Perswell, wife of the superintendent, taught art classes. Children showed a keen interest in cultural offerings. Ruth Snell taught foreign language courses. These included Spanish, Latin, and French.

Religion Was Official

From the very beginning, religion was an official part of high school activities. Every Wednesday morning, students and faculty spent an hour singing hymns and listening to a spiritual talk by a minister, visitor, or teacher. Usually the program included a vocal solo.

While Oilton attracted teachers, it had difficulty keeping them. On the average, teachers stayed only two years and then apparently sought a more placid life somewhere else. The high school was like a revolving door for superintendents. Eastham stayed only a year and was succeeded

Oilton's First Schools

by N. Lloyd Morriset, probably in the fall of 1916. He remained until the spring of 1918. He was succeeded by Paris Perswell, who appointed Eugene Kile principal. Perswell left in the spring of 1920. E. L. Lounsberry took over in the fall and appointed a war hero, Ben Arnold, as principal as Kile became superintendent at Jennings.

Oilton changed superintendents again in 1923 as E. H. Lennox took over. The date of his departure is uncertain, but it is believed that Eugene Kile became superintendent in 1925. Kile had been a very popular teacher and principal. He kept the position until 1929 when he was succeeded by L. W. Taylor, a name familiar to many Oiltonians today. Taylor may have the longest tenure of any Oilton superintendent as he remained until the outbreak of World War II in 1941. Taylor was a leader in the Methodist church and other community activities. Taylor was succeeded by Harry Bradford, who had taught in the Drumright system for many years.

Outstanding Athletes

Much of the history of both the town and the schools went unrecorded because during many of the years Oilton had no newspaper and the high school had no yearbook. This was especially true of the achievements of high school athletic teams. Oilton often played the role of giant-killer. Even after the population diminished to 2,000, it was still playing Drumright, Cushing, Stillwater, and other larger towns in addition to Pawnee, Cleveland, and arch-rival Yale. While no records exist, Oiltonians still have some vivid memories.

These include:

— The early 1930's, when Robert J. (Bob) Troxel, bruising 200-pound fullback, tore up defensive lines of Panthers' opponents. Troxel was one of Oilton's first all-state players and is considered by some to be the Panthers' greatest player of all times.

— Two Oilton players, Otis Rogers and Jim Thomas, who helped lead Oklahoma University to an undefeated season in 1938 and its first trip to the Orange Bowl January 1, 1939. Rogers was a halfback and Thomas a tackle.

— The 1938 basketball team that went all the way to the finals in the championship play-offs. The Panthers lost to Norman in the finals. The team included Jack Lebrecht, Ralph Alworth, Marvin Moore and Robie Biggs.

— Leroy Flynn and Leroy Henderson, who starred in football for Central State University.

— Ted Corbin, all-state center of 1927.

— Backs such as Russell Childers, Pete Witt, Jim Todd, Marvin Moore, and the Peck brothers, Lloyd and Paul. The latter won all-state

Drumright II, A Thousand Memories

These five Oilton teachers taught a total of more than 150 years. They are l. to r. Ruth Chappell, who was honored in 1952 for 36 years of service, Jewel Phillips, wife of Dr. J. W. Phillips, Irene Collins, Faye DeGeer, and Ada Jackson. In the background is Roosevelt School. *Photo courtesy Irene Collins.*

honorable mention in 1924, although he weighed only 130 pounds.

—The Hulsey, Terrill, and Rogers families that provided a stream of talent for Oilton's teams for many years. The Terrills included Jess, Valus, Omer and Floyd. The Hulsey brothers were Howard, Oren, Garley, Buren, Beul, and Ed. The Rogers were Otis, Delmer and Edwin.

—Basketball talent such as George Daniels, Buster Andeel and J. D. Giddings.

Undoubtedly achievements of many other athletes would be recorded had there been yearbooks and a local newspaper.

Oilton's early schools, Wilson, West Side, and Junior High, have been torn down. The high school is still in use. In 1964 a new John F. Kennedy elementary school opened on the east edge of town with Ada Jackson as principal. In 1986, Dr. Dan Parker, superintendent, reported that Oilton had 210 high school students, and 191 pupils in the lower grades. The teaching staff numbered 21. Parker is a 1950 Oilton graduate.

What It's Like Today

Oiltonians Talk of the Past But Prefer the Present

Oilton is no longer the rough town it was in the boom days. At this writing, much was still there to remind one of the past. Descendants of early-day families still lived in Oilton. Paul Peck carried on the undertaking business his father, Albert, started in 1915. His wife, Fern Doolin, was a daughter of Wallace Doolin, who owned the big ranch east of town. Another Doolin daughter, Beulah, also lived there. Burnie Mann came to the oil field in 1915. His eating places were widely known for years. Mann was spending much of his time playing snooker at the senior citizens center on Main Street.

Lewis Lindsay, who lived in Markham in the boom days, was in Oilton, as was J. D. Tyree, one of the first pupils of old Buckeye school. R. E. (Sonny) Pope, whose father, F. E. Pope, operated the Blue Front Pop Stand at Crow lived in a new housing addition in Oilton, and his mother lived in the family home on First Street. These and others keep the history of Oilton alive.

Some of the old buildings were still around. The early First State Bank became the city hall and police station. The old Bob George grocery at the other end of the block was still there. Over the years it became the J. B. Hunt Grocery, Willie Pope Grocery, and Ballard Grocery. In the boom days, Hunt kept several monkeys in the display window. The Phil Hall building was still standing, as was N. Simon's building across the street. L. L. Scott's Baptist Church, was still in use.

On the south edge of town was a stone building that in the 1930's once housed a notorious gambling den called the Ledo. The American Legion occupied the building. A city park covered the corner on Main where the Oil Exchange and red light district once prospered. The historic Ku Klux Klan Building that had been an Oilton landmark for more than 60 years is gone. It collapsed during a 1985 spring storm.

In 1986, Oilton still had a neat Main Street with several thriving businesses. In the center of the block was a modern new First State Bank operated by R. A. (Dick) Sellers, Jr., the son of the man who wa co-owner of the Citizens Bank in Shamrock and later Drumright. An attractive modern drug store and two auto supply stores attracted people to the street. A new post office was built in 1961 next to Scottie's Baptist Church.

Drumright II, A Thousand Memories

Burnie Mann's Barbecue at the northwest corner of Broadway and A Streets was known for miles around, but the building is even more historic. It's the old Crow school building, which Mann moved to Oilton in the late 1930's. *Photo courtesy Burnie Mann.*

The First State Bank was completed in 1915 at the southwest corner of Main and B Streets. It now serves as Oilton's city hall. *Photo courtesy Frankie Jo Posey.*

What It's Like Today

In 1915, N. F. Cheadle built the Royal, Oilton's finest hotel. It lasted until the late 1930's when it was torn down and a new high school gymnasium was built on the site. *Photo courtesy Frankie Jo Posey.*

These men selling bonds during World War II were some of Oilton's best known citizens. L. to r., Dr. J. W. Phillips, Leonard Lauener, Jack Brazil, James Todd, L. W. Taylor, O. E. Wade, Dr. D. W. Humphreys, Bill Cook, and Anderson. Lauener was still operating a store on Main Street at this writing. *Photo courtesy Mr. and Mrs. James Todd.*

Drumright II, A Thousand Memories

New brick homes are around the outskirts of Oilton. The population was estimated at 1,000.

Oilton people are proud of their town and boast of its colorful past. Life is now centered around the churches and schools. The people follow the Panthers everywhere. A major center of activity is the senior citizens center where from 40 to 50 gather daily for lunch and games. Often they talk of the wild past, but most seem content with the peace and tranquility of the present.

Memories — Olive

First on the scene, where people came to stay

Susie Lacey, (l.) attended a log school and the first stone school in 1910. Loy Ann Gibson Carroll's grandparents, Roy and Maude Hallman, came to Olive in a covered wagon in 1913. She is a 1961 O.H.S. graduate.

Chapter V

Olive — First on the Scene

It Barely Missed Being a Great Rail and Trade Center

Pioneers of Olive take pride in displaying old maps of western Creek County that show no trace of Drumright, Shamrock, Oilton and sometimes even Bristow. These maps have "Olive" in bold face type. Although the community was never incorporated, it had its beginning before the turn of the century. There were no fences then and roads were wagon trails. Olive had a post office 15 years before the Wheeler well discovery started the Drumright oil field. In 1986, there were still residents of the Olive area who arrived in 1900 and they recalled Olive as the "metropolis of the prairie."

Olive received both a name and a post office on November 20, 1896. The post office was located in a double log house a mile west, two miles north, and another half-mile west of present Olive on the Charley Hayes farm. It was named for Olive Shelton, small daughter of Warren Shelton, the first mail carrier. The girl later took the name of her stepfather, and became known as Olive Didlake.

Mail came to Olive twice a week from Red Fork by horseback over the Old Red Fork Trail that went all the way to Guthrie. W. R. (Roy) Whitehead, who wrote a history of Olive in 1968, said that Washington Irving traveled this trail and through Olive on his exploration of the West. The first postmistress was a Miss Wharry.

With the turn of the century, immigration increased and the population grew. New residents settled to the south of the post office and it was moved one-half mile east and one and one-half miles south to near the northwest corner of the Frank Spencer farm. It remained there for a short time and then it was moved to the H. G. Matherly farm one-half mile east. About two years later, it was set up at the present site of Olive.

In about 1902, Olive was surveyed and platted. Lots were sold to business people of the town and the main business area was located at its present site about two miles north of the Happy Corner intersection of Highway 33. In his history, Whitehead wrote:

> Olive was the first town in the territory to have hard-surface streets. "Mother Nature" paved the streets with sandstone. Incidently, she forgot to smooth them. As a result, no one ever broke the speed limit nor did they get stuck during the spring rains.

Olive—First on the Scene

With the town center established, Olive became a thriving agricultural community. It boasted a cotton gin, blacksmith shop, hotel, hardware, drug store, doctor, saw mill, grist mill, dentist, pool hall, barber shop, four grocery stores, a justice of the peace, and a constable.

In the years that followed, postmasters included Jim Holeman, P. L. Baker, Sam Castleberry, G. G. Holcomb, Ruth Holcomb, H. G Matherly, Joseph W. Woods, and Mrs. Mary Mahan. Matherly was postmaster for many years and also operated a general store and filling station to serve Model-T Fords. Woods was Olive's last postmaster on permanent appointment. He served from February 1929 until May 1938. Mary Mahan then was temporary post mistress until September 1938, when the post office was closed and mail service was provided through Drumright Route 1 delivery.

School in a Log House

The first school in Olive opened in 1901 in a crudely-built log house one mile north and one mile west of the present community. Seats for children were made of split logs with a small shelf beneath for books. W. R. Whitehead recorded that the teacher, a Mr. Martin, was supplied and paid by the U.S. government. School terms then were only about four and a half months. Students who attended the first school were the children of Bill Glanders, Joe Spencer, John Whitehead, Monroe Hazlip, John Hillis, Armen Rusco, Mat Didlake, Walt Southward, David Hallman, Jim Holman, Lewis Staton, and John Newman, Oscar Terry lived in the community but had no children in school.

Olive's second school house was built in February 1905, about one block north of the present Baptist Church. Fathers of the school children cut logs and hauled them to a sawmill nearby. Then they hauled them to the building site. Classroom seats were made of 1 x 12 boards.

As the community grew, the buildings became too small, and in about 1910, a two-story, four-room native stone building was erected on the site of the present Olive grade school building. The community was proud of the new facility, but when cracks appeared in the structure, it had to be condemned.

Ethel Cook Campbell taught school in the stone building in 1916. She was valedictorian of Drumright High School graduating in 1916 when the first class graduated from the red high school on North Penn. Shortly after that she took an examination and received a teaching certificate. In the fall, she began teaching at Olive. In 1986, she still had many memories of Olive and community life:

> The school was a two-story building with two rooms upstairs and two downstairs. In 1916, we had three teachers, Mrs. Gayman, Miss Hall, and I. There was no teacherage so teachers roomed and boarded with a family in the community.

Drumright II, A Thousand Memories

Olive was named for this child, Olive Shelton Didlake. Her father, Warren Shelton, carried the mail to Olive on horseback from Red Fork in the late 1890's. She later took the name of her stepfather.

> Expenses were quite cheap then and so were our salaries. I received $60 a month, which was probably more than I was worth.
>
> Some of the prominent families there then were the Matherlys, Spencers, Holcombs, Woods, Cadenheads, Laceys, Daileys, Mahans, and Coils. Susie Lacey was a pupil then but not in my class. Hampton Dailey was county commissioner for some time.

Social life for the Olive young was limited in 1916 because few cars were available but as Mrs. Campbell recalled, the youths had good times anyway:

> There were many young people in the Olive community. We had good times at parties, etc. Some of the young men had teams and buggies, and sometimes we enjoyed an evening at a movie, or attending a "literary meeting" at a nearby rural school. The literary group served the rural community with entertainment, usually some music, recitations,

Olive—First on the Scene

The John Calvin Whitehead home near Olive still stands, although it has been modified since it was built at the turn of the century. Tom Slick and B. B. Jones stayed there frequently when they were exploring for oil in the Olive area. A family picture shows (back row) Herbert, Ray, Earl, Blanch, and Ralph, and (front row) Raymond, John, Margaret (Maggie), Howard, and Gona in her mother's lap. *Photo courtesy Myra Whitehead.*

and finally a debate on some silly subject. It had its purpose in the early days when other forms of fun were not available. It held a community together.

The school was torn down in 1923 and the stones were used in the foundation of a new red brick one-story building that is now used as a grade school. This was a milestone in Olive school history because in 1923, high school work was offered for the first time. In 1926 the school boasted its first graduating class. The four seniors were Daisy Hayes Hayter, Flossie Bruce Prince, Forest Holcomb and Stanley Holcomb.

In 1923 Olive's schools began to serve a wider area. Liberty School was annexed to Olive that year. Since then, other rural Creek County schools that have been consolidated with Olive include Rockdale, McClintock, Sand Creek, Cottonwood, Eureka, Pine Hill, Victors Chapel, and Buckeye. Some pupils from U.G. 5 and Shamrock transferred to Olive when their schools closed.

Olive rejoiced when a new high school building and gymnasium were completed in 1954. The old building became a grade school. On June 8, 1974, the high school was reduced to a shambles by the worst

Drumright II, A Thousand Memories

Olive had two log schools before this stone building was completed in 1910. Three pupils in this 1910 picture, Lonetta Cadenhead Whitehead, Susie Staton Lacey, and Ruby Trueblood Box, still live in Olive. Other pioneer names above include Holcomb, Rusco, Holeman, Dailey, Hazlip, Coil, Mundell, Matherly, Cadenhead, Smith, and Chandler. *Identifications by Ruby Trueblood Cox and Susie Lacey.*

tornado ever to hit the Drumright area. The gray swirling cloud about a mile wide hit first at Oak Grove School west of Drumright about 5 p.m. From there it tore through Drumright destroying more than 100 homes. It then moved eastward to Olive where it struck the Olive school buildings. Once again the community rallied and built a very attractive new high school and a beautiful gymnasium.

The Churches

At this writing, Susie Lacey had lived in Olive for 83 years. Her parents, Mr. and Mrs. Moses Lewis Staton, came to the Olive area in 1900 with the Armen Rusco family. Traveling from Newkirk in a covered wagon with two cows tied behind, the families forded the Cimarron River and arrived at a tract of land about two miles north of Olive. Staton chose the south side of the tract and the Ruscos took the north side.

Mrs. Lacey recalled how her mother, Jennie Staton, with the help of her 15-year-old brother, Oscar, started Olive's first Sunday school. At first, a group of about seven met under a tree, but after the log school was completed, it was used for Sunday School. One day in 1901 a Baptist minister came from Cushing to perform a wedding, and Mrs. Staton

Olive—First on the Scene

These "chicken coop" buses, named because the windows were covered with chicken wire, served early-day Olive pupils. At far right is Harve Matherly, perhaps Olive's most prominent pioneer. He was a rancher, farmer, legislator, retail merchant, postmaster, and school board member for 18 years. Denied schooling in his early life, he went to the stone school as a young adult and learned with small children. He came to Olive in 1897 and died in 1967.
Photo courtesy Okemah and George Matherly.

persuaded him to start a Baptist church in Olive. As the group became more organized, Willis Hurd became the first Sunday School superintendent. An itinerant Methodist minister named Sullens walked through the oil field and among the farms to reach those who chose not to attend church.

The Baptist Church became more firmly established in 1936 with the construction of a frame building in the heart of the community. This building lasted until 1974 when it was damaged by the June 8 tornado. The congregation went to work immediately and built a modern brick structure at the same location that is still the center of religious activity in Olive.

Olive—Then and Now

Except for a few quirks of fate, Olive might now be the principal trade center of western Creek County. In the early 1900s, several rail lines contemplated a route from Bristow to Jennings with a stop at Olive. This dream was forgotten almost overnight when the Drumright oil field opened in 1912. The principal concern became getting rail facilities into Drumright, Oilton, Shamrock, and Pemeta to service the great field. Olive was forgotten.

Olive also missed the impact of the oil boom. Some exploration

Drumright II, A Thousand Memories

and drilling took place in the area, and Thomas B. Slick used the John Whitehead farm as his headquarters periodically while exploring around Olive. Slick had little luck and neither did the others, and Slick told them success would come further west. It was he who discovered oil on the Frank M. Wheeler farm near Drumright in March 1912.

While it missed the benefits of the boom, Olive has remained one of the most stable communities in the county. Names of those who attended the first school are still familiar in Olive. The pioneers or their descendants are still around after more than 80 years. Such names include Whitehead, Rusco, Spencer, Lacey, Cadenhead, Hazlip, Mahan, Matherly, Holcomb, and Hayes. Probably their descendants will be tilling the land another 80 years hence.

Old timers can remember the businesses that once served the community — Doc Johnson's Drug Store, Granville Holcomb's hardware, Jim Frank Cadenhead's grocery, Dumus General Merchandise Store, Furman Mahan's Grocery, and the Winchester Hotel. All recall Harve Matherly's big general store of the 1930s, and some remember Matherly's filling station that serviced Model-T Fords.

All of these are gone now as is the post office. The nearest store in 1986 was at Happy Corner at the Highway 33 intersection. However, Olive has become a commuter community for a number of residents who drive to Tulsa and back. This has offset some of the loss.

Life in Olive is built around the school, the farms, and the church. The school, like the community, has remained very stable. Enrollment has fluctuated from 475 to 525. In 1985, Superintendent Tom King reported that 470 were enrolled. The beautiful Olive school gymnasium was the envy of other schools. Olive people are proud of their heritage, their community, and their school. They get along well with their neighbors. It has been thus for nearly 100 years and this is likely to continue for the foreseeable future.

Memories — Drumright

Very Special Moments, Historic Homes and Buildings, Babe Ruth & Sports Memories, The First School Days

The first school built in the great oil field still stands majestically atop the hill—a storehouse of Drumright memories.

Chapter VI

Very Special Moments

The Ice Wagon, Big Fires, Jackson Barnett, Etc., Etc.

Drumright was unique, even among boom towns. Out of hilly bare ground, a swarm of people searching for instant wealth created a new community, carved out streets across farms and pastures, lived in tents and shacks, and fought to survive without comforts that most citizens now take for granted.

Their experiences have been recorded in pictures, anecdotes, and even in poetry. In 1915, Mrs. Flora Snyder, one of the early arrivals, wrote what may have been the first poem about Drumright. Published in the April 2, 1915 issue of the *Derrick*, it told how proud even then the people were of their exciting new town:

DRUMRIGHT

There is quite a town named Drumright
   Mid a sea of derricks stands.
And you couldn't find her equal
   If you'd search through all the lands.
Less than three short years have seen her
   With her first white tent in view
When the oil which came so freely
   Gladdened all the working crew
How we've grown from few to thousands
   Is a wonder of the day.
Ah! how the pretty homes are growing
   Where the tents were in display.
And the new stone buildings towering
   Up toward the azure blue,
Tell of prosperous business people
   And their faith in Drumright, too.
Oh! they're coming! coming! coming!
   Spite o'heat, or mud or snow,
Coming ever on to Drumright,
   Helping us to grow and grow.
There are others taking pleasure
   Boasting of their wealth in oil
But there's none that can beat our town
   Nor can they the people foil.
So we'll sing a song of oil wells
   Rivers full of oil,
Great tanks, made of steel, full,
   Lakes dug in the soil.
See the eager workers, how they toil and toil.

>   Listen! pumps are pumping
>   Oil out of the earth.
>   Listen! gas wells blowing
>   And what are they worth?
>   Money! Money! Money!
>   Hear its jingling mirth!
>   Ha! Ha!
>
>   Mrs. Flora A. Snyder

While the poem offered a humorous view of Drumright, many of those who lived in the boom era cherish memories of specific incidents and scenes. In the early days of Drumright, truth was often stranger than fiction. This chapter seeks to preserve through rare pictures and interviews, many of those real moments.

The Ice Wagons Started Early

January and February were bitterly cold months during the oil boom days from 1913 to 1917, and there were cracks an inch wide in most oil field shacks. Sometimes the wind whistled around Roy Hulsey's house and through the cracks, and the snow was falling outside, but when his alarm clock jangled at 3 a.m., Roy Hulsey knew he had to get up. It was time to start delivering ice along Drumright's dirt Main Street.

The present generation may find it difficult to understand life without electric refrigerators and freezers, but in 1913 even business houses had to buy chunks of ice to preserve food and to keep water cool. Roy Hulsey was a Drumright ice man longer than any other individual. He started during the boom days and for 29 years delivered ice to homes and businesses. Each day he arose in time to trudge to the ice dock and start his delivery route by 4 a.m. His typical work day was 14 hours often ending at 9 p.m.

At the ice dock, Hulsey and his co-workers loaded the wagons, hitched the horses, and delivery began. Some of his fellow employees included P. R. Armstrong, Silas Stracener, and Harry James. Armstrong had been a friend since boyhood in Missouri of ice plant owner Pat Badger. He later operated a grocery store for many years next to the Tharel Hotel.

The ice company was first known as Petty & Badger and was located behind the 100 block of East Broadway which later became the site of the Oklahoma Gas & Electric Co. power plant. It soon moved to the edge of Tiger Creek not far from the old Santa Fe Depot.

Ice for the Kids

The wagons were usually loaded with 300-lb. blocks of ice, but there was an exception. One block was chopped up near the back of the wagon. This was for the children. On almost every block of Drumright

Drumright II, A Thousand Memories

Ice wagons and their drivers line up near the dock beside the railroad tracks. Dock is in the background. The long building in the foreground is part of the National Supply Co. Jokes about ice men and women customers aren't true, said driver Roy Hulsey. *Photo courtesy Patty Badger Hickman.*

streets in the summer, children watched for the ice wagon. As it came by, first one and another hopped on to ride a ways and pick up a chunk of ice. Some brought small red wagons and ran happily away as Hulsey placed a small block of ice in them.

Ice men delivered every day on Broadway and every other day to residences. Delivering ice to business houses was no great problem in the early days. "Most of the town was on the east end of Broadway then," Hulsey said, "and everything downtown was wide open. There were people on the streets, and stores were busy at 5 a.m. I usually had one load delivered by daylight."

From 1912 until World War II, Drumright citizens left their homes unlocked, even at night. If they wanted ice, they placed cards in their front screens that specified how many pounds. Often the family was still in bed as Hulsey entered the door nearest the ice box and made his delivery. He never saw most of his customers more than once a month. They left money on top of the ice box.

"All the jokes about ice men and women customers aren't true," Hulsey said, "They never flirted with me. I was too busy to get involved anyway. I didn't stay in one place long enough to talk to anyone. I just didn't have time."

Some Lacked a Dime

Many people came to the dock to pick up ice because it was

Drumright—Very Special Moments

A close-up of one of Pat Badger's ice wagons. Ice deliveries were made to business houses every day starting at 4 a.m. Some people needed ice to keep milk cool for their children but lacked a dime to buy 12½ pounds. *Photo courtesy Patty Badger Hickman.*

usually a nickel or a dime cheaper. They came in cars, wagons, and even on horseback. Some pushed wheelbarrows to the dock. Ice was 20 cents for 25 pounds off the wagon and 15 cents for 25 pounds at the dock.

In spite of the prosperity many enjoyed from the oil boom, times were very hard. "I knew lots of people who desperately needed ice to preserve milk for their children, but they couldn't buy it, Hulsey recalled. "They could have bought 12½ pounds for a dime, but they didn't have a dime."

To help these people, Pat Badger had his crew take leftover small blocks and chips and make a pile of ice shavings. It resembled a pile of snow. People came with buckets and small containers for the shavings. Some stayed near the dock and grabbed chips of ice as they flew from large blocks being cut up.

Hulsey delivered ice from 4 a.m. until 4 p.m., then worked on the dock every other night until 9 p.m. It was usually 10 p.m. before he returned home to set his alarm again for 3 a.m. "But," he said, "it was good money for those days."

The Courtship of Jackson Barnett

Of all the multi-millionaires who emerged from the Drumright

Drumright II, A Thousand Memories

Jackson Barnett continued to live in his tumble-down shack even after his Drumright wells made him the "richest Indian in the world"—until everybody else started fighting over his money. *Photo courtesy Archives/Manuscripts Division, Oklahoma Historical Society.*

oil boom, one name was publicized more than any other. Jackson Barnett was hardly aware of the commotion about him after he became known internationally as the "world's richest Indian" and everybody started fighting over his money. His "instant romance" and marriage were in the national headlines from 1920 to 1939.

Jackson Barnett was a fullblood Creek Indian who became owner of land on the southeast edge of Drumright when the Creek nation was broken up about 1900 and tribal members received individual allotments of land. After oil was discovered on his land, his wealth approached $10 million. The Jackson Barnett No. 11 well just off present Highway 16 not far from the Tidal Refinery became the first well to produce one million barrels. In 1918, F. A. Gillespie, who held a lease on the Barnett land, paid the largest internal revenue tax of anyone in Oklahoma, and Barnett bought nearly $10,000 in Liberty bonds.

All of this was exciting to the oil industry, but it never fazed Jackson Barnett. He was scarcely aware of it. He was illiterate and had been judged mentally incompetent by the Creek Indian Agency. Barnett lived on a small rocky farm on the outskirts of Henryetta. His abode was a one-room log cabin where he slept on the floor rolled up in a blanket. His only friends were his packs of hounds. He was an orphan and had little recollection of his past life, his parents, or whether he had ever been married, and he didn't care. He didn't know his age but he was believed in his sixties when the oil strike came on the Wheeler farm.

Drumright—Very Special Moments

When wealth poured in from his Drumright wells, Barnett paid little attention. He kept on living on his small farm. He had no interest in a car, clothes, or a fine home. But if Barnett didn't care about his money, everyone else did. Churches, organizations, lawyers and even the State of Oklahoma looked for ways to dip into the Indian's millions.

'I Love Jack Dearly'

Then on Friday, January 31, 1920, The Creek Agency received a call from Okemah. A middle-aged woman was applying for a marriage license and the man with her was Jackson Barnett. When the court clerk asked Barnett how long he had known his prospective bride, he replied, "Oh, I got acquainted yesterday. I liked her pretty well so I thought we would get married."

The agency persuaded the court clerk not to issue the license and a state-wide search was begun for Barnett. Another call came from Holdenville, where a license was also refused. The Agency, the guardian, and all those trying to get Jackson Barnett's money breathed a sigh of relief when the Indian and his intended bride returned to the farm Sunday after they were unable to find a place to get a marriage license.

It was then they learned that Barnett's fiancee was Anna Laura Lowe, divorced wife of the late Judge Thomas Lowe of Guthrie, former Secretary of State of Oklahoma. She had also been married a second time. She was involved in oil leases and said that was what brought her to Jackson Barnett Thursday. "He asked me to marry him and I told him I'd think it over and let him know," she said.

Then, at 8:30 p.m. on February 23, Jackson disappeared again, and another frantic search began. But this time, love apparently triumphed over all obstacles. Anna Laura and Jackson slipped across the border into Kansas and were married in Coffeyville. Jackson's guardian, Carl J. O'Hornett, and the superintendent of the five civilized tribes, Gabe Parker, were furious and pledged a fight to annul the marriage. They looked first at a Kansas statute that prohibited marriage between a feeble minded person and a person 45 years or younger of age. But Anna Laura had listed her age as 51. "And she doesn't look a day over 30," O'Hornett said. Jackson's age was given as 68 on the marriage license.

The new Mrs. Barnett denied she had kidnapped the Indian. "I love Jack dearly," she told a *Muskogee Times-Democrat* reporter. As Barnett sat by her side smiling happily, the reporter asked, "Do you reciprocate your wife's affection?"

"Sure you do, don't you Jack?" Mrs. Barnett prompted. "Uh huh," the Indian replied, and he made it plain he would not go back home without her. To make sure the knot was tied properly, Mrs. Barnett took him to Neosho, Mo., a few days later and married him again.

Drumright II, A Thousand Memories

Jackson Lives It Up

Thus began a legal fight that lasted for 19 years over Jackson Barnett, his marriage, and his money. Shortly after returning to Henryetta, the Barnetts built a new home in Muskogee and furnished it elaborately. Barnett began to smoke high priced cigars. Sometimes he was seen in a suit, white shirt, tie, and even shoes. He enjoyed rolling up in his blanket and sleeping in front of the fireplace. Often he napped there in the daytime. Jackson was learning what the Italians mean by *la dolce vita* (the sweet life), and what money can do. He appeared content.

After three years as legal skirmishes continued over the marriage, Mrs. Barnett moved the couple to Los Angeles. They purchased a $300,000 home on fashionable Wilshire Boulevard and a ranch in Coldwater Canyon. Here Barnett seemed happy as he divided his time directing traffic on the busy boulevard and tending his ponies at the ranch.

As years went by, efforts continued to keep various organizations and institutions from getting Barnett's money, and in 1928-1929, the old

Bert Wheeler came from the Bartlesville field and built the well-known Wheeler Hotel, which opened June 1, 1914, in the 300 block of East Broadway. He offered sleeping quarters for 50 people. He boasted the hotel stayed full and that it was "nothing to clear $250 per month." In 1916, he joined the police force and sold the hotel to James and Maude Salisbury.
Photo courtesy Ruth Salisbury Ruyle.

Drumright—Very Special Moments

Indian, now in his eighties, was called before a United States Senate Committee. The purpose was to ascertain whether or not he was feeble-minded and whether he had been duped into marriage. Although illiterate, Barnett made it clear to the committee that he was content with his marriage and said he wasn't ready to go back to Oklahoma.

Then in late March, 1934, U.S. District Judge William P. James declared Mrs. Lowe's marriage to Jackson Barnett void. He said the Indian was incompetent and didn't know what he was doing when he gave the marriage vows. Mrs. Barnett was furious.

"If those birds in Washington try to separate me and the chief, they'll think they've got revolution on their hands," she said in an Associated Press interview. "You bet I'm going to appeal." Mrs. Lowe said she would act as her own attorney. She ridiculed the government's contention that her marriage was illegal. "Humph for that. It was just as legal as any wedding ceremony ever performed. I just dare anyone to try and have it annulled."

And as for Barnett's mental status, she said, "The chief incompetent? That's a lot of baloney. He's not half as incompetent as most

The Wheeler Hotel dining room was considered one of the better places to eat while it was operated by the James Salisburys from late 1916 to 1919. All meals were family style. The Salisburys moved their baking and ice cream company to Drumright from Eldon, Mo., in March 1916, and set it up next to the Hotel. They later became known for their berry farm in Pemeta. *Photo courtesy Ruth Salisbury Ruyle.*

Drumright II, A Thousand Memories

of those who have been hounding us for 14 years. They said the chief is old and childlike—he's good for 50 years yet and I'm going to stay right with him as his legal wife and the guardian of his person. The chief thinks it's a bunch of hooey and I quite agree with him."

Mrs. Lowe lost her appeal but she was permitted to remain in the house and given a $2,500 a month allotment to care for Barnett. Then on May 29, 1934, Jackson Barnett died. He arose as usual at 5 a.m. and collapsed while dressing. The Associated Press gave his age as 92.

His Money is Divided

The legal battle over Barnett's money was mild compared to what it became after his death. He left no will, and hordes of people named Barnett emerged to claim his estate. Once Barnett's wealth had been $10 million, but now it had dwindled to about $1,500,000. All of a sudden, Barnett after death acquired nephews, nieces, brothers, and uncles who wanted part of his estate. One man claimed to be a son by an earlier marriage. Relatives said Anna Laura Lowe would seek half of the estate. The State of Oklahoma indicated it might try to get all of it.

It was five years before the case was settled. On December 16, 1939, U.S. District Judge Robert L. Williams announced the division

Broadway was alive with wagons hauling construction materials for new buildings in this scene, probably in early 1916. The water tower has been built, and the railroad is operating but has not yet crossed Broadway going south. Continental Supply Co. is in center at left. The first two buildings on the right are the Salisbury confectionery and the Wheeler Hotel.
Photo courtesy Drumright Oil Field Museum.

of the spoils. Anna Lowe was denied any of the estate. Judge Williams ruled that Barnett had never been legally married to her and that she was not entitled to inherit although she had lived with him for 14 years. The court used Dawes Commission records to ascertain that Barnett was the son of Siah Barnett, a full blood Creek Indian, and of Thiesothle, a full blood Creek woman. The estate was divided among three groups of descendants of this pair.

Justice may have been impossible in such a complicated case, but there was some irony in the outcome. Whether Barnett was kidnapped and dragged into marriage as the government claimed or whether he actually proposed to Anna Laura during their first meeting, his most contented years were those he spent with her. A considerable amount of his money was spent on him and the things he enjoyed. Those who claimed kinship after his death and who received shares of the estate were people whom he had never seen or heard of and who never came by when he lived alone in poverty on the old rocky farm near Henryetta.

The Jackson Barnett name is still well-known around Drumright. Water-flooding, a secondary process for recovering oil, has been employed in the last few years on the Drumright lease that bears his name. The No. 11 well that made history has disappeared but people remember it. Old-timers of the boom area still remember and talk about the courtship of Jackson Barnett and how it made national headlines for many years.

1916 — The Year of the Fires

It was at three o'clock on the cold morning of February 5, 1916 the fire whistle broke the stillness. Within a few minutes, the southeast corner of Penn and Broadway had become an inferno. By daybreak, three city blocks of business had been destroyed, three persons had burned to death, and 15 businesses were in ashes. This was the worst fire in Drumright's history and one of the three that made 1916 known as the "year of fires."

On the southeast corner of Penn and Broadway then was Ed Thomas' City Drug Store and above it the Lewis rooms. Down the hill to the east were the Klinger Cafe and H. L. Cohen Tailor Shop. The fire started in one of the latter establishments and moved quickly to the corner. The To-Ho-Ya Medicine Show cast that had been performing in Drumright was trapped in the Lewis Rooms, but finally escaped down the stairway. Dr. C. C. Cherry carried his wife through the flames to safety. Mrs. G. B. Wallace, a housekeeper at the Lewis Rooms, stood at the window screaming. A group of men formed a net below and pleaded with her to jump, but she fell backward into the flames and was killed. Fred Olwilder, a roomer from Erie, Pa., also perished.

Within a short time, the flames engulfed the big Western Supply Co., on South Penn where Dr. O. W. Starr's Clinic was later located.

Drumright II, A Thousand Memories

The most tragic and devastating fire in Drumright history started at 3 a.m. on February 5, 1916 and destroyed the entire 100 block of South Penn on the east side. Three were killed. *Photo courtesy Drumright Oil Field Museum.*

The company was operated by William Foerster, a former harness maker who settled in Drumright after buying a merry-go round and traveling with a carnival through Michigan and the South. At first he operated a two-story grocery store on Tiger Hill near the Stubblefield Funeral Home, but later he moved it to South Penn. The Foerster family lived above the store, but Mrs. Foerster was not at home at the time of the fire. In the confusion someone tried to save the furniture and a dresser became lodged at the top of the stairway. Trapped behind it was 12-year-old Hervey Foerster. Several men finally dislodged the dresser and rescued the boy just before the building collapsed.

2,000 Spectators Gather

As the blaze turned into an inferno, glass store fronts on the north side of Broadway began to explode. For a time, it appeared the fire might spread across the street. By 5 a.m., 2,000 spectators had formed a semicircle around the fire. Drumright had no fire trucks or professional fire fighting equipment. Firemen sought only to contain the fire. They saved the Majestic Theatre and the First National Bank.

As daybreak came, survey of the losses showed 14 businesses

Drumright—Very Special Moments

destroyed. On Broadway, those destroyed were the City Drug Store, Lewis Rooms, Klinger Cafe, H. L. Cohen Tailor Shop, Kentucky Rooms, Alifer's Candy Shop, Mertie's Pool Hall, and the Sanitary Barber Shop. On South Penn, the fire destroyed Western Supply Co., Star Electric Co., Gourley's Tailors, and Gillespie's Grocery & Meat Market. As it spread down Fulkerson Street, it burned the Rockhold Rooms and the Killum Rooms. None of the businesses was insured.

One charred body was never identified. For a time, firemen thought that Frank Glease of Shamrock, whose Horseshoe Cafe had been destroyed in a similar fire two years previously, was lost in the fire, but he was later found alive.

The Miracle of the Morrow Fire

Drumright's second great fire of 1916 also occurred in the early morning hours. The fire whistle sounded at 1 a.m. on Sunday morning, October 8. The town was still alive with Saturday night activities at The Hump, the Savoy Hotel, and other favorite hangouts. In a half hour, 5,000 people were watching Drumright's finest building, the Morrow Hotel, go up in flames. In another 30 minutes, the building was a heap

After daybreak, onlookers gather to view the ruins. The three who lost their lives were in a rooming house over the City Drug Store. *Photo courtesy Drumright Oil Field Museum.*

Drumright II, A Thousand Memories

of ashes and ruins. Along with it went the Western Union Office and Sullivan's Pool Hall.

The miracle of the Morrow fire was that six patrons jumped from upper stories, four of them from the third story, and all survived without serious injury. Bob Mayo received an injured hip in his third-story jump. Dr. S. W. Reynolds, his roommate, broke both of his arches. W. D. Hadley, broke four bones in his right foot. Before he made his jump, S. E. Settle, pianist for Ruby Darby, was severely burned about the chest and head as he saved $750 in cash and $1,500 worth of diamonds. Tom Ferguson leaped from the third floor and Mrs. Chris Glackin jumped from the second. Neither was seriously hurt. The only fatality was Gould Wright of Kankakee, Ill., who made his home at the Morrow. He was afraid to jump and he perished in the flames.

Once again the Drumright fire department with its primitive equipment was helpless. Fire chief Jake Marcus was visiting relatives in Texas and the assistant chief, Jim Klinglesmith, took over. The Strand Theatre, hotel, and confectionery were on the opposite end of the block. Windows in the building burst from the extreme heat, but it was saved.

The loss of the Morrow was felt widely in the oil industry. The hotel was a favorite stopping place of oil people and it had not had a vacancy for 90 days previous to the fire. The hotel boasted a restaurant, dry cleaning shop, steam laundry, ice and electric company, and a pop factory. Built in early 1915, it had everything but a fire escape. Its decor and apartments were considered elegant.

R. J. (Bob) Morrow, a co-owner, was visiting in Oklahoma City when the fire occurred. He and his wife lost all their possessions. He was carrying only $15,000 insurance on the supposedly fire-proof building and could not rebuild. The only reminder of the hotel today is Morrow Street, named for the hotel and for Bob Morrow. In 1918 the Morrow was replaced by the Roberts Hotel.

The *Derrick* Gives Warning

The Drumright *Derrick* was angry at the loss of the Morrow and adjacent buildings:

> This is not the first disastrous fire and the city and business men have been warned time and again. There has been enough property destroyed here by fire to pay for a hundred fire engines of the latest type. With the memory of thousands of dollars loss and at least one human life, and perhaps more, still fresh in their minds, how much longer will they procrastinate? Who knows when we will have another big fire and more lives will be lost? It is a proposition that should have attention, not tomorrow or next week, but today . . .

The *Derrick's* warning was prophetic, for on November 16, 1916,

Drumright — Very Special Moments

The Morrow Hotel was the pride of Drumright and the oil field. In its last 90 days it never had a vacancy. The Morrow had elegance and class in 1916. It had almost everything but a fire escape. *Photo courtesy Drumright Oil Field Museum.*

Drumright II, A Thousand Memories

Within 30 minutes after the fire started, the Morrow Hotel was enveloped with flames and collapsing. In an hour it was a heap of ruins. At least seven people survived after jumping from the third story. *Photo courtesy Drumright Oil Field Museum.*

One of Drumright's favorite eating places in 1913-14 was the Horseshoe Cafe on the south side of the 100 block of West Broadway, but it went up in flames on the night of February 12, 1914. Frank Glease was owner. *Photo courtesy M. H. Billingslea.*

Drumright—Very Special Moments

One of the clearest pictures of Drumright's most destructive oil fire also shows on the right The Leader, a department store, and Logan-Elliott, one of the first grocery stores. The picture says August 27, 1914, but the *Derrick* reported the fire started on August 24. *Photo courtesy of Ruth Salisbury Ruyle.*

Firefighters of Prairie Oil & Gas Co. rallied to fight the big blaze. Company officials drove up and down Broadway offering men fifty cents to come out and lend a hand. *Photo courtesy Drumright Oil Field Museum.*

Drumright II, A Thousand Memories

Smoke billows over Drumright on a stormy night as lightning strikes a 55,000 barrel tank. Electric storms were the frequent cause of oil field fires. *Photo courtesy Don and Cecil McKnight Corbin.*

just five weeks later, a fire that started in the Tony Rooms east of the railroad tracks, spread quickly and destroyed 10 buildings on East Broadway. The 1916 fires were tragic, but the town finally learned its lesson. In 1917, it built a city hall and bought modern fire equipment.

Where Streets Got Their Names

For a time after the oil strike in 1912, Drumright had only one identifiable street. Sometimes it was called Tiger Creek Avenue and at other times Main Street. The serious naming of streets began in January 1913 when Aaron Drumright and J. W. Fulkerson met with several other citizens to begin platting the new town. As Drumright's population grew rapidly, the town spread in all directions and many new streets were created in the new additions.

The main business street separated the farms of Fulkerson and Drumright. They decided to call the street Broadway. The first street south of Broadway was named Fulkerson and the first on the north was named Drumright. Harley Fulkerson's farm bordered on both of the other farms and the dirt trail running north to the Wheeler Camp was named North Harley. This later became the old highway to Oilton. As the town grew, other streets were named for oil men, oil sands, states, trees, and numbers. It was not possible to trace origins of all streets, but some are as follows:

Drumright—Very Special Moments

Artist Jack Allred used this view of the Roberts Hotel and Tiger Hill for the cover art. The hill was the northern border of Tiger Town. *Photo courtesy Corine Peterson Gaines, daughter of George Peterson, pioneer cafe operator, and Billie Linduff Collection.*

For Early Day Citizens:

Jones Street: Bernard B. Jones, Tom Slick's partner on the Wheeler No. 1 well, established his offices in that area. His brother, Montfort, was his associate. They called the street Jones.

Bristow: Bernard and Montfort Jones were joined by four of their brothers. All were from Bristow. And the next street east of Jones became Bristow.

Dale: Dale Shaffer and his wife lived at the end of North Penn where it now curves and becomes Dale Street. Shaffer was a brother of Charles B. Shaffer, who financed the discovery well. He maintained several horses and vehicles at his shotgun house to help transport workers to the oil field. He named the street Dale.

Shaffer: Shaffer was also instrumental in the naming of the street south of Dale. Whether he sought to honor himself or his brother, Charles, is uncertain, but possibly both.

Drumright II, A Thousand Memories

Bernard B. Jones, Tom Slick's partner in the Wheeler No. 1 well, was largely responsible for naming Jones and Bristow Streets. He and his five brothers were from Bristow. *Photo courtesy Velma Jones Collins.*

Stiner: Edward Steiner was an oil speculator who came from Chicago with Charles B. Shaffer. He died not long after the field was discovered. Over the years the "e" disappeared from the street name.

Smather: Smathers was the partner of Charles B. Shaffer in his Chicago office. His first name does not appear in accounts of Shaffer's activities.

Morrow: In 1915, construction began on the elegant new hotel called the Morrow. It was built by R. J. Morrow and "Doc" White. The street running north and south beside it became Morrow.

For oil sands:

Layton, Skinner, Tucker, and Bartlesville Streets all bear the names of oil sands. The Layton sand was established in the Cleveland field, Tucker came from a strike on the Fred Tucker farm east of Drumright, and Bartlesville from explorations just at the turn of the century near that town, which was named for Jacob Bartles.

For states:

The principal street intersecting Broadway was called Pennsylvania because so many early arrivals at Drumright were from the Pennsylvania oil fields. Streets east of Penn running north and south, except for Harley, were given the name of other states. These included Ohio, Kentucky, Virginia, Texas, California, Maine, and Oklahoma.

For trees:

Streets north of Drumright to Shaffer Street running east and west were named for trees—Walnut, Oak, Hickory, Cherry, Maple and Pine.

Numbered Streets:

Streets on the south part of Drumright are numerical, from First to Sixth. The author was unable to ascertain the origins of Federal and Noble Streets just south of Broadway or of Duke Street on the east side. Wood was believed named for T. J. Wood, oil explorer and father-in-law of W. E. Nicodemus.

Tiger Town Streets

In the beginning the southwest part of Drumright was called Tiger and Tiger Town, named by William E. Dunn. The steep hill leading to the area became Tiger Hill. It is possible that Dunn was responsible for the naming of Cimarron, Grand, and Creek Streets.

Later Names:

In January 1950, work began on Drumright's first major housing addition in many years, Country Club Heights. John Chronister headed the Drumright Development Co., which also included M. J. (Jim) Barris, J. D. Gibson, and John Griffith. When the project was completed, streets were named Chronister, Barris, Gibson, Griffith, and Clara Lee. The latter was Barris' wife, who had taught in Drumright elementary schools. Barris was a Santa Fe agent, Gibson an automobile salesman, and Griffith and his wife operated a boarding house at the Tide Water refinery. Chronister was formerly in the car business and also built Drumright's first motel.

The latest street named was Lou S. Allard Drive, which extends from South Pennsylvania southwest to the city limits. Originally it was called the "old Cushing Road" and Fairgrounds Drive. It was later changed to honor Lou S. Allard, Jr., who died in 1974. Allard's father owned the Drumright *Derrick* for many years, starting in 1916. Lou, Jr., was associated with the *Derrick* for many years and was a publisher from 1946 to 1974.

For many around the state, Allard's name was synonymous with Drumright. He had been president of the Oklahoma Press Association, president of the state Junior Chamber of Commerce, and a member of the state legislature for many years. He had also headed many organizations in Drumright.

J. M. Haggar in Drumright

Of the thousands who passed through Drumright at the peak of the oil boom, many later achieved prominence for the roles they played in the oil industry. But there were also those who went on to fame and fortune in other enterprises. Among these was Joseph Marion Haggar. Haggar became known as the dean of the textile industry in the United States, and his company the largest producer of men's dress slacks in the world.

Drumright II, A Thousand Memories

J. M. Haggar and Rose Wasaf at their wedding in Bristow in 1915. He introduced "wash 'n wear" and "double-knit" to the clothing industry. *Photo courtesy J. M. Haggar.*

In late 1914, Haggar was employed in the K. Wasaf clothing store in Drumright. It was probably romance that brought him to Drumright. In St. Louis he met Rose Wasaf. When her family came to Drumright, Haggar followed them. He and Rose were married in 1915. He was 23 at the time.

After leaving Drumright, Haggar was associated with Ely & Walker, one of the nation's largest dry goods companies, in St. Louis, and with King Brand Overall Company in Dallas. At age 34, Haggar decided to try for his dream, which was to manufacture separate dress slacks by mass production that could be sold at lower prices. He introduced the words "wash n' wear," and "double-knit" to the clothing industry.

A native of Lebanon, Haggar came to America in 1905 at age 13. He was penniless and unable to speak English. In 1976, he received the Horatio Alger Award and an honorary Doctor of Laws degree from Notre Dame. At age 91, Haggar's memories of Drumright were vague, but he had some advice for success: "Don't expect to get something for nothing. You've got to work hard, be honest, and accept opportunities that come to you. And you've got to have faith in God, in your country, and in people . . . It's work, honesty, and faith that make for success."

Drumright—Very Special Moments

The strain of pulling heavy oil field equipment caused horses to collapse and die. This occurred often on Drumright's muddy Main Street in the early days. They were dragged to a ditch and covered with dirt. *Photo courtesy Don and Cecil McKnight Corbin.*

This early bathroom facility was one of Drumright's more expensive types, especially reinforced. It probably cost $15. Other models were available for as low as $5. *Photo courtesy Drumright Oil Field Museum.*

Drumright II, A Thousand Memories

Drumright's first undertaker (and also first fire chief) Jacob Marcus, and the Strand Theatre, the town's finest, were on the opposite end of the block from the Morrow Hotel. The sign on the utility pole at left in this 1916 scene announces that the First National Bank is moving to the northwest corner of Ohio and Broadway. *Photo courtesy Drumright Oil Field Museum.*

Drumright's first veterinarian, Dr. L. H. Cravens, had offices in the Tri-State Livery, one of the town's best. It was next door to the Masonic Temple. With from 800 to 1,000 teams operating in the oil field, the veterinary practice was good from 1912 to 1917. *Photo courtesy C. W. Spangler.*

Drumright—Very Special Moments

Labor Day in Drumright once meant a parade and celebration. In 1919, East Broadway was a busy part of town although it had not converted to brick buildings. *Photo courtesy Billie Linduff Collection.*

This impressive new building once stood on the site of the present Drumright post office. On the ground floor was Williams Grocery, one of the first, and above it was the well-known Travelers Hotel. The building was torn down in the 1930's. *Photo courtesy Drumright Oil Field Museum.*

Drumright II, A Thousand Memories

Titsworth's, the first variety store, was described as the busiest place in town in 1914. It had as much merchandise on the sidewalk as inside. Business at the tent store next door was beginning to lag as new arrivals were moving into wooden shacks instead of tents. The stores were in the 100 block of East Broadway on the north side. *Photo courtesy Wilma Kincaid Allard.*

Drumright—Very Special Moments

The Hughes Tool house served as a church for the First Baptist congregation in 1916, but plans were underway for a new brick building on the same site. In center is Rev. R. W. Lackey, the new pastor. In front of him are Gladis, Dorothy and Zola Dix. Far right is Hubert Rust and his sister, Lois. To their left is Mrs. W. F. Tannehill. Leaning against post is Clyde Robb and next to him wearing cap is Bill Shibley. Upper left with moustache is W. L. Dix, an original board member. *Photo courtesy Gladis Dix Brill.*

BEWARE!

All ye people of the Earth: There is but one and only Ku Klux Klan; therefore,

SHUN

as a poisonous serpent any other organization of similar name. We warn you,

BEWARE!

IMPERIAL
PALACE
INVISIBLE EMPIRE
Knights of the Ku Klux Klan
ATLANTA
GEORGIA

INVISIBLE EMPIRE
Knights of the Ku Klux Klan
(Incorporated)

The following is taken from the Constitution and Laws of the Order
OBJECTS AND PURPOSES.
ARTICLE II.

Section 1. The objects of this Order shall be * * a common brotherhood of strict regulations for the purpose of cultivating and promoting real patriotism toward our Civil Government; to practice an honorable clanishness toward each other; to exemplify a practical benevolence; to shield the sanctity of the home and the chastity of womanhood; to maintain white supremacy; to teach and faithfully inculcate a high spiritual philosophy through an exalted ritualism, and by a practical devotedness to conserve, protect and maintain the distinctive institutions, rights, privileges, principles and ideals of a pure Americanism.

Section 2. To create and maintain an institution by and through which the present and succeeding generations shall commemorate and memorialize the great sacrifice, chivalric service and patriotic achievements of our original Society—the Ku Klux Klan of the Reconstruction period of American history. * * *

Section 3. This Order is an institution of Chivalry, Humanity, Justice and Patriotism; embodying in its genius and principles all that is chivalric in conduct, noble in sentiment, generous in manhood and patriotic in purpose; its peculiar objects being: First—To protect the weak, the innocent, and the defenseless, from the indignities, wrongs and outrages of the lawless, the violent and the brutal; to relieve the injured and oppressed; to succor the suffering and unfortunate, especially widows and orphans. Second—To protect and defend the Constitution of the United States of America, and all laws passed in conformity thereto, and to protect the States and the people thereof from all invasion of their rights thereunder from any source whatsoever. Third—To aid and assist in the execution of all constitutional laws, and to preserve the honor and dignity of the State by opposing tyranny, in any and every degree attempted from any and every source whatsoever, by a fearless and faithful administration of justice; to promptly and properly meet every behest of Duty "without fear and without reproach."

Officially adopted September 29, 1916, A.K. L.

These brochures distributed in Drumright in 1921 were "an urgent call to real men from the Imperial Palace of the Knights of the Ku Klux Klan." They purported to bring "Words of timely Wisdom from the soul of the great Imperial Wizard, who out of Mystic Darkness, brings light." Hundreds of oil field men apparently heeded the call.

Historic Homes and Buildings

If Only They Could Talk, What Stories They'd Tell

Homes built by Drumright pioneers from 1913 to 1929 are still among the most impressive in town, and old buildings are among the sturdiest. Many of them are still in use today. They are silent witnesses to the oil field's past.

No stone or brick buildings existed in Drumright until 1914. Then came the conversion from frame structures to permanent buildings at the top of the hill on East Broadway. The Aaron Drumright building, the Drumright State Bank, and Burney Brasel's Drug Store led the way and others followed quickly. In 1916, as a result of many fires, the city required that new street buildings be stone or brick.

By 1915, the J. W. Fulkerson building at Ohio and Broadway was completed. A year later the new post office on North Ohio Street on the west side was ready for use and the First National Bank building was completed. Harley Fulkerson began construction on his new office building.

Tents, box car houses, and shotgun houses were the abodes of even the most affluent Drumright citizens until late 1914. The Drumright *Derrick* wrote on May 2, 1913, ". . . the home building spirit has begun and rapidly our little rag homes will vanish . . . until every street will show the sign of thoroughly progressive home builders." By late 1914, impressive homes were appearing on Tiger Hill and in Tiger Town.

Drumright women were deliriously happy in 1914, when the city built a sewer system. Two of them, Mrs. H. W. Slover, and Mrs. W. E. Nicodemus, announced plans for twin modern bungalows on Wood Street. They were even more ecstatic when P. J. Stephenson and Andy Reid brought to town impressive contraptions called bathtubs. Until then, everybody bathed in a wash tub. The *Derrick* was overjoyed and asked that Mrs. Slover and Mrs. Nicodemus be adored with special laurels for "construction of the first modern homes in Drumright, the fountain of oil and pride in Oklahoma."

In this chapter are pictures of many early structures, some dating back to 1913. Homes occupied by Aaron Drumright, J. W. Fulkerson, P. J. Stephenson, W. E. Nicodemus, and other pioneers are still in use. Pictures of other historic buildings are included in the Ben Russell collection in another chapter. Still others were in the first Drumright book. Lack of space prevented including many others.

Drumright II, A Thousand Memories

Obscured by shrubbery and almost forgotten is this historic building across the street south of Second Ward school at South Cimarron and Wood Streets. On one end of the building in 1913 were the offices of Gypsy Oil Co., and on the other was the office of Thomas B. Slick, who brought in the Wheeler No. 1 well. The structure existed before the school was built in 1914. After the boom, it was converted to apartments. *Photo by author.*

Historic Homes and Buildings

After the 1916 fire demolished the Lewis Rooms at Broadway and Penn, C. K. Lewis sold the lots to G. W. Canfield of Yale, who built the Canfield Building. Once a bowling alley and later the Drumright *Journal* operated in the basement. The appendage on top may be as historic as the building. It served as a beacon light for police before their cars had radios. When the light was on, it meant, "There's trouble. Hurry back to the station." *Photo by author.*

Two historic Drumright buildings stand side-by-side. Harte-Ashwell operated a dance studio in the frame building at 212 West Broadway and next to it was the Salvation Army "citadel," dedicated in 1921. It cost $9,000. A brief history of the studio and Salvation Army are in the first Drumright book. *Photo by author.*

Drumright II, A Thousand Memories

Drumright's first hospital opened in 1915 on California street, but a second one in this building at 400 E. Broadway was a much bigger facility. It boasted a dozen physicians headed by Dr. S. Woodson Reynolds, and modern surgical facilities. Across the street west was B. F. Miller's Norfolk Hardware, established in 1916. *Photo by author.*

The J. W. Fulkerson family lived at this home at 508 E. Broadway even before the 1912 oil discovery. A smaller home was here when Fulkerson arrived in 1907 and he replaced it with this one. Most of the 11 Fulkerson children lived here while attending Third Ward school. *Photo by author.*

Historic Homes and Buildings

The dedication of R. J. Massad's new brick Boston Store in 1916 was a big event in Drumright. The building was changed in the intervening 70 years but it's still standing at 121 E. Broadway. At the dedication are Joe Solon, Shoy and Jimmy Massad, two children, R. J.'s mother, Mrs. R. J. (Lemya) Massad, and R. J. *Photo courtesy Tom J. Caldwell.*

At the crest of Tiger Hill were many impressive early-day homes. The C. B. Stubblefield Funeral Home was the first in Drumright not a part of some other business. East of it were the homes of B. F. Miller, who started the Norfolk Hardware in 1916, Elmer J. Campbell, who, with Leroy Brown, operated a furniture store next to the J. W. Fulkerson building, and James G. Bennett, owner of the Idle Hour and Strand Theatres for many years. *Photo by author.*

Drumright II, A Thousand Memories

Aaron Drumright first lived in a home at Maple and Smather Streets, but in 1916 he sold the home and took his family to Colorado for several months for his wife's health. He returned a few months later and purchased this home at 128 E. Dale near the new red high school. The family lived here for several years. *Photo by author.*

Several generations of the DeBakey family, early-day merchants, lived at 605 East Broadway, but before that Stokes Jones, one of the six Jones brothers from Bristow, owned a mule barn there operated by Millard McGinnis. *Photo by author.*

Historic Homes and Buildings

Several prominent Drumrighters lived in this imposing home at 403 South Creek. Dr. C. E. Kahle, one of the earliest physicians was first. Aaron Drumright later moved there from Dale Street. When Drumright decided to move to his farm in Parsons, Kansas in 1937, L. E. Shanks, long time real estate and insurance agent, purchased the property. The Shanks family lived there for many years. *Photo by author.*

A landmark is this stone home built on the west edge of Drumright in 1925 by Mr. and Mrs. Harry Moore. It is near the former site of The Hump. After a year, the Moores traded the home to Dr. O. W. Starr. Present owner (in front of house) is Howard Huff, former druggist and civic worker. Mrs. Moore, now Mrs. Arnold Scheer, recalls how large centipedes were attracted by the stones for a time and tried to invade the home. *Photo by author.*

Drumright II, A Thousand Memories

This home at 203 N. Jones once was at the corner of North Harley and East Drumright Streets on the site of the present Church of God. Harley Fulkerson built it and lived there in 1916 while he operated a wagon yard. At the time of the oil discovery, Fulkerson's farm extended from North Ohio Street east to California Street and from Broadway north to Oak Street. *Photo by author.*

Still one of Drumright's most attractive homes is this residence at 115 South Creek. The house was originally planned for W. C. French, who became superintendent of schools in 1917, but he decided to build on South Bristow. W. E. Nicodemus, Drumright's first mayor, then became its first occupant. When he left Drumright in 1931, John Paul Jones purchased it. Jones came to the oil field in 1913 with Charles B. Shaffer. The Jones family remained through most of the 1930's, and then it became the home of Mr. and Mrs. R. A. (Dick) Sellers. The Edgar Vice family resided there at this writing. *Photo by author.*

Historic Homes and Buildings

Most Drumrighters remember this building at 323 East Broadway as the Paul Wallman Battery Shop but it was actually the first Church of Christ, built in 1917. *Photo by author.*

This home and yard at 505 N. Cimarron were as elegant in 1986 as in 1917 when it was built by P. J. Stephenson, Sr., Drumright's first city clerk and co-owner of the first retail store in 1912. Living there and maintaining the beauty of the property was P. J. Stephenson, Jr. *Photo by author.*

Drumright II, A Thousand Memories

This place at 121 N. Creek was considered home to six generations of one Drumright family. A. J. (Andy) Reid built it in about 1917. It's indoor bath facilities made it a rarity. Above with Reid is his daughter, Mae Reid Harrington, his wife, and his granddaughter, Lorene Wood Davenport, mother of June Blackwell and Wilma Mills. Four generations of the family attended Drumright High School. The sunburst above windows had to be covered during World War II because of its Japanese look. *Photo courtesy June Blackwell.*

Well-known Drumright families have lived in this home at 128 E. Cherry since it was built in 1917 by C. I. Maxwell, early-day grocer, a founder of the First Christian Church, and one of the first city councilmen. Later residents have been the P. C. Beardsley and D. C. (Coin) Sellers families. Present occupants are Cleo and Cora Lee (Corky) Hutchison. Hutchison is also a grocer and served as mayor of Drumright from 1949-1961. *Photo by author.*

Historic Homes and Buildings

The former home of Fred Way at 115 N. Cimarron overlooks the city park that bears his name. Way owned the Chevrolet agency in the early 1930's and devoted much of his time to working for the betterment of Drumright. *Photo by author.*

Pat O'Tracy, early day peace officer and justice of the peace, lived at 501 South Skinner. He also managed the Tidal baseball team in the early 1920's. Trimming the shrubs is David Hart, present resident. *Photo by author.*

Drumright II, A Thousand Memories

The Tidal Refining Co. (later Tide Water) was Drumright's biggest employer for years. It was built in 1920. Its superintendents, Harry Beck, Rowland Stanfield, L. M. Jagou, and Ralph Boyd lived in this company home near the office southeast of town. It was vacant at this writing. *Photo by author.*

The Cities Service Co. rooming and boarding house north of Drumright was one of many in the oil field, even into the 1930's. Once a row of lease homes were adjacent to it. In 1986, Northeast Central Pipeline Co. owned the property and Don Rickner, district operator, lived in the house. *Photo by author.*

Historic Homes and Buildings

A few houses still remain on the Cushing Gasoline Co. and Pure Oil camp on the southeast edge of Drumright. Fred Robinson made a nostalgic visit to the site where he lived while attending high school 50 years ago. Family names on the lease included Ed Fox, C. A. French, Cole Downing, H. C. Cooper, L. B. Lankford, Everett Bump, Bill Shepherd, W. H. Penland, Sherman Uptegraph, Marvin Robinson, and Clarence Carnahan. *Photo by author.*

One of Drumright's finest early homes was built by Boyd L. Blackstock at 528 N. Ohio in about 1914 or 1915. Young Blackstock camped in a tent at Bald Hill near Tiger School when he arrived in 1912 from Resaca, Ga. Hundreds of horseshoes are in the concrete around the home. Blackstock obtained them from the Tri-State Livery and used them to reinforce the concrete. He helped build the Roberts Hotel and many other Drumright homes. *Photo by author.*

Drumright II, A Thousand Memories

A good time was being had by all at this party at the Bart Foster home at 320 West Oak in 1928. Foster was Drumright's second city clerk, an early-day county commissioner, and interim D. H. S. football coach during the 1918 flu epidemic. Party-goers, front row, include P. J. Stephenson, Jr., Bob Foster, C. B. Stubblefield, V. C. Arnspiger, and P. J. Stephenson, Sr. Second row, (left) is Lawrence (Stevie) Stephenson, and behind him Schley Ferguson. Far right, second row, is Pat Cawley, and on top row are Dr. O. W. Starr and Homer O'Dell. Others include Mrs. Ruth Williamson, Second Ward teacher, and her sister, Pearl Head, and Elmer J. Campbell. Mr. and Mrs. James L. Shanks lived in the home at this writing. *Photo courtesy Jennie Houser and Mr. and Mrs. Cleo Hutchison.*

Babe Ruth and Sports Memories

And Eph Thomas, the 20-Mile Race,
D. H. S. Iron Men, the Old Gym, Etc.

Drumright was a hotbed of baseball activity in its early days. Its high school teams were state champions, and it had several community teams that drew large crowds. Drumright's first baseball park was on South Ohio Street on the J. W. Fulkerson farm, but the one that most remember was the park on the site of what later became the high school football field southwest of town at the intersection of South Jones Street and Lou S. Allard Drive. This was for many years called Drummers Park, named for one of the early baseball teams. Previous to that it had been known as American Legion Park.

The biggest moment in Drumright baseball was the day Babe Ruth played for Drumright and another Yankee great, Bob Meusel, played for Shamrock. Several members of the Yankee club who were members of the New York Legion of Honor agreed to come to Drumright on Wednesday, October 25, 1922. The pitcher for Shamrock was Chief Moses Yellowhorse of the Pittsburg Pirates.

Several hundred fans from Drumright and surrounding towns quickly filled the bleachers and others bought standing room only tickets to see Babe Ruth in action. They were happy to know he would be playing right field and batting in clean-up position. The *Derrick* said, "The day was wonderfully fair and the fall sun was strong enough to make a seat in the sun almost uncomfortable."

As Ruth came to bat in the first inning with a runner on base, the fans roared. The Babe responded by doffing his hat and waving to the bleachers. The crowd waited in great anticipation. It was only a few moments before their feelings were deflated. Yellowhorse, unawed by Babe's reputation, sent four pitches whistling across the plate. The Babe missed three of them and struck out.

But the big moment came in the third inning when Ruth again came to the plate. This time the bases were loaded and the Babe was batting clean-up. It was a situation the fans had dreamed of. Again, Ruth received a great ovation as he stepped to the plate, and again he waved confidently to the fans. They were still with him.

As the first pitch came across, Babe "took a wicked swing." Had he hit it, they said the ball would have wound up in Shamrock, but he

Drumright II, A Thousand Memories

missed. Babe let a low outside pitch go by, and then took another vicious cut at the third pitch. Strike two. The Babe stepped back as a low inside

Drumright and Shamrock lined up just before the big baseball game. Babe Ruth is in the center to the right of John Fields, the man in the black suit. Fields used the game to further his candidacy for governor. To the left of Fields is Bob Meusel of the Yankees. *Photo courtesy Drumright Oil Field Museum.*

154

ball brought the count to 2-2. Then Yellowhorse sent a sizzler down the middle. Ruth saw it coming, poised for it, and swung with all his might. He didn't even come close. Strike three. For a moment there was a hush in the stands. There was no joy in Drumright that day. The mighty Bambino had struck out with the bases loaded, and Drumright lost to Shamrock, 7-5.

Ruth batted twice more. He managed a single and then another strikeout, and the *Derrick* said, ". . . when Babe fanned again and again you'd be sure he was the rottenest baseball player in the United States from the way the crowd hooted him. It was a downright shame."

What the fans probably didn't know and what the *Derrick* didn't mention was the real reason the Babe was such a disappointment. Chester Ferguson was watching closely that day and he recalled, "Babe had had a few drinks that day, maybe more than a few. He sent balls out to the fence in practice, but he wasn't steady during the game. It was a fun day for him. Even though he didn't hit well that day, most of us knew he was still the greatest."

The OU Coach Said, "*You,* Thomas?"

Those who lived in Drumright in the 1920's and even into the 1930's speak of Eph Thomas as the greatest all-around athlete in Drumright High School history. He was captain of the football and basketball teams and as a track star he was undefeated running the 100-yard dash against Bristow, Cushing, and other area trackmen. In 1924 he was a widely publicized all-state halfback. Thomas played in a colorful era that produced many other outstanding backs, including Bill Saffa, Perry McCoy, Roy Berry, Leo Davis, Lazelle White, and Kaki Love.

In 1986, he had his own memories of the early days, including how he acquired his name. Few people knew it but his name was really Everett. Before coming to Drumright he lived in Arapaho in Custer County, where his father, Ed, was sheriff. In the early 1900's, prisoners often served sentences in county jails instead of being sent to the state penitentiary. In jail at Arapaho was a black man named Ephraham serving life sentence for murder.

Often Ed was too busy to look after young Everett. His solution was to let Ephraham out of his cell long enough to take the boy around town. At first people complained, but Thomas explained, "Ephraham didn't do anything really bad. All he did was kill another nigger." Ephraham and Everett were seen together so often that people began to call the boy Eph. The name stayed with him forever.

One of Thomas' lasting memories is the day he reported to practice at Oklahoma University in the fall of 1925 when Bennie Owen

Drumright II, A Thousand Memories

Eph Thomas squares off against Eddie Murdock, lightweight champion of the West Coast in 1927. The two fought to a draw. The fight was in the red high school building. Second from right is Sam Whitlock, the promoter, and dimly in center background is Ed L. Thomas, who seldom watched his son play football because he thought it was a silly game. *Photo courtesy Mrs. Eph Thomas.*

was football coach. Eph weighed less than 150 pounds and appeared almost lost among the 250-pound lineman. Owen saw him standing off to one side and sent an assistant to find out what such a small individual was doing on the field. "I'm Thomas from Drumright," Eph told him. And the coach gaped and exclaimed, "My God, are you Thomas?"

But Thomas stayed and made the first team. In 1926, he married Beulah Vinson of Drumright and decided not to remain in school. For a brief time he tried his hand at boxing. He never lost a fight and in 1927 fought to a draw with Eddie Murdock, lightweight champion of the West Coast.

How his father came to Drumright is also entrenched in Eph's memories. In 1912, Ed Thomas was in Wyoming operating a ranch owned by him and Clint Strong, former Oklahoma State University business manager. One day Strong called him and said, "Ed, my brother has gone off and left his drug store in Drumright. Why don't you come to Drumright and take it over?" Thomas knew nothing about the drug business. Eph remembers his mother's words that evening. "Son, Dad's drunk again. He's traded the ranch for a drug store in Drumright, Oklahoma." Thomas' City Drug Store became one of Drumright's best-known establishments for more than 30 years.

Eph Thomas, at 81, said his health was good. He had fond memories of his coach, Lee K. Anderson, and his teammates, including Kaki Love, Leo Davis, and a fellow all-stater, tackle Lee Brisendine. His house at this writing was in Belton, Texas, but his home, he said, will always be in Drumright.

Drumright High's 'Iron Men'

The young men who became Drumright High School's first interscholastic athletes often walked two miles over dirt streets to school, bought their own uniforms, had a cobbler attach cleats to their street shoes, and played both offense and defense. In spite of this, the years 1916-1920 in the red high school on North Penn set an example for future years and produced two of the outstanding athletes in D.H.S. history.

The school hired Clifford Capshaw as coach as the new high school opened in 1916. With only 11 starters and two substitutes, the Tornadoes had rough sailing the first year. Sometimes the starters played entire games without substitution, but Cecil Albert, one of the substitutes, said, "I don't think we had a serious injury all that time."

Another problem plagued the pioneer D.H.S. athletes. Often teams from Bristow, Cushing, and Pawhuska sent in players who weighed from 185 to 200 pounds and who appeared to be 21 or 25 years old. V. Clyde Arnspiger, who coached the 1919 team, sometimes stopped the game to protest. An investigation showed the men were not even attending school, but were oil field workers being used to beef up the teams. In spite of such handicaps, Drumright defeated Cushing 46-7, Bristow, 26-0, upset Stillwater, 12-7, and tied Shawnee 0-0.

Drumright's early programs had a strong Oklahoma University flavor. Capshaw, a drop-kicking specialist for the Sooners, became coach in 1916, and he was followed by another Sooner, Jack Frost, in 1917. The two were impressed, not only with the high salaries at Drumright but by several of the young players.

Two Tornadoes became stars for D.H.S. and then for Oklahoma. Lazelle White, a great natural athlete, lettered four years in both baseball and football at D.H.S. and was football captain in 1919. On offense he was a great power runner. On defense he switched from fullback to tackle and crashed through opponents' lines.

His teammate, Herbert Shaffer, was considered one of the outstanding Oklahoma high school centers in 1917 and 1918, and was captain in 1918. Shaffer was a nephew of Charles B. Shaffer, who financed Tom Slick's drilling of the Wheeler No. 1 well. White and Shaffer attended O.U. together and were starters for three years on the Sooner team.

Hervey Foerster, another star of the 1919 team, and Cecil Albert, also went to O.U., but did not play football. Sixty-six years later, the

Drumright II, A Thousand Memories

Lazelle White (shown) and his teammate, Herbert Shaffer, were starters for the Oklahoma Sooners for three years. Shaffer was captain of the Tornadoes in 1918 and White in 1919 when they played on the rocky ground back of the red high school on North Penn. Both also played on the state championship baseball team of 1917.
Photo courtesy Wilma Kincaid Allard.

two still had vivid memories of the first D.H.S. athletes. "We were proud of our beautiful new high school," Albert said. "No one on the team smoked, drank, or broke training. Our school spirit was high."

The team played its home games on the rocky ground northwest of the school where goal posts had been erected. There were no bleachers. The few fans who came followed the teams up and down the field. Dr. O. W. Starr was named team physician in 1916 and attended all games. They traveled to out-of-town games in Model-T's or Dodges.

Drumright's official school songs had not yet been written. Albert recalled one song whose words were, "Dear D.H.S., dear D.H.S., you are the school that is the best." And Foerster recalls the students singing, "our boys will shine." Most Drumright citizens today never saw the red high school building on the hill, but it is still foremost in the memories of those who were a part of it. To them, Drumright is still home.

Babe Ruth & Sports Memories

On June 17, 1928 Drumright held its great marathon race. Forty-three men and one boy participated in the 20-mile run, which consisted of 80 laps around Drummers Park, where the high school football field is now located. Promoters were Sam Whitlock, grocer and later mayor, and John J. Pargen, known as Drumright's "Pork and Bean King." Tom Hamilton of Bristow finished in 2 hours, 18 minutes and 30 seconds to win the event. *Photo courtesy James Crabtree.*

Drumright II, A Thousand Memories

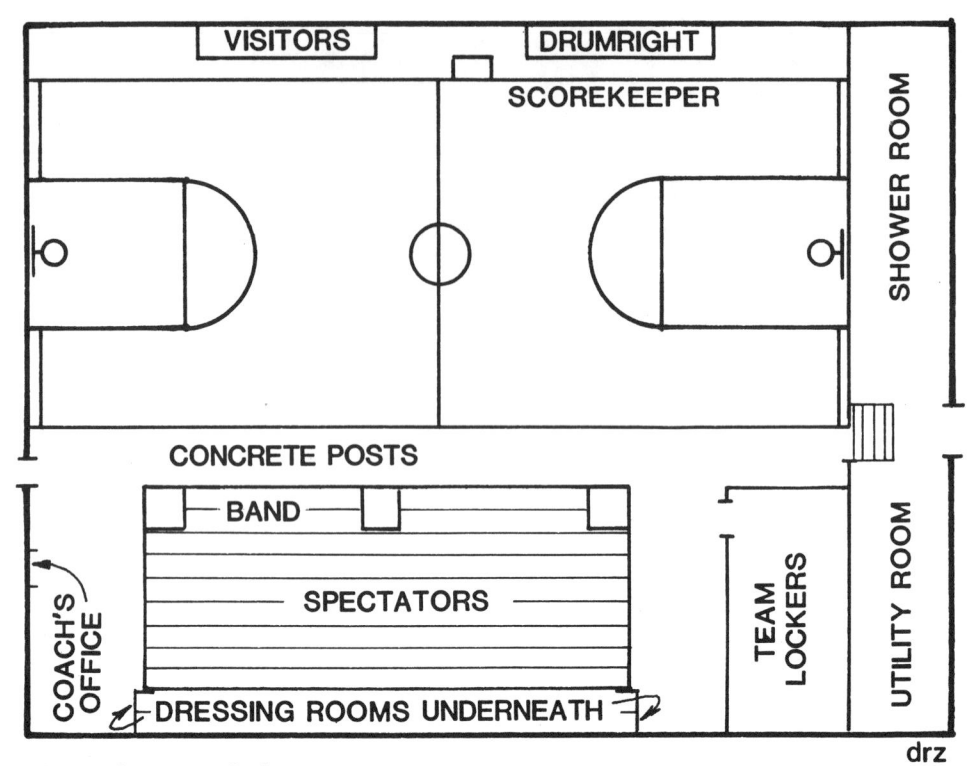

It was almost an early-day version of "streaking," (running in the nude) when basketball players in that historic first gymnasium had to scurry from their dressing rooms under the stands to the showers on the east end after games. They waited until they thought fans were gone but sometimes they got caught. *Drawing by Dwight Zimbelman.*

That First Gymnasium

When the second new high school opened in the fall of 1920 on South Pennsylvania Street, it brought joy to the hearts of those who transferred from the old red school on North Penn. It meant for the first time they would have a gymnasium and an indoor basketball court. It mattered little to them that competing schools considered the gym an abomination and it never occurred to them they might acquire lifetime scars.

The gymnasium was actually an oversized basement. Its walls and floor were solid concrete. The court was about 36 by 66 feet in size compared to the present standard size of 50 by 94 feet. For 17 years, Drumright high school teams competed in the enclosure against Northern and Cimarron Valley conference opponents. Memories of some of the players are still vivid, sometimes even stark, of those days.

Wayne Johnson, a 1934 graduate who lettered four years in basketball, believes the old gym may have produced the first version of

In spite of the old gym's facilities, D. H. S.'s 1933 basketball team won the district championship and went to the finals of the regionals during the state play-offs. Front row: Arlin Taylor, Glenn Frazier, Ted DeShan, Capt. Floye Largent, Joe Horn, Howard Dysart, Lee McCoy. Back row: Manager Nolen Matts, Wayne Johnson, Sam Trout, Otis Brown, Harry Simpson, and Coach John Brand. *Photo 1933 Gusher.*

streaking, a term used in 1960's for running in the nude. Dressing rooms were under the stands and showers were on the east end of the gym. After games, players shed their uniforms and then scurried nude across the court to the showers. They waited until spectators were gone, but often as they made the run, they heard screams and sometime catcalls from girls and women who had not yet departed.

So close was the court to the wall that Johnson can remember hitting the light switch as he drove for layups. Neither the fans or the referees could tell whether the shot went in. In spite of such handicaps the 1933 team won the district championship and went to the finals in the regional tournament. Among Johnson's teammates were Ted Deshan, Alfred Minnear, Captain Floye Largent, Arlen Taylor, and Joe Horn.

An all-district forward that year, Horn also remembered well the old gym. "People called it the cracker box," he recalled. "It was so crowded that when you stood out of bounds you were right up against the seats. I'll never forget the day we beat Stillwater 18-17. We had lots of sprained ankles from those games, but even more happy memories."

Boys' troubles were minor compared to those of girls' teams. The Bartley sisters, Faye, Elsie, and Hazel, were on teams from 1924 through 1928, and Hazel was captain in 1928. In those days, there were no showers. Girls dressed at home before the game or in a classroom. After the game, they bathed at home. Girls laundered their own uniforms, and Elsie made her uniform.

The first girls' teams wore navy colored bloomers with middie blouses and sailor collars. "The bloomers hung down so much they looked like skirts," Hazel Bartley Murphy recalled. "In 1925 they started pleating

Drumright II, A Thousand Memories

The 1938 Dunbar High basketball team was so proud of winning the state championship in its class that it send a picture to Joe Louis, heavyweight boxing champion of the world. Front row, l. to r., N. E. Adams, Sammy Crowell, Chester Smith, Elza Wallace, Lonnie Smith, Troy Beck, and Charles Randle. Back row: Robert Waught, assistant coach; Stanford Lyons, Talbert Adams, Elvin Wallace, Leslie Adams, and Henry Crowell, coach. *Photo courtesy Mrs. Gretchen Johnson.*

the bloomers and we switched to red flannel so we would be wearing the school colors. We wore red socks up to our knees and high-top tennis shoes. A big year for us was 1929 when they let girls wear shorts."

Those Rough Oilton Girls

The worst time for girls in the old gym was when Oilton came to play. "Those Oilton girls were the roughest of all," said Elsie Bartley Allshouse. "They were big rough farm girls and they didn't like Drumright. They would really knock us around. We hated to see them come in the door."

The Drumright-Oilton feud came to a head in a game at Oilton in 1915. Push came to shove and then a female gang fight. The boys teams joined in as did some spectators. After that, the schools did not play for a year or so. In spite of such incidents the Bartley sisters agreed, "Those were the best years of our lives."

For 17 years, the concrete gym was the center of D.H.S. activities, but in 1937 construction began on a separate building that would house both the athletic and band activities. It was completed in time for the 1938 basketball season.

Babe Ruth & Sports Memories

Among former athletes still in the area in 1986 was Jack Carnahan, a basketball starter in the new gym after playing in the old one. "I'll never forget my first look at the new basketball court," he said. "It looked so large I thought we would lose our way. And those elaborate showers and dressing rooms."

As he spoke, Carnahan rubbed his elbows. "Anyone who played in the old gym had chipped elbows," he said. "The goals were so close to the walls, you could hardly shoot. When you came down the court, you always put one foot up to hit the wall. Visitors didn't know this and many of them really banged into the concrete. The floor was uneven, too, and you never knew which way the ball would bounce. I was glad that in those days players wore knee pads and high top shoes. That protected us some." Like the others, Carnahan has memories that make him forget the scars and reminisce about the days in that first gymnasium.

Those Very First School Days

Students Recall Hardships, Tragedy, The Paddle, Fights, and Prayer

From 1912 through 1916, the most trying years of the oil boom, nobody argued about prayer in schools or whether a teacher could spank a student. The paddle and prayer were a part of the accepted scene, and those who started on the opening days of Drumright's first schools said almost without exception, "I knew if I got a whipping at school, I'd get another when I got home." Their favorite memories are of trying to outwit teachers who employed the paddle, even if they got caught once in a while.

One such teacher was Frank Peters, the first superintendent. He might have been forgotten had he not considered the paddle as the cure-all disciplinary implement for pupils of all ages. Drumright's schools started in 1912 in a tent on Broadway and about a dozen shacks throughout the oil field. In 1914, when Peters came, he started a "subscription school." Parents paid a monthly fee for their children's grade school education. Few high school students were in the new town. Peters and his wife were the teachers. Some classes were held in the open air where Way Park in now located. Then, they were moved to the Methodist Church, which was completed in 1914.

Dr. Hervey Foerster was a prominent Oklahoma City physician and lecturer at the University of Oklahoma School of Medicine for many years, but in 1914 he was a pupil in Drumright's subscription school. He recalled how Peters pounced on students even for not having their lessons. The superintendent had a peg leg and had difficulty chasing students, so he kept his paddle handy. "We had a spelling bee every Friday," Foerster said. "One day during the bee, someone stole Peters' paddle. Peters was very upset and when he finally found out who it was he made him go outside and cut a hickory switch, which he used instead of the paddle."

When Fourth Ward opened in 1915, pupils marched into their schools to the tune of a patriotic song such as "The Stars and Stripes Forever." In many rooms, a prayer came before classes began. Almost all who participated say it was a good thing.

Sometimes school memories reveal more of a town's history than do historical data. This chapter combines factual data with memories of those present as oil field schools opened from 1912-1920. Many of these

Those Very First School Days

This 1929 "kavalkade" may be the last hurrah for the Ku Klux Klan in Drumright. Hooded figures are followed by a line of cars enroute to the red high school atop the hill on North Penn. The school was the favorite KKK meeting place. *Photo courtesy Drumright Oil Field Museum.*

people went all the way through the smaller schools and then to Drumright High School.

    Some names recur throughout the chapter and for good reason. Everett F. Drumright, for instance, may be the only living person to attend little Wheeler school just north of his father's farm. Frank M. Wheeler donated land for the one-room frame school. For a time in 1913, classes, pie suppers, and other activities were held there, but the school disappeared from the scene early. Drumright later attended Second Ward, Fourth Ward, the red high school, and the present high school. He could probably have written this chapter.

    Foerster and Alva Bartley both attended the subscription school and then were at ward schools and the red high school. Cecil Albert was a pupil at Tiger in 1914 and is probably the only surviving individual today who spent four years at the red high school. Ethel Cook Campbell was at Fourth Ward in 1915, the first valedictorian at the red high school in 1916, and then taught at Olive and Pleasant Hill. Chester Ferguson was at Second Ward on opening day in 1914, went to junior high at the red high school, and graduated at present D.H.S. Winifred Stayton, at this writing retired in Edmond, taught at Silverdale, Pemeta, Third Ward, and Fourth Ward in the early days. It seemed remarkable to the author that a town could still have so many living witnesses to its schools and to its town from the very beginning.

Drumright II, A Thousand Memories

Tragedy at the Red High School

At this writing, 66 years had gone by since the closing of Drumright's red brick high school on North Pennsylvania Street. Yet, a surprising number of former students were still around to share memories of the school that lasted only four years. This was actually the town's first high school. In 1914, the stone Second Ward school served all 12 grades and the first commencement exercises were held there. But already on the drawing board were plans for a first high school building. It was completed in time for the class of 1916 to hold its commencement there.

While former students recall many happy days, the memory of a tragedy is still vividly with them. It was a cold winter afternoon in 1920 and the cast had gathered in the auditorium to rehearse the forthcoming operetta, "The Gypsy Rover." This would be the last major activity for the senior class and the group was excited at doing a dress rehearsal. The auditorium was cold but to the side of the stage was an old-fashioned gas heating stove with open flames.

Between scenes in which she was involved, one member of the cast, Mildred Faye Parcher, backed up toward the stove to get warm. The flames from the stove seemed to suddenly reach out to her hoop skirt costume. In a moment, she was engulfed in flames. As she ran across the stage, Cecil Albert and several others grabbed her and extinguished

The red brick high school just before it opened in 1916. School spirit was high and alumni still speak proudly of their alma mater. *Photo courtesy Drumright Oil Field Museum.*

Those Very First School Days

the flames. She was taken to a doctor's office but died the next day. The 1920 yearbook was dedicated to her

A happier memory is of the first graduation exercises in the red high school in the spring of 1916. Things were done differently then. All eight members of the graduating class sat on the stage with the principal and superintendent.

Ethel Cook Campbell was valedictorian, the first in D. H. S. history, and at age 88 she recalled the 1916 exercises. "I had to make a talk about all the good things that happened that year," she recalled. "I was so nervous that when I glanced at our principal, Estelle Nichols, I almost forgot my speech. Only a few townspeople came to the 1916 exercises."

After the program, the class members walked a half mile down the dirt trail in a group to the Morrow Hotel. There they were joined by the four 1915 graduates and the first alumni banquet in Drumright's history was held. It was the only one at the Morrow, which was destroyed by fire in October that year.

Frank D. Albert rented a boxcar and brought his family to the oil field in 1914. On one end of the boxcar was a horse and buggy; on the other end were the family belongings. His son, Cecil, was 11 then. The family settled on the Powell farm near Oilton and Cecil walked to Tiger school. Later the Alberts moved to a farm west of Tiger, and Cecil became one of a few students who attended the red high school from the time it opened in 1916 until it closed in 1920. His memories at age 86 were still vivid.

Albert did not have to walk to the red high school. His father bought him a paint pony. And as he rode to and from school, Sinclair Oil Co. paid him to stop by the tank farms and pick up run tickets. Each day, gaugers stuck a long pole in the large tanks to measure the oil. At the end of the day, they repeated the procedure. The difference in oil levels showed how much oil had been taken out and placed in pipelines that day. The figures were recorded on run tickets and Albert picked them up from a can each day and took them to the Sinclair office as he went home from school.

Albert kept his pony in a barn across the street east from the school. Near the barn on North Penn was the home of the superintendent W.C. French, and a grocery store operated by W. W. Walls. Pennsylvania Street was so narrow, rough and muddy that cars seldom tried to get to the high school except on graduation day. A board sidewalk was built all the way from Broadway to the school on the east side of Penn so students could walk to school.

"Most of us didn't even know the name of the street then," Albert recalled. "Broadway was about the only street that was marked. The others were just trails."

Ethel Cook Campbell was the first valedictorian in D. H. S. history and perhaps the only living individual to attend the first alumni banquet at the Morrow Hotel in 1916. In 1986, she returned for a nostalgic look at Edison School, where Fourth Ward once stood. She was also a student at Fourth Ward in 1915. The new Edison opened in 1949. *Photo by author.*

Although the oil boom was at its peak during the existence of the first high school, and the town was rowdy, the students were well behaved and found joy in the school's orchestra, dramatics, art, and athletics. "In all my four years there, I never knew of a single student who got into trouble," Cecil Albert said. "Our principal, J. G. Deininger was a stern fellow and rather aloof, but we respected him and never really caused trouble." And Ethel Cook Campbell recalled:

> Social life for teenagers in 1916 was limited . . . it consisted mostly of parties in the homes, weiner roasts, swimming parties and school activities. To these affairs we always went in a group. Drifters came to the oil field and preyed on people and it wasn't safe to go out alone. Once in awhile we could attend a movie at the Idle Hour or go down and listen to the small band that always played outside the show. My father, O. T. Cook, was a member of the band. The Idle Hour was operated by the J. R. Snodgrass family then. Young people couldn't go to the Strand Theatre because its stage productions were considered too risque.

The favorite hangout for boys and men was the New Smoke House. It was started by Billy Roberts and Bob Achterman, but in 1920 it was operated by Ben Russell, the town's first photographer, who for a time had worked part-time at the Smoke House between picture-taking trips in the oil field. Located in the 100 block of East Broadway on the north side, the Smoke House boasted a barber shop and a lunch counter in front that featured chili and cherry nut sundaes. In the back were pool tables. In front until 1916 taxis lined up and drivers beckoned prospective passengers with the familar "Take you over the Hump." They would not leave until they had a full load of passengers.

Boys sometimes wandered into the black community on the northeast corner of Drumright and bought choc beer, a drink made largely from potatoes. And sometimes if a high school boy wanted to be particularly daring, he sneaked into a house of prostitution on the edge of Morrow Street and Broadway and danced with the girls to the tune of a player piano.

"We had a fine high school," recalled Hervey Foerster, a 1920 graduate and football star. "It had two stories and a sub-basement, and we entered from the side door on the south. We had well-equipped facilities for manual training (taught by V. A. Pleasant), typing, chemistry, and art. Our auditorium on the first floor was really nice. Foerster was the first Drumright boy to graduate from the University of Oklahoma School of Medicine.

"For a town the size of Drumright, it was indeed an imposing building," said Everett F. Drumright, son of Aaron Drumright who attended the red high school when the family moved to nearby Dale Street. "What I recall most was the impressive auditorium on the rear of the building. Unfortunately, the building was poorly constructed and had the disadvantage of being remote to most of the students."

The school graduated its last class in the spring of 1920 and the new high school on South Penn opened that autumn. The red school became known as First Ward School, but it lasted only a few years. Then it became the favorite meeting place of the Drumright Ku Klux Klan. Hooded figures carrying a fiery cross and plodding slowly up North Penn were a familiar sight in the 1920's. City officials, prominent business men, and even school men were among those who gathered in the auditorium to discuss ways of enforcing community moral standards. During the depression it served as a cannery for the needy, and for a time the A. L. Kirkwoods turned the ground floor into a home. In 1940, it was demolished without fanfare and faded from the memories of most Drumrighters except its former students.

Second Ward (and the Hump)

When Tom and Katie Dix moved to Drumright in 1913, their small children had a close-up look at the town's most noted institutions, the first school in the oil field and the notorious gambling den, The

Drumright II, A Thousand Memories

Hump. The dirt Cushing road then was not straight. It curved to the south near present day Haven Hill Drive, made a sweeping semi-circle past a beautiful ravine called Cedar Canyon, which was known for an artesian well and sparkling brook, then headed west again.

Around the first bend of the road sat The Hump, facing south. A short distance from there a small road wound eastward into the woods. The Dix boxcar house with its rounded roof sat there. Just beside The Hump was a windmill, a large water tank, and a stable. The Hump became not only an oasis for muleskinners but for men. They came from miles around to drink, rest, gamble, and fight.

So wild was life at The Hump the Dix children were not permitted to play at Cedar Canyon or even to walk to the home of their uncle, Arthur Dix, who lived less than a block the other side of The Hump. But Gladis, oldest of the Dix children, remembers the fun they had watching officers raid the den. County lines were not as distinct in those days. The Hump sat near the Creek-Payne County lines.

Officers of both counties often conducted raids, but The Hump owners were seldom caught unaware. "They had their whiskey bottles in gunny sacks," Gladis recalled. "If the officers came from Creek County, they would flee into Payne County with their gunny sacks on their backs. If the officers came from Payne County, they ran into Creek County." Gladis remembered The Hump as being much like the artist drawing by Pat McCartney in the first Drumright volume, except that it had an

Clara Spellman Landrum, (right) one of the first D. H. S. graduates in 1915, sits at the foot of a slide on the northwest corner of Second Ward grounds. With her is a friend, May Fowlkes. Northwest Drumright was sparsely settled then and the oil tank in the background is in town. The pipe fence is gone. *Photo courtesy Drumright Oil Field Museum.*

Those Very First School Days

upper floor where teamsters rented rooms. "The Cushing road was like a day and night parade of wagons going back and forth to Cushing," she said. "The teamsters stopped at The Hump to refresh themselves and their animals."

Second Ward Opens

The town was excited when the first new school in Drumright opened in September 1914. Pupils walked over hill and dale from all directions to the new school atop the hill. All 12 grades were taught there while a new high school was being planned.

Gladis Dix was among those from near The Hump who walked to the school. She joined a few playmates and they walked through thick woods down paths to town. Usually, they emerged on Skinner street near the present day ball park. But there was no park then, only a large Sinclair Camp south of there. On the Whitlock Park site was a teamsters barn. The northwest area of Drumright was then called Tiger Town.

The school, itself, was an impressive sight, appearing almost as a stone bastion looking at oil derricks all around it. Even in its earliest days, the iron fence made of oil field pipe surrounded it. And Zola Dix, Gladis' sister, recalled, "Little girls kept the pipes shiny swinging on them. When they 'skinned the cat,' you could see their flour-sack panties, even some of the brand names."

The stone building was still not completed when Gladis started to school, and children attended classes in a long, two-room wooden building on the south edge of the grounds that faced the offices of Gypsy Oil Co. and Tom Slick across the street. On the grounds were swings, a teeter-totter, a volleyball net, and a basketball court. Children spent much of their time throwing rocks off the playground. Even after construction was completed, the school was so crowded children could attend only half a day.

Across the street north in a small candy store was a familiar figure to Drumright school children for many years, A. L. "Nor" Norwood, and his wife Sarah. The Norwoods operated a similar store near the high school when it opened in 1920. The Second Ward store was taken over by Mrs. Myrtle Gibson, who remained in business until Second War closed it permanently. About a block south of the school in 1914-15 was a baseball park where children often went to eat lunch. This may have been Drumright's first ball park.

Tom and Katie Dix moved from The Hump location to a boxcar house on South Grand. Six of their children attended the stone school. In addition to Gladis and Zola were Dorothy, Bill, Richard, and Don. All were later involved in many Drumright High School activities. In 1986, Gladis returned for her 60th D.H.S. class reunion. With her was her senior class sponsor of 1926, James A. Brill, whom she married in 1966.

Drumright II, A Thousand Memories

Second Ward Was Peaceful

Among other pupils as the school opened was Chester Ferguson, who later spent many years employed in the Drumright post office. He arrived in town in 1913 and lived with his family in a tent on Tiger Hill. The Hill was a busy place then with several grocery stores, a drug store, and for a time even a post office. "Tents and box car houses were everywhere," he recalled. "For a time we lived in a tent with another couple that had seven in the family. Then we moved to a shotgun house on Fulkerson Street. It had an outside privy, gas mantle lights, and a water well. A lot of people then had only lamps for lighting."

Ferguson remembered the stone building being fairly peaceful, although he watched his little brother, Virgil, "fight all over the yard." Boys and girls both played jacks, but the favorite games for boys were marbles, spiking tops, and leap frog. Boys often ate their lunches in trees that sprung up all over the grounds. One of his special memories was of the day a talented fifth grade violinist, Wilma Kincaid, came to his classroom and played a solo.

Old Second Ward School, later named Washington, still stands proudly atop the hill on South Cimarron between Federal and Wood Streets. It is the only ward school that has not been torn down. Classes

Fourth Ward, Drumright's second school, opened in 1915. Boys here were considered rowdy and Frank Peters, the first superintendent, had difficulty chasing them because of a peg leg. *Photo courtesy Drumright Oil Field Museum.*

are no longer held there and it has been designated a state historical landmark. At this writing it was a senior citizens center and some of its alumni returned there daily to be among friends and to relive the past.

4th Ward—No Place for a Sissy

The red brick school at the corner of present-day Harley and Pine Streets was Drumright's second public school. The school board envisioned it as a learning center for youngsters in the northeast part of town, but for the first few years it was regarded as more a corral for rowdy oil field youths.

Originally, Fourth Ward, later called Edison, was thought to have opened in the fall of 1916, but Ethel Cook Campbell said she attended school there in 1915 while waiting for the new high school on North Penn to open. She had moved to Drumright from Davenport. Although Fourth Ward offered classes only to the eighth grade, Ethel was a junior in high school and was permitted to take high school work until the new high school opened.

Harley Street was a dirt trail and Pine may not even have existed when Fourth Ward began. The school was surrounded by tents and boxcar houses. The oil boom was at its peak. Everett Whorton, one of the first students, said, "Kids saw many gruesome things. Sparks from Model-T's set off natural gas explosions and people in the field were burned. They saw stabbings and fights."

Whorton lived with his parents and two other children in a small house that sat on a large rock behind the present post office. The house was so small the family hung chairs on the walls when they were not in use so there could be room to move about. Once, he said, a big nitroglycerin explosion in Cleveland shook the house and knocked all the chairs off the wall.

"Everybody had outdoor privies then," Whorton recalled. "People would sneak in and use others' privies. Some owners would run out and lock intruders inside their privies."

In the eight years he spent at 4th Ward, Whorton said nearly all boys wore overalls and went barefoot as long as weather permitted. They had fun climbing 50 feet up oil derricks or swimming in the large wooden tanks which oil companies kept full of water to cool machinery. The water was always warm.

Fourth Ward was two stories with as many as 700 students in 1915. Two grades were taught in each room. It had indoor toilets with a large elevated tank of water that tilted to flush the stools all at once. Classrooms had desks, not just chairs, as in some schools. Pupils marched in while the teacher played a patriotic song on the piano. They stood by their desks until told to sit. In the afternoon, they marched out again,

Drumright II, A Thousand Memories

Roy Townsley holds a collapsible drinking cup such as each Third Ward pupil was required to carry during the great flu epidemic of 1918 that killed more than 50 Drumright people. Townsley was at Third Ward when it opened in 1916. *Photo by author.*

remained in line until the teacher banged a triangle, and then headed for home.

Fourth Ward was noted for its rough pupils "Kids were always fighting," Whorton said. "One family of boys beat me up nearly every day." And Winifred Stayton, who was principal there 1924-1926 said, "It was a wild situation. The upper grade children were rough and undisciplined. They were the worst in town for behavior. Almost all boys in the upper grades were hoodlums."

Such conduct may have been why Frank Peters, the first superintendent, spent much of his time at Fourth Ward making a big show of his long wooden paddle. The boys were undaunted. Peters had a peg leg and the boys taunted him into chasing them. Then they took delight as his peg leg sank into the dirt or mud. Not all the boys escaped. Among those caught was Everett F. Drumright, who was frolicking in the building as the bell rang. "I never told my father about being taken to the office and having a paddle administered to my backsides," he said. "I was told to mend my ways if I wished to stay in school."

As years went by, the boom subsided and Drumright's wild life became more subdued, but things never changed at Fourth Ward. In 1916, Ed L. Roberts came to Drumright from the Wilson oil field as a pumper-gauger for Charles B. Shaffer. He and wife, Eula, settled across

Those Very First School Days

the street from Fourth Ward School, less than half mile from the Shaffer camp. Six Roberts children, Leona, Sam (Son), Harl, Gene, Dale, and Gwen, made their way through the school one at a time over a 20-year-period. For 70 years a member of the Roberts family has lived across the street from the school.

In 1986 Dale Roberts was living in the family home and recalled, "Fourth Ward was still tough in the depression days 1929-40. Clothes were all torn up and boys were always covered with scabs and scars. Kids at Fourth Ward came off farms and oil leases. They were rough and tumble. When they weren't fighting, they played football in tennis shoes and overalls on the rocky ground. They tore each other up. Nobody had any spending money and about all boys had to do was fight."

The school was not spared, even during summers. "When school was out, kids would gather up and throw rocks at the windows," Roberts recalled. "It was a miracle if any windows were left by fall." Thus, from its beginning in 1915 until 1970, and when it became a school for sixth, seventh, and eighth graders, Fourth Ward was no place for a sissy.

Third Ward Kids Were Big

The opening of a new school at Duke and Fourth Streets in September 1916 to accommodate children in the southeast part of Drumright was chaotic at first. Roy Townsley was there on the first day and spent the next eight years attending what was known as Third Ward

Third Ward elementary school on the southeast edge of Drumright opened in 1916 and closed in 1969. It produced many outstanding Drumright High School athletes. Pearl Head was its best known principal. *Photo courtesy Drumright Oil Field Museum.*

Drumright II, A Thousand Memories

and later as Lincoln School. At this writing, Townsley was still living on East Wood Street in the third ward area.

"There were hundreds of children and many of them were big kids," he said. "The school had a gymnasium but it was partitioned in the middle and used for classes. The school was so crowded that one class was held in the hall upstairs. Children had chairs but no desks and two children sat in each seat. In addition, three frame outside buildings were all full, too."

Drumright had reached its peak in population with an estimated 18,000 in the town limits. The children who came to Third Ward were large because many of them did not start school until they were 10. Their parents had been on the move from one oil field to another. "I was a runt and everybody picked on me and pushed me around," Townsley recalled. Third Ward had two full-time truant officers.

Water for the new school came from a well on the southeast corner. Also outside the building were toilet facilities. The school offered grades one through eight. Early principals were Ruth Coyner and Oliver Akin. Children marched into the building and out of it after school.

One of Townsley's profound memories is of the 1918 flu epidemic. "Every morning one or more children did not show up at school," he said. "The flu took many of them." The epidemic was so bad that each child was required to bring his own drinking cup to school. Townsley still has his cup. The 1921 tornado also claimed the lives of several Third Ward pupils.

For many years J. M. (Jimmy) Dover was associated with Drumright theatres and operated other business enterprises, but in the late 1920's he was a pupil at Third Ward. Things were much the same as in earlier years. Pearl Head had become principal. The school was still overflowing but had inside facilities and drinking water. Pupils still appeared to be rather large for grade school, but discipline problems were few.

"There was a good reason," Dover said. "Pearl Head ran a tight ship. She wore tweed skirts and other clothes that made her look stern. When she said jump, students moved."

One big change had come about. The seventh and eighth graders were moved to the high school. Along with them went pioneer teacher Lou Ann Pinkston. Dover remembers one other teacher. "Frances Tucker spanked me about every day for mischief and then we'd both cry. We wound up good friends, though." Schoolground games then were marbles and jump-for-down for boys and jacks and jumping rope for girls.

Boys formed gangs on the schoolground. Some of Dover's group included James Matts, Lavern and Paul Ridenour, James Overdeer, James Tucker, C. F. Moore, J. P. Bankston, John (Hap) McPherson, and J. C. Wilson, and Harding Lawrence, who later became president of

Those Very First School Days

Braniff Airlines. Many Third Ward pupils became outstanding athletes at Drumright High School.

All Drumright grade schools felt the impact when the Tide Water refinery closed in 1955. Soon, consolidations were necessary. Third Ward was closed in 1969 and the building was later torn down to make way for a public housing project.

The only visible remnant of old Third Ward is a concrete marker near the entrance to the Oil Field Museum, but former pupils exchange memories during the high school reunions and sometimes during morning coffee breaks.

Silverdale — Terror at School

Sometime in 1918 or 1919, a small school called Silverdale was built to accommodate oil field children living in camps east of Drumright. It was on the north edge of the Pat Badger farm just east of town. The Badger family still owns the farm.

Soon a community of transients formed around the school. Some were employed at a nearby oil company vacuum plant, but others were drifters who moved from one oil field to another. They used Silverdale as a base for stealing, robbing, and preying on nearby communities. Sometimes they killed, and bodies were found the morning after in tanks or under culverts. Most belonged to a fanatical religious sect and felt their actions were justified. When newcomers came to the community, they exerted great pressure on them to become a part of the sect.

It was into this situation that Dee L. Stayton moved in the fall of 1920 as an employee of the vacuum plant. Soon after that, his daughter,

After enduring "terror" at Silverdale, Winifred Stayton found teaching at Pemeta in 1920 less of a strain, although she walked nearly three miles every day down the railroad track to school. *Photo courtesy Drumright Oil Field Museum.*

Winifred, was hired as Silverdale teacher and came to live with him. Stayton and his daughter were ordered to join the sect or "take the consequences."

Winifred taught all eight grades in one room at Silverdale. Sometimes there were as many as 50 to 60 students ranging in age from five to 16. At the front of the room was an elevated platform and a bench on which students sat to recite. Toilet facilities were behind the school.

The terrorism of the community carried over into the school. Some of the older boys were rough and tried to close the school. Winifred carried a hickory limb to defend herself. Once a seventh grader threw a book at her and she asked him to pick it up. He pulled a knife with an 8-inch blade and moved toward her. She broke his hand as she swung hard with the hickory limb and then threw him into a corner.

"After that, I was warned to leave within six weeks," she recalled. Then my father was transferred and I was alone. I rented a room in a nearby shack for a time and had to sleep with three of the family's children. But as threats increased, I gathered up all the school's records in April, took them to Superintendent French, and closed the school."

At Pemeta, They Chewed Tobacco

Having escaped the terror of Silverdale, Winifred Stayton became a pioneer teacher in another oil field community, Pemeta in September 1920. In 1986, sixty-six years later, she was possibly the only individual who could remember Pemeta's first school located on the edge of Tiger Creek. Although Pemeta was still a lively oil town, Miss Stayton was so overjoyed to find the children well-behaved that she was willing to overlook the fact that many of them smoked and even the 5-year-olds chewed tobacco.

Teaching at Pemeta was a grueling existence. Each day Winifred arose early and walked more than two miles, most of it down the railroad track to be at the school by 8 a.m. She lived with her father, who had been transferred to the Stanolind No. 2 plant a mile north of Drumright just east of the old Oilton Highway. She lived next to the J. A. Parcher family. Other family names on the lease were Jett, Thomas, Gooch, Ryan, Hann, Warner, Duncan, Woods, and Wharton. All the homes had gas lights and outside privies.

The railroad followed Tiger Creek out of Drumright and came within a fourth of a mile of the Stanolind camp as it crossed the Oilton road. Miss Stayton walked from the camp to the railroad tracks and then plodded down the tracks through Frey and on to Pemeta.

On arrival at the school, she taught from 8:30 a.m. until 4 p.m. without a break. By 4:30, she had put away supplies, straightened up the room, and walked down the tracks to home. Her schedule was so

Those Very First School Days

full that during the two years she taught at Pemeta, she never once visited the business district.

Pemeta's first school had two rooms. She taught four grades in one room and Harvey Grubbs, the principal, taught the other four grades in the other room. On a platform at one end of her room was a teacher's desk, but she never sat down all day. During recess and noon she supervised children in the schoolyard or helped serve them hot soup made by the home economics class. Miss Stayton had never seen a basketball game, but in the spring of 1921 she was ordered to coach a Pemeta team which was made up of both boys and girls. She was surprised when it won the district championship.

School records have been lost but sometime in the early 1920's a new Pemeta school was built just off Main Street a short distance from the Santa Fe Depot. For a time it offered work for all 12 grades, according to Mrs. Emma Akin, wing school supervisor. In 1925, William T. Hatch succeeded Grubbs as principal.

Activities expanded after that. Operettas were produced indoors or under gas lights outdoors. Picnics, pie suppers, and Hallowe'en parties were held. Students competed in spelling bees, debates, and athletics. The boys played marbles and the girls' favorite game was jacks.

Some names that became well-known in Drumright attended Pemeta. These included Salisbury, Jones, Hicks, Dysart, Barr, Terhune, and Thompson. One of the pupils, Maggie Jones McClary, has one special memory of the school. "We started every day with the Lord's Prayer and a flag salute," she recalled. "It does no harm and it never did. I'd be glad to vote it back in. Kids had a lot more respect for others then."

Tiger — Where It All Began

Tiger School's history has been clarified since the first Drumright book. This is important because Tiger was the prototype for Drumright's later wing schools. A few oil wells had sprung up around the school even before the oil strike of 1912. Small stores existed there as early as 1909, and it was the site of the first oil field post office in June 1910. From 1912 until 1939, several hundred oil field children from the little school came to Drumright High School.

The Drumright *News* said in March 1915 that Tiger School was built by William E. Dunn in 1908 or 1909. This is not verifiable, but Dunn had moved to that scene in 1908, hoping to establish a town called Tiger.

One pupil who attended Tiger in 1910 survived at this writing. Blanche Wheeler Kersey, daughter of Frank M. Wheeler, on whose farm the oil strike occurred in 1912, walked about two miles across open fields to school from the Wheeler farm a mile north of Drumright. Her memories are vague, but she recalls Tiger as a one-room frame building

Drumright II, A Thousand Memories

One boy pumps so others can drink at Tiger School's outside water fountain. Many Tiger pupils walked long distances. They headed home quickly as classes ended in the afternoon. *Photo courtesy Drumright Oil Field Museum.*

with one teacher for the dozen or so pupils. In the spring of 1911, Tiger School burned and remained closed for a year.

Originally, it was believed the school was brick when it opened again in 1912, but when Cecil Albert arrived in 1914, it consisted of two frame buildings. Cecil was 11 when his father Frank, moved from Avant and became a head roustabout for Wolverine Oil Co. The family settled on a farm owned by Tom Slick four miles south of Oilton and Cecil walked to school every day after someone stole the family's horse.

A Tobacco-Chewing Professor

His most vivid memory 62 years later was of the Tiger principal. "He always chewed tobacco," Albert recalled. "He kept the cuspidor not far from his desk. He would talk awhile and then spit. He was a tall angular man and the pupils watched in awe as he unwound almost like a baseball pitcher and took aim at the cuspidor. He was very good."

Everyone walked to school and everyone was poor, Albert said. Pupils never got to know one another. As soon as school was out, they all hurried home to their oil field shacks or tents.

Things were about to modernize at Tiger when Ivan Weaver arrived in the fall of 1920. Weaver in 1986 was one of the few living pioneers to have ridden on the first oil field "school bus," a covered wagon that picked up pupils at the Stanolind Gasoline Plant east of Drumright and took them to Pleasant Hill.

As he moved to Tiger, the new four-room brick building was almost completed. It had one room for beginners, first, and second grades,

Those Very First School Days

Familiar Drumright names are in this Tiger School picture of the early 1930's. Front row: Genevieve Wilburn, Raymond Carriker, Bob Bump, Elda Poole, Doris Lee Pennington, Maxine Winkler, Theda Bob DeGeer, Rex Starkey, Everett Reed, and Raymond Youker. Second row: Rosalie Hoggatt, unidentified, Marie Wise, Letha Fern Fisher, Hortense Youker, Lloyd Matherly, Ruby Bevins, Juanita Wilburn, Clarence Dodd, Russell Powell, Dick Wise, Mrs. Eula Thompson Melott, teacher, and Lucian Mills. Top row: Hughie Lilly, Kenneth Gooch, Merkel Mansell, Alvin Combs, Dan Kelly, and Loren Horrell. (Identifications by Lucian Mills, Cletolee Kelly Harrell, and Margreat Hoggatt Sweet). *Photo courtesy Rex Starkey.*

Drumright II, A Thousand Memories

one for the third, fourth and fifth grades, and another for seventh and eighth graders. The fourth room was for assemblies. The latter had a roll-up wall between it and another room. About 80 pupils were at Tiger then.

In the early 1920's Tiger was also a place of worship. "We had a non-denominational Sunday School every week that gave us religious training as well as education," Weaver recalled. The school also had basketball, baseball, and track teams, even in the early years. Mr. and Mrs. Bert C. Balch were Tiger's teachers then.

The Late, Great Years

Tiger's last 10 years of existence may have been the greatest. Enrollment through most of the 1930's fluctuated around 150. Many Tiger patrons had large families and their children moved through school in stair-step order and then on to Drumright High School. One could be sure that at any given year in the '30's there would be at least one Kelly, Hoggatt, Pennington, Starkey, Mansell, Wilburn, Wise, or Winkler. (See picture.)

Dan Kelly was one of five A. C. Kelly children whose era at Tiger extended from the early 1920's to the mid-1930's. Kelly was possibly Tiger's

Steel is raised for a big tank on the first tank farm in the Tiger School area in 1913. Teamster Pete Hoggatt was one of the builders. Hoggatt may have set a record by sending nine children to Tiger School. *Photo courtesy Margreat Hoggatt Sweet.*

Those Very First School Days

most noted graduate. After graduation from Drumright High, he eventually became president of T. G. & Y., a national variety store chain.

The Kelly family first lived on a farm near Tiger and later on the Minnehoma lease across from the well-known ball tank. Dan Kelly had retired from T. G. & Y. and in 1986 he and his younger brother, Jim, were operating three variety stores. His memories of Tiger School indicate that some things had changed and some had remained the same in the later years.

"Almost everyone walked to school and almost everyone was still poor," he recalled, "but we were together more. From the fourth grade on we got to compete against Pemeta, Fairview, and other schools in athletics. We all looked forward to the holiday season and free Christmas candy."

The Pete Hoggatt family may have set a record at Tiger. Hoggatt came to the oil field as a teamster in 1913. Nine of his children, starting with Mildred in 1916 and ending with Billy when the school closed during World War II. In between were Bryan, Joe, Philip, Rosalie, Geneva, Ethel, Eldon, and Margreat. Four of the children were born in a tent south of the Cities Service camp.

Cecil Albert, Ivan Weaver, and Dan Kelly all consider Tiger School days as an important phase of their lives, and Kelly adds, "For anyone raised during the depression, it was a great opportunity to be in the Tiger area. The teachers were so kind and helpful." School records show Tiger closed officially on November 5, 1942, but the 1938-1939 year may have been its last year of instruction.

Reincarnation

Dry Hill, one of the first two schools in western Creek County, was resurrected in this home built by Harry Reasor in the late 1930's. It is at the entrance of Country Club Heights west of Drumright. *Photo by author.*

Drumright II, A Thousand Memories

Mr. and Mrs. Ancil Settle, Sr., built this home west of Drumright from the stones of Fairview School shortly after World War II. *Photo by author.*

Old wing schools never die; they come back in other forms. The two bungalows above in the 400 block of North Broadway, Edmond, were once little Litchfield School southeast of Drumright. L. C. (Demont) Townsend, former U. G. 5 superintendent, did the moving and rebuilding in the 1940's. *Photo by author.*

U. G. 5, Markham, and Vida Way

They were Surrounded by a Forest of Derricks

Most Drumright people never saw U. G. 5 School, but its pupils were nearly all children of oil field workers who were known in the area. U. G. 5 was located about two miles southeast of Shamrock. It was housed in a very attractive brick building and offered work in grades 1-12.

Patrons and pupils manifested an almost fierce loyalty to the school and they struggled for years to keep it from being annexed by Shamrock. The loyalty and pride in the school apparently had not diminished years after the school closed, since more that 200 attended the first U. G. 5 reunion held on September 15, 1985, in the Drumright Community Center.

In the 1920's, a number of schools were established in the state with uniform system of operation and grading. These were called Union Graded Schools. U. G. 5 was one of several in Creek County. Another, U. G. 6 was located near Bristow. U. G. 5 was opened in the fall of 1926 and at first it was called Central. In the beginning, it had four rooms and included grades one to nine. Later two more classrooms and a gymnasium were added and grades 9 through 12 were taught.

Howard Touchatt, one of the first students, recalled that although U. G. 5 had a very attractive brick building, it started with outside toilets, and a well outside provided drinking water. Then someone devised a pump that made it possible to have drinking water inside.

The school competed in basketball and baseball with Slick, Depew, Pleasant Hill, Gypsy Corner and other schools in the area. Sometimes girls played on the basketball team when not enough boys were available. Among coaches at U. G. 5 were Haskell Paulding, who also coached at Shamrock, and Glen Potts.

L. D. (Demont) Townsend was superintendent of U. G. 5 from 1930-32 and 1938-40. "Students who came to U. G. 5 were smart and well-mannered," he recalled in 1985. "We never had a boy or girl who did not make a high grade on entrance exams at Oklahoma State or Oklahoma University. Most made very high grades."

U. G. 5 pupils took great delight in participating in county contests against "city kids" at Bristow. They won many contests in spelling,

Drumright II, A Thousand Memories

poetry, speeches, arithmetic, reading, and history. Enrollment fluctuated at U. G. 5 but the school had about 125 students at its peak.

In the first graduating class at U. G. 5 in 1930 were Alice Wassom, Eula Thompson, Francis Ray, Ruth Bailey, Delbert Clemens, Scott Clemens, and Jeff Carruthers. Among the first teachers at U. G. 5 were Mr. and Mrs. Fred Witly and Clara Davis. Among those who taught later were John Burns, Jeff Watson, Haskell Paulding, J. E. Webb, L. D. Townsend, Glen Potts, Audie Maples, Carl Wendt, Eula Melott, Ella Duke, Thelma Bach, Gladys Neal, Marjorie Moore, Sarah Clark, Oma Rich, Mildred Nichols, Marline Toalson, Edna Fletcher, and Mrs. Leroy Brown.

The Big Fire

In spite of the happy atmosphere at U. G. 5, patrons always felt that a dark cloud hovered over the community. This was the threat of annexation by Shamrock. The threat about became a reality in 1937. Late at night on March 18, Maxine Barnes, a pupil, looked out the window of her home and saw flames rising as high as 25 feet above the school. An alarm was sounded but aid was too little and too late. U. G. 5 was burned to a rubble.

The community was stunned and many pupils and parents still believe the fire was deliberately set. For a time, junior high students were sent to the old Litchfield school building. Haskell Paulding held classes for others in the teacherage, but the fire forced U. G. 5 to hold election to decide whether to rebuild or to become part of the Shamrock system. On June 22, 1937, in a bitter election, U. G. patrons voted 96-89 to rebuild.

Some of this retaining wall and a part of the fountain are all that remains of once attractive U. G. 5 School. Its pupils excelled in county contests competing against Bristow, Drumright, and other larger schools. For forty years it fought annexation by Shamrock. *Photo courtesy Frank Butler.*

A U. G. 5 class in the late 1920's. First row: Thelma Parker, Sterling Stafford, John Grooms, Oda Rodebush, Minnie Mustard, Nita Arnold, and Marguerite Renfro. Second row: Elwood Wasson, Trual Latting, Carl Wheeler, Kathareen Morton, Vivian Barnheart, Evelyn Matherly, Fred Jordan, and George Jester. Third row: Dorothy Weaver, Mildred Renfro, Fern Williams, Ella Duke, Lula Woolem, Elsie Meskimen, and Clifford Thompson. *Photo courtesy Paul Jordan.*

Drumright II, A Thousand Memories

In the fall of 1938 a new U. G. 5 opened with a combination gymnasium-auditorium, well equipped laboratories and a large lunch room. But the school never fully recovered from the loss and the changes it brought about had a traumatic effect on some of the pupils. The school maintained its independent status only until 1940, when it was annexed by Shamrock and disbanded. The brick in the new building was purchased by a Bristow church and the school was torn down. Remnants of the foundation and retaining wall still stand.

In the last graduating class in 1940 were James O. Tucker, Willard McClain, Berrill Forbes, Lorene Matherly, Christine Dickerson, Mary Hooper, and Alma Lottie Hart. Names of the U. G. 5 patrons familiar to many in Drumright included Jess L. Barnes, Charley Clemens, Everett Dickerson, Ernest Frazier, Gene Hart, William Hooper, LaRue (Buster) Jordan, Ernest McClain, Roy Matherly, Joe Morris, Ed Hart, Mac Meskimen, George W. Oldenstadt, Bill Pixley, Orlin Phillips, Otis Rodebush, Bill Renfro, Otis Shelton, Raleigh Stafford, James I. Tucker, Frank Wheeler, John Weaver, Charley Williams, Cale Patton, and George Thompson.

Memories

U. G. 5 alumni who gathered for a reunion in 1986 are now in their 60's, 70's and even 80's, but they still treasure special memories. Among them was how L. D. (Demont) Townsend kept order with a belt. Said one, "He could yank his belt off in a split second and let you have it." When a student was guilty of misconduct, Townsend would put a mark on the board. Every so often, he held students accountable. Students found joy in watching their classmates suffer.

Paul Jordan, who later played on Drumright's 1941 championship football team, recalled a day that every student in the class but him had a mark and Townsend was settling the score. He showed so much glee that Townsend grabbed him and included him with the others. Jordan got even one day. He threw a handful of .45 bullets into the wood stove and watched pupils scamper through the door and windows just before the bullets began exploding.

Students also have fond memories of the custodian, George William Oldenstadt. A native of New York City, Oldenstadt left home at the age of 12 to work on a ship. After 14 years on the high seas he returned but his family had disappeared. He never found them and he came to the Drumright oil field. Children gathered around him often in the schoolyard to hear stories of his adventures. He died after a stroke in 1933. His son, George, became a graduate of U. G. 5. A list of U. G. 5 former pupils who attended the 1985 reunion is in the appendix.

U. G. 5, Vida Way, and Markham

Vida Way School was in the heart of the north pool action near the Cimarron River. During the oil boom, night classes were held for oil workers to help them learn to calculate depth of nitroglycerin charges and to fill out reports. *Photo courtesy Frankie Jo Posey.*

Vida Way—Surrounded by Derricks

Vida Way's past is especially colorful since the school was in the very center of the great north pool of the Drumright field. It was surrounded by pumping wells, gasoline plants, drilling companies, and leases. It was only a short distance from the Cimarron River and the Markham Ferry. The school was founded almost immediately as the oil boom moved northward from Drumright and Pemeta, probably in late 1914 or early 1915. It was built on the oil lease of Vida Way.

In the immediate area were holdings of oil companies that included Sun, Prairie Oil & Gas, Carter, Sleurian, Gulf, Deep Rock, and Texaco. While Vida Way was a distinct community with company homes lining the dirt road leading to the school, it never had a business district except for two grocery stores operated by Mrs. A. Dean Scott and the James Palmer family. In the early days, people walked to Markham three miles away or into Oilton about a mile further.

From Drumright today, the route to Vida Way would be north on Highway 99 about five miles to a blacktop intersection. A turn west leads to the Cimarron River, and a short distance beyond the river bridge is a dirt road leading south. The foundation of Vida Way school is still visible about a mile and a half south and east. Across the road from the school site was the Mable Dale lease and in the immediate area were leases or farms of Jess Bruner, Amy Simpson, Ambrose Miller, Everett Wilson, and Frank Ryan.

Vida Way was a four-room frame school with a teacherage just behind it. Toilet facilities were outside. Its principals included A. Dean

Drumright II, A Thousand Memories

Scott, who later served several terms in the state House of Representatives. C. R. Costello, E. E. Patton, Clell Scott, Carl B. Kime, George Cunningham, R. A. Fielding, and Maizelle Brown, who was the last principal when the school closed in 1960.

Many oil workers were without even grade school training and Scott held adult night classes to teach them enough arithmetic to fill out production reports and to calculate depth for shooting with nitroglycerin.

Social life centered around the school. Pie suppers, ice cream socials, and basket dinners brought the people together. Nearby, Texaco built a park which became a center for both Vida Way and Markham. Large crowds came to baseball games, horseshoe contests, and other games. Vida Way reunions were held for many years and attracted from 200 to 300 former students.

Although located in Creek County, Vida Way was under the jurisdiction of Payne County until the Markham school closed in the 1940's. A school bus came from nearby Yale to Markham to pick up high school students. In later years, some Vida Way pupils went to Drumright for high school, but patrons voted to transfer to the Oilton system. Vida Way was packed with enrollments of 100 or more for many years, but the number had dwindled to about 30 when it closed. A list of former Vida Way pupils is in the appendix.

A remnant of Markham School and its teacherage, built in early 1915 still stands. The teacherage was remodeled in 1986. Once a road existed from the school to the Markham business district about a fourth mile east. *Photo by author.*

U. G. 5, Vida Way, and Markham

Markham—A Thriving Town

Looking at the sparsely populated Markham area today, one may wonder why it is necessary to have two schools within three miles of one another. That was the approximate distance of Markham school from Vida Way. A look at the pictures of activity along the Cimarron River makes this understandable. From late 1914 to 1919, oil derricks and

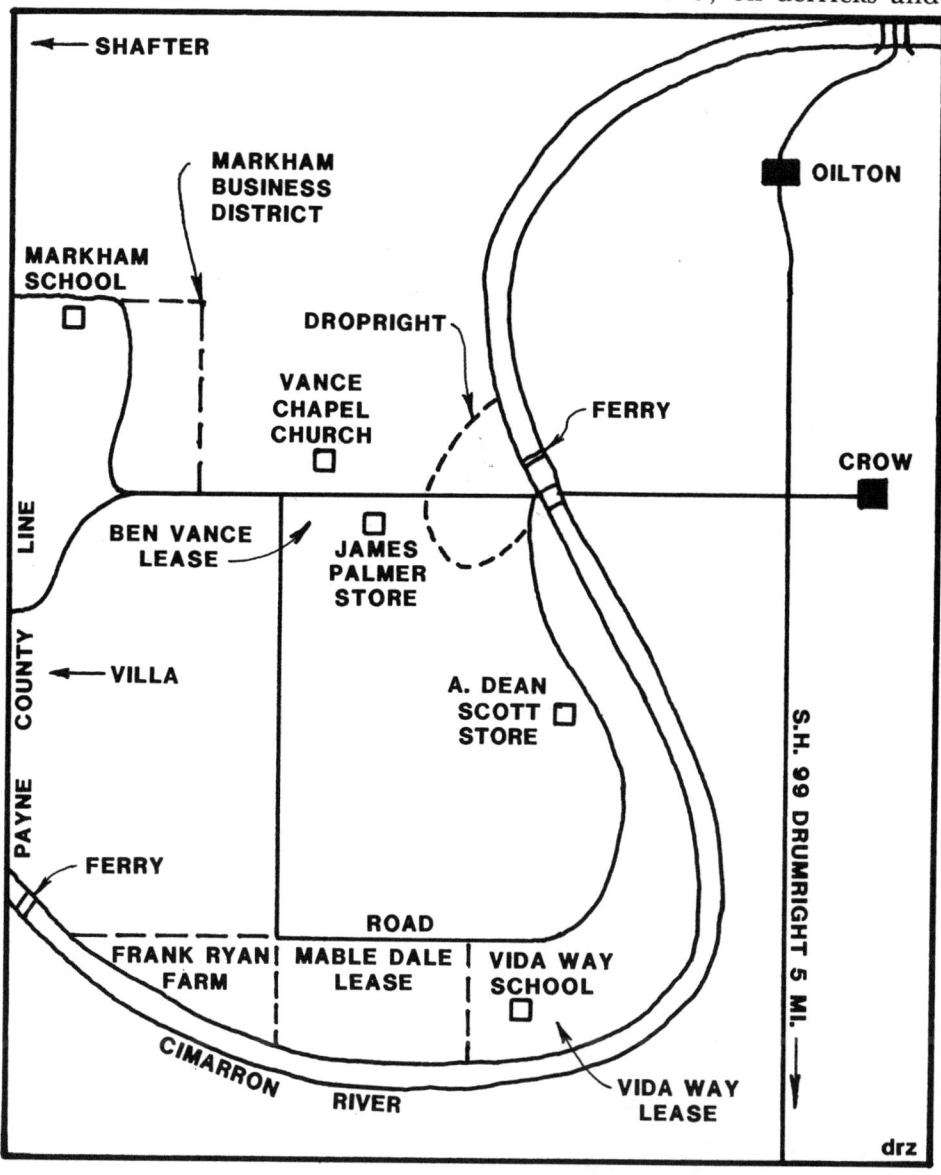

Communities long forgotten—Dropright, Crow, Villa, Shafter, and Markham are shown on this map of the Markham area. Once oil derricks were like a dense forest throughout the north pool. It is 2.4 miles from Highway 99 to the old Markham school. (Sources: Lewis Lindsay, Frankie Jo Posey, and W. C. (Bill) Bedingfield.) *Drawing by Dwight Zimbelman.*

Drumright II, A Thousand Memories

auxiliary equipment covered the banks of the river. Homes lined the dirt roads leading to both schools, and were in rows on oil leases. Some people lived in tents and dugouts. At least a dozen major oil companies and scores of smaller operators pushed frantically into this area called the north pool. Probably more of them became millionaires here than in any other of the oil field domes.

Even two schools could not accommodate the children who were part of the rush. Markham dreamed of being the center of the north pool. It was originally called Dropright. After oil was found on the John H. Markham, Jr. farm, the name of the town changed, and plans for a new city were made. Among those who helped layout the town was S.W. Colvin, who later operated an automobile agency in Drumright for many years.

Oil field people built a school they thought would grow with the town. It was a two-story brick with two classrooms downstairs and two more upstairs. As the population influx grew, an annex, also brick, was added on the west. The latter still stands as does the teacherage next to the school.

Andrew Knapp Ralston was the last superintendent of Markham school, which closed in about 1944. Ralston had been the first Cherokee County superintendent of schools after statehood, and a lawyer and deputy sheriff at Tahlequah. He and his wife, Nora Mae, had also taught at Sand Creek, another small Creek County School. *Photo courtesy Sandra Still.*

U. G. 5, Vida Way, and Markham

The school's entrance was on the east and it faced the Markham business district about one fourth a mile away. In 1915, the dirt road that runs east and west beside the school intersected Markham's Main Street. Now, what was once the main part of town is an open field. All traces of the Main Street are gone and the road from the school curves around it. Once on the corner of the main intersection was a large water well, then a bank, a grocery store, a hotel and post office. On a side street were several other stores. Near the area was Free Will Baptist Church.

Lewis Lindsay was a pupil at Markham during its peak years. Living in Oilton at this writing, he recalled how the school was the center of activity. It was also the major communications medium. "When they wanted to get news around or announce a community meeting, they would pin notes on the kids at school for their parents," Lindsay said. "Quite a few meetings were held to talk about town problems."

Lindsey also had vivid memories of one of his first teachers, young Hugh Maroney, son of an Oklahoma A&M College history professor, whose first teaching job was at Markham. Maroney lived at a rooming house and Lindsey's mother did his laundry. "He'd get right out and play games with the boys at recess and during the noon hour. We had no swings, teeter totters or other such things. We just had a dirt playground. He'd get so dirty he had to change clothes once or twice a day, but he had fun. He was crazy about photography and tried to

At least a half-dozen families are in this tent settlement near Markham in late 1914. Oil workers in grimy clothes, housewives showing the strain of primitive living, and children watching in awe make up the typical oil boom scene. *Photo courtesy Mrs. M. L. (Clara) Marrs.*

teach it to us. Once he climbed to the top of an oil derrick and had me take his picture from a high bluff of the Cimarron. We were at about the same height. Then he stood on his head on the railing of the bridge in the middle of the river and had me take another picture."

Markham, like Vida Way, was under the supervision of Payne County, possibly because it was close to Yale and possibly because it and Vida Way could be reached without crossing the Cimarron. Markham school closed shortly after World War II as enrollment declined and its few students transferred to Vida Way. The town had disappeared long before that. John H. Markham, the man for whom the town and school were named, had also departed long ago. He moved to Tulsa with offices in the Exchange Building, undoubtedly taking with him the $7 million he received for his holdings in the Drumright field.

Memories —
The Founding Fathers

Personal glimpses of
Aaron Drumright, J. W. Fulkerson,
Harley Fulkerson, W. E. Nicodemus, and
P. J. Stephenson, Sr.

Harley Fulkerson (l.) founded Drumright's first skating rink in 1914. The building later became Cain's Academy and the American Legion Hut. With him are brothers Albert and McKinley.

Chapter VII

Aaron Drumright—

'If They Can't Call It Drumright, Tell 'em To Name It Aaron'

By Everett F. and Florence Drumright*

I was my father's first son and I may well have been a disappointment to him. Even after I became Ambassador to the Republic of China, he could not understand why anyone would choose to live "over there with those heathen Chinese" rather than live on a farm in Oklahoma. And he asked, "Why in the world would anyone want to spend all that time learning a language like Chinese?"

Sometimes during my career I was referred to as a "minister," and that also puzzled Dad. How could anyone be called a minister if he didn't preach and never went to church?

Dad never reproached me about my career. He knew how much it meant to me. I had traveled extensively as a youth and I loved it. Shortly after I graduated from the University of Oklahoma in 1929, I chanced upon a booklet on foreign service careers. I knew immediately that's what I wanted. After taking a written exam in Denver and an oral exam in Washington, I was astonished in late 1930 when told that I had been selected for a probationary appointment in Mexico. That was the beginning of a 31½-year career climaxed by an appointment as Ambassador to the Republic of China.

Once when I came home to the farm for a visit, Dad and I went out and worked together for several hours in the cornfield. As we walked back he turned to me, sweat streaming from his brow, and philosophized, "Well, in your job you will never have to work hard to get on in this world."

Certainly I and most other men could not endure the physical labor Dad imposed on himself year in and year out. With him the earth came first. He planned his year, his month, his week, and his day to best care for his land. Rarely would he let anything interfere with his farming routine. If it was the day to plant corn, nothing was important as getting the seed in the ground. The same was true for hoeing and picking the ripened ears. One day when friends tried to persuade him to return to Drumright for a special celebration honoring the town's founders, he

---

*Everett F. Drumright was one of several Oklahomans to hold distinguished positions in the U.S. government. A 1925 graduate of D.H.S., he spent 31½ years in foreign service, including four as Ambassador to the Republic of China. With the help of his wife, Florence, he provides intimate glimpses and memories of his father, Aaron Drumright, for whom the town of Drumright was named.

looked on his calendar and shook his head. "I can't get away that day," he said. "That's the day I plow the corn."

And when I came home once after a four-year absence for him to meet my wife, Florence, Aaron, Jr. met us. "Dad's out hoeing corn," he said. "He said you will still be there when he comes in." Instead, we walked to the field where he was working. There he stood, tall, raw-boned, bronze-faced in blue overalls. "You should have waited until I came in and washed my hands," he said, greeting us with a warm but almost critical smile.

When he lived on the farm he always wore overalls, shoes, and shirts from J.C. Penney Co. His dresser drawers were full of unopened gifts of white shirts, ties, and other dress clothes.

Florence prepared a nice family dinner that night, but Dad wouldn't partake. His breakfast was always a fried egg on toast, his lunch a ham sandwich, followed by a bowl of ice cream and a few cookies, and dinner was a bowl of cornflakes. As the rest of us ate the big dinner, Dad ate his cornflakes. His routine must have been good for him, since he lived to age 86.

A Builder and A Worker

I recall a favorite story Dad told us about Drumright. It was in the earliest days and the town still had no official name. Dad owned the farm that covered most of the north half of Drumright and he wanted the town to be named for him. But even after oil was discovered he went right on with farm chores. One day when he was in the barn milking, a friend came rushing in and shouted, "Sorry, old man, we can't name the town Drumright. There's already another Oklahoma town by that name." Dad kept on milking but looked up smiling and said, "Well, if they can't name it Drumright, tell 'em to just call it Aaron."

Dad worked as hard in Drumright as on the farm. He helped organize and was president of the Drumright State Bank. He built the first stone building and was in many other enterprises. In 1923, he established a service station on East Broadway just across the railroad tracks.

He got right out on the driveway and went to work. I doubt that many of the people who came in for gasoline realized that the attendant washing their windshields and checking their tires was the man for whom the town was named. But even after he became moderately wealthy, he never considered himself above doing menial chores. He pumped gasoline, checked oil, washed cars, and swept the driveway. He liked to work, he liked people, and he was proud of whatever business he was operating.

My father was essentially an unschooled farmer before oil came his way. He never went beyond the fourth grade in an Ozark country school. But he surprised everyone by taking to business in Drumright like

Drumright II, A Thousand Memories

Aaron Drumright (r.) shakes hands with M. L. (Mike) Marrs, a pioneer Creek County oil man who drilled on the Drumright farm. This picture was taken on one of Aaron's rare visits back home.
Photo courtesy Drumright Oil Field Museum.

a young duck to water. He amassed a small fortune. His most unsuccessful project — in which he participated with four partners — was the Roberts Hotel, which was never a financial success.

He Moves to the Farm

In spite of these successes, Dad still remained a farmer at heart. As soon as he accumulated royalty money from his oil in 1915, he bought a good 240-acre farm near Parsons, Kansas. He held on to it through thick and thin. He never said much, but we knew his dream was to go back to the soil. Twenty-two years later, he abandoned all ties to Drumright, taking with him his sons, Fred, who was slightly retarded, and Aaron, Jr. He began a second farming career that lasted into the 1960's when he sold all but about four acres to the city of Parsons for a water reservoir.

Aaron Drumright was born June 22, 1882, in West Plains, Mo. He first came to Oklahoma in 1900 and farmed near Coyle. After a short time in Coyle, he moved to Kansas, then Colorado, and then back to

The Founding Fathers — Aaron Drumright

His humble farm home at Parsons, Kans., was a far cry from his impressive two-story home in Drumright, but Aaron Drumright was happy there because it brought him back to the soil. His son, Everett, Ambassador to the Republic of China, is at his side. *Photo courtesy Drumright Oil Field Museum.*

Oklahoma in 1905. For nearly four years he rented a farm near Euchee Creek, then moved to a farm near Isabel, South Dakota. This venture was also short-lived and he returned to Creek County and settled on the farm that was to become the town bearing his name.

My father was essentially a good family man. He had a harmonious union with his two wives, and he was good to his children. He tried to instill in them the virtues of truth, honesty, and industry. As a matter of fact, Dad had once thought of becoming a minister. His grandfather was a minister in the Ozarks. Dad often quoted chapters in the Bible and expounded on righteousness. Having been exposed to slight education, he stressed its value to his children and assisted three of us to attend universities. He was a moderately firm disciplinarian. More than once he applied a light paddle to me and my brother, Aaron, Jr.

Rarely would he talk about his family but once when Florence asked about Mother, he did soften and smile. "Mary Gertrude was a good woman," he said. "We never had a fancy wedding, just went off and got married. I guess you might say we eloped."

He was proud of a painted photograph taken by an itinerant photographer of four of his children barefoot and standing at attention. Dad had the black and white photo enlarged and colored, and had shoes painted on all the bare feet.

He Comes Back Home

The day came when Dad was in his eighties and had to stop driving to town. It was a blow to his pride but after a few landings in a ditch, he agreed. He became more of a recluse, his only welcome company consisting of his three dogs. For years, he had his hair trimmed

Drumright II, A Thousand Memories

every two weeks. Now he began trimming it himself. "No one ever looks at an old codger like me. Why go to a barber shop?" he said.

Often we tried to persuade Dad to go back to Drumright to see his old friends, but he declined. "What would I want to go there for," he asked, "No one there I know any more. But you better go along and see the cemetery where your mother is buried. See that they are keeping it in good shape. When the time comes, I'll go back to Drumright but not before."

And so it was on February 21, 1969, we all went to Drumright, to the fine old Methodist Church he had helped build. Dad's friends came from all over the oil fields and surrounding county to bid farewell to the town's pioneer. Even in his death, his jaw was set firmly and with his eyes closed, one missed the warmth of those blue-blue eyes. He had given his name to his town and he had given many years of work in laying it out and making it grow. He was buried in the South cemetery in the family plot beside his two wives, Mary Ryan, who died in 1920 after a prolonged illness, and Lydia Parker, whom he married in 1922 and who died of a brain tumor in 1925. Aaron Drumright had come home to stay.

J. W. Fulkerson

His Greatest Dread: The Saturday Night Bath

By Carrie Fulkerson McLain*

Someone said there were 16 oil wells brought in on my father's farm, but even if there had been 100, it would have made no difference in him.

My father always preferred simplicity in life. Before and after oil was discovered on his farm, he centered his life around his family and his church. He took little part in the hustle and bustle of the boom town. As a matter of fact, he moved away from it for nearly three years because he thought it would be best for his children.

Neither did he care for the expensive homes or cars. As long as he had a front porch where he could sit in the evenings and read the Bible and enough room for his children to play, he was satisfied with a plain home. He once owned an old Studebaker, and sometimes he seemed irritated when the children could outrun the car.

Dad was born in Elizabethtown, Ky., on October 16, 1859. When he was 29, he married Lucinda Floyd. When doctors told him he should leave Kentucky for his health, he rode all the way to Oklahoma in the winter on a white mule to explore. Later he and his wife struck out in a wagon for the West, and eventually made the run into Oklahoma in 1889. After living for awhile in Lincoln County, Dad bought the farm in Creek County where Drumright is now located. My parents moved there in 1907, five years before the oil boom.

Corralling Eleven Children

When Mother died in 1909, my father became dad and mom to eleven children and at the same time looked after the cotton farm. One can imagine the challenge in a small house without modern conveniences, but Dad set up a few rules to try to keep us under control.

First, he did something about shoes. One can imagine that with eleven children around, there were shoes everywhere—from one end of the house to the other. He told us always to put our shoes under the bed

---

*J. W. Fulkerson owned the farm that became the south half of Drumright when oil was discovered in 1912. For a time the new town was called Fulkerson. He and Aaron Drumright met in January 1913 to plan a general layout of the town. His daughter, Carrie, is the only surviving member of the immediate family at this writing.

or we would find them out in the street the next morning. I don't think he ever really did that, but the threat was enough to make us obey.

At mealtime, Dad always made the children eat everything on their plates. And if one complained he didn't like something, Dad would say, "If you get hungry enough, you'll come to like most anything." And as soon as the meal was over, some of us had to wash the dishes right away. "If you go anywhere, you won't want them still there when you get back," he would say.

Sometimes Dad would chide me about my cooking. Once when I cooked some biscuits especially for him, he said, "Be sure and don't feed any of these to the dog. They might choke him." He never had much education himself, but he always looked at our report cards. He seldom commented about low grades in subjects, but if any of us had a low grade in conduct, he would say, "Well, at least you could behave yourself."

He Supported Lackey

It wasn't long after Drumright took form in 1912 that churches began to organize. Dad was a life-long Baptist and beyond his home and family, the church was his first concern. In May 1915, he was one of a group that met and organized the First Baptist Church in Drumright. W. L. Dix, another member of the group, was one of his best friends. The two men were among the first deacons of the church.

The present Baptist church is on the land that was once a part of my father's farm. He donated the lots for the church and made a substantial contribution to help finance the building. His name is among those on the cornerstone of the building.

When Mother and Dad went to church, she would always wait until just before she arrived at the church to put on her shoes and stockings. Quite a few women did that in those days. We were very poor then and Mother did anything she could to make her good shoes last a little longer. As the family grew, Dad took us all to church every Sunday.

Rev. R. W. Lackey was pastor of the church during most of the early years and Dad liked him very much. He told me that Lackey had quite a temper and wouldn't take much from anyone. Once the preacher got into a bitter argument with a prominent Drumright business man. Finally Lackey turned his head for a moment and then knocked the man down. "The Bible says to turn the other cheek," Lackey said, "but it doesn't say what to do afterwards." Dad supported Lackey in his fight against liquor and gambling.

He Dreaded Saturday Baths

J. W. Fulkerson had a few unusual habits. He always slept with his feet sticking out the end of the bed, no matter how cold the weather.

The Founding Fathers — J. W. Fulkerson

The Fulkersons were a prolific clan. Here the family poses before a tank on the Fulkerson land in 1917. J. W. Fulkerson stands head and shoulders above his descendants. *Photo courtesy Carrie Fulkerson McLain.*

Even after he acquired money from oil, he always wore dime store glasses. He never went to an eye doctor for tests. Even though he would sometimes sit for hours and read the Bible, he would never sit in a rocking chair. He always sat in a straight-back chair, even on the front porch in the evenings.

 The biggest fights the family had with J. W. Fulkerson were during efforts to get him to take a bath. Pioneer families bathed in metal wash tubs and Dad resisted even the traditional Saturday night bath. Usually we shamed him into a bath by holding our noses and pointing at his feet.

 I know Dad was sometimes lonely after Mother died but he never seriously considered remarrying. Once, one of his secretaries asked him to marry her. He teased her and said, "Now you wouldn't want an old man like me." But he told me later, "If you ever love one woman dearly, you will never want another." And he loved Mother very dearly.

His Money Disappeared

 Dad was not an astute business man. When we went to Kentucky shortly after the oil boom, he placed much of his money in the hands of a trusted friend, and when he came back most of it was gone. He built

Drumright II, A Thousand Memories

the J. W. Fulkerson building in 1915 and over the years many well known lawyers, doctors, and dentists had offices there, including Grace Arnold, Dr. William J. Neal, and the first dentist, Dr. M. C. Lovell. But when the building sold, it went for only $5,000. If Grace Arnold had been handling his affairs that would not have happened.

In March 1931, Dad had been ill for several weeks and he knew the end was near, but he seemed content because he had achieved the most important goal of his life. "I only wanted to live to raise my family," he told us. "If I could go on and be with all my loved ones, how happy I would be." He died on March 15, 1931, and Reverend Lackey came from Wilburton to conduct the services.

These are some of the memories of J. W. Fulkerson, but my most precious memory of all is that he was a wonderful father.

Harley Fulkerson

A Restless Builder, He Loved to Flirt

By Clarence G. Fulkerson*

It's sometimes hard for me to believe that my father, Harley, was a Fulkerson. Most of the family, starting with my granddad, J. W. Fulkerson, lived a quiet, peaceful life built around home, family, and church. They got married and stayed that way. They seldom got involved in the busy life around them.

Harley Fulkerson never fit the mold. He never went to church. He flirted with women and they flirted with him even more. Divorces were rare in the oil boom days of Drumright, but he married three times and was divorced twice. He was a restless bundle of energy. He worked from daylight until after dark on the cotton farm until the oil boom came, then he started one business after another. When anything new came along, he just had to be a part of it.

Dad never got real rich like some of the others but he accumulated about a quarter of a million dollars. His wealth began flowing in early during the boom when the first well on his farm was discovered just behind the present Masonic Temple. He told me later his money may have done him more harm than good. Women became much interested in him when he acquired wealth. I think he was sorry that he and Mother were divorced and that it might not have happened if he had remained poor.

Our farm home was located on what is now the 200 block of East Broadway right on the edge of Tiger Creek. It sat back from the dirt street about 50 feet between where the Paul Wallman Battery Shop and the Drumright Auto Supply are now located.

Fishing in Tiger Creek

Tiger Creek was then a much bigger stream than it is now. On a bend in the creek just a stone's throw from the house was a water hole about 20 feet by 50 feet in size. This was our water supply, as we drew the water out in buckets. Fishing was good on Tiger Creek up to 1912, and we used to pull 2-pound catfish and lots of perch from that water

---

*When the oil boom began, Harley Fulkerson owned land that extended from what is now Broadway to East Oak and from N. Ohio to California Streets. His son, Clarence, recalls vividly the early Drumright days. Clarence played on the 1928 Bristow High School football team, was a combat veteran of World War II, and for many years operated an ice company in Oklahoma City. At this writing, he has retired in Drumright and looks after wells on the Fulkerson land.

Drumright II, A Thousand Memories

hole. Tiger Creek used to overrun its banks and flood the area during storms, and once Dad slipped and fell into it. It was nearly an hour before he made it back home, and we were afraid he had drowned.

Our farm covered much of the eastern half of Drumright. It started on Broadway and North Ohio and extended north to Oak Street. Then it included everything east to California Street. Among the important buildings at this writing in that area are the post office, Masonic Temple, Harley Fulkerson building, the old Santa Fe depot, and the businesses on the south side of Broadway east of the depot.

Across the street from Dad's farm was the J. W. Fulkerson farm. Granddad came to the area in 1907, riding a white mule all the way from Kentucky. Dad bought the 40 acres north of him shortly after that when he was still in his early 20's.

In Lincoln County, Dad had been a champion bronc buster. He was lithe and wiry and never weighed more than a 120 pounds in the old days. He could really cling to a bucking bronco. He was also a champion cotton picker. He was so quick they measured his pickings and found that he was averaging more than 500 pounds per day.

When he acquired his own farm in Creek County near Tiger Creek, he worked just as hard. He was up before daybreak doing chores. I remember days when he would put me on an empty cotton sack and drag me to the cotton patch. I'd watch while he picked cotton. He nearly always picked 500 pounds. Then he'd come to the house after that and chop a cord of wood. He never put anything off until tomorrow.

Clarence G. (Tex) Fulkerson, Harley's son, looks after Fulkerson No. 2 well and the tanks behind it just north of the Drumright Oil Field Museum. This area was part of his father's farm in the boom days. *Photo by author.*

The Founding Fathers — Harley Fulkerson

He Was Tough and Strict

Hard work made him strong. I've seen him knock a cow down with his bare fist. He'd get mad when they messed up the barn. He wanted his boys to be tough, too. He planted watermelons in the cotton patch so they would have shade. Sometimes we exercised by rolling melons up the hill. He bought us boxing gloves when we were very young and taught us how to use them. My brother, Bill, and I milked seven cows every day. Dad was strict with us. When he said something, he meant it, and we never crossed him. But he had a sense of humor, too. He told lots of funny stories, and he took it in good spirits when we slipped a bunch of live crawdads into his bath water one Saturday night. Everybody bathed in wash tubs then.

Dad loved his own father, J. W. Fulkerson, and they got along well except for one period. Dad had six brothers and one day he and Asa got into a real fight. When he thought it had gone far enough, Granddad told Harley to stop, but he just kept pounding Asa. Granddad then tried to pull him off. When that failed he just picked up a club and banged Harley over the head with it. That stopped the fight, but they didn't speak for awhile.

After the oil boom, Dad turned to other things and I think he started more businesses in Drumright than almost anybody. He had a wagon yard at a new home he built on the corner where the Church of God now stands. Then he started a grocery store and delivered groceries throughout the oil field. After that came a pool hall, located on the corner of South Ohio and Broadway. his next venture was a skating rink he built where the Santa Fe depot and the oil field museum were later located. When the trains came to Drumright, the skating rink building was moved to East Fulkerson street and later became Cains Academy and the American Legion Hut.

Watching the Girls Go By

Dad's most lasting achievement was probably the Harley Fulkerson building that is still in use at the northeast corner of Ohio and Broadway. He was really proud of that building and he stood in front of it often flirting with women who walked by. He really liked to do that and most of them seemed pleased. At first the Guaranty Bank rented the first floor of the building. The upper floor was divided into rooms and rented to single women, most of them school teachers. He used to flirt with them, too, and he said some of them wouldn't pay their rent unless he came in an courted for awhile.

When anything new came on the scene, Dad couldn't wait to try it out. He brought a player piano to Drumright, the kind you pump with your feet. We stayed up all night for awhile having fun with it. Then

Drumright II, A Thousand Memories

he heard about the new phonographs, the ones with the picture of a bulldog on them. He brought the first one to town. After that came a Reo Speedwagon, which was considered a fancy car in those days. I think Dad may have had the only windmill ever in the city of Drumright. He set it up at his wagon yard. We furnished water to everyone in the neighborhood.

Dad died in Drumright in 1939 at age 53. That seems a rather young age now, but this happened to many who lived in the early days and it is understandable. People today have no idea of how hard life was back then. Work was backbreaking for both men and women. Families lived in shacks and for a long time they had lamps for lighting and wood stoves. No one had ever dreamed of automatic washing machines or refrigerators. Food was scarce for many. Lots of times I saw people eat lard sandwiches. They would spread lard between two slices of bread and put salt and pepper on it. People would scrape up oil that had built up on the railroad tracks, take it home, and make lard out of it some way. It's a wonder many lived as long as they did.

My father left behind many reminders of the oil days. The Harley Fulkerson building is still in use, mostly as an office building. Several wells are still pumping on the land that was his. Fulkerson No. 2 is just a few yards from the old Santa Fe Depot. Fulkerson No. 3 is on the edge of Tiger Creek near where our old fishing hole used to be. This is near the cotton patch and not far from the old home. I think of him and the oil boom days often as I visit these places.

Mayor W. E. Nicodemus

Each Day 'Hookie' Miller Said, 'I'll Kill You, You S.O.B.'

By W. E. (Edgar) Nicodemus*

My father, Warren Edgar Nicodemus, was the first elected mayor of Drumright in 1916 and the eight years he served were the most trying times not only for him but for the city council and others who were trying to build a new town. The town was wild and citizens were concerned about crime.

His life was in danger most of this time. Both he and Jack Ary, the chief of police, received threats constantly that they and their families would be killed if they tried to stamp out crime, and they were threatened almost as much if they did not. They carried a gun everywhere they went.

Like many Drumright pioneers, Dad could have had a life of ease had he stayed in Pennsylvania. He was born in Martinsburg, Pa., on November 28, 1874. He received an excellent public education there and then his father sent him to a private university where he learned a great deal about law and government. My grandfather owned four banks in Pennsylvania and he already had a banking career laid out for Dad. But Dad was restless and adventuresome. For him banking was too routine and dull. He wanted something with action. He eventually may have gotten more than he bargained for in Drumright, for once during the great turmoil, he threw up his hands and said, "Worst mistake I ever made." But when others tried to get him to leave for other opportunities elsewhere, he wouldn't go. "Drumright is like a magnet to me," he would say. "I want to stay here and build a great town."

When he left Martinsburg in 1898, Dad first went to Terrell, Texas, where he bought a cotton gin and warehouse. In November 1907, he married Ida C. Wood. They stayed in Terrell until 1910 and then moved to Oklahoma City. There, his father-in-law, T. J. Wood, told him about exploration for oil in Creek County. This excited him, and he was among the first on the scene in 1912 when the oil boom began.

Drumright was so wild at first that he did not bring his family until 1914. He set up business in a tent on East Broadway and lived in

---

*W. E. (Edgar) Nicodemus is the son of Drumright's first mayor, W. E. (Nick) Nicodemus. He lived in Drumright until he completed his junior year in high school, then moved to Oklahoma City where he graduated from Classen High in 1931. He was associated for 34 years with Kerr-Lynn Oil Co., which later became Kerr-McGee. When he retired he was Kerr-McGee purchasing manager for drilling, production department, and refineries, pipeline and marketing. He attended Oklahoma City and Kansas State Universities.

Drumright II, A Thousand Memories

the back of it. The whole family lived in the tent for awhile and then Dad built a shotgun house a short distance from the tent.

Because of his education and his background in finance and law, he quickly became involved in organizing a city government. Among those who worked with him in preparing a city charter were Bart and Earl Foster, P. J. Stephenson, Ben Russell, E. W. Holland, and Aaron Drumright. These men remained his close friends for years, and other friends included Dr. O. W. Starr, Pat Cawley, Loyd Zumwalt, Oliver Akin, and Dr. William J. Neal. His work on the charter and his contributions to help laying out the town caused many of the leaders to want Dad to be the town's first mayor, and in 1916 he agreed and was elected.

Problems: Crime and Crime Fighters

Problems he had to face as soon as he took office were gambling, sale of liquor, and prostitution, plus fights and killings. Other problems included the International Workers of the World (I.W.W.), the Ku Klux Klan, the W.C.T.U., and Reverend Lackey of the First Baptist Church. The crusade of Lackey and the W.C.T.U. in trying to clean up the city was as bad as all the crime element.

Lackey and the W.C.T.U. were badgering the mayor and council about letting things run wide open. Dad has said a thousand times these

W. E. Nicodemus' first business in 1912 was in this tent on East Broadway. Later his family lived in the back part of it. His education and background in law led to his becoming the first mayor. *Photo courtesy Drumright Oil Field Museum.*

The Founding Fathers — W. E. Nicodemus

people did not realize the city officials were outnumbered 300 to 1. The oil field was alive with robust men who had not had feminine companionship for a long time. To cut off all their entertainment sources might have brought about even more serious crime.

To combat all the trouble, Dad in 1917 appointed Jack Ary chief of police and gave him full power to try to keep the peace. Jack had come from Texas and Dad thought he was the man for police chief. Jack, like Dad, was a very blunt person, and neither of them was afraid of anything. Jack told Dad, "I'll enforce the law if I have to kill every S.O.B. in the city."

Both Dad and Jack Ary were held to blame for not ending crime in Drumright, but what most people did not know was that money from back east and from Kansas City was behind criminal operations in the oil field. Jack Ary would raid a house of prostitution, close liquor joints, and raid gambling houses. But no sooner were the operators arrested than they were given a fine and released to go on with their operations. Dad and Jack carried guns all the time because they were told if they caused too much trouble, their families would be killed.

Ary Raids a Bawdy House

Almost every day Dad ran into "Hookie" Miller on Broadway. I remember him. He was the meanest looking man I ever saw and he was just as mean as he looked. He was the town bully and the most feared man in town. He was tied in with The Hump and the out-of-town interests. Each day as Dad passed by, Miller would snarl, "I'll kill you, you S.O.B." Dad kept his hand near his gun and would answer, "Any time you're ready, Miller."

I remember one night when Dad and Jack Ary planned a raid on one house of prostitution and gambling den, and no one knew but the raiding party. How surprised they were when they discovered that about a third of those arrested were business leaders and members of Reverend Lackey's crime fighters.

All hell broke loose as Dad had them all brought to his office. Some were his friends and some were not, but this was the best thing that could have happened to all. Dad told them if they wanted to drink and play poker, "For God's sake, do it in my office, not in a gambling den. You can have anything here but prostitution." They took him up on his offer, and some of them came around frequently for poker and drinks. As Dad said later, some would call it blackmail, but he really got their attention and all agreed to help him clean up Drumright, even The Hump.

Wearing Guns to Church

Some of my most interesting memories are of Dad and his

Drumright II, A Thousand Memories

associations with ministers, especially Reverend Lackey. Lackey wanted all gambling and liquor dens and houses of prostitution closed up. Dad believed in closing up the most flagrant violators such as The Hump, but he did not believe it possible to close up all dens in a wild oil town of 18,000. The unusual fact of this was that Dad and Mother attended the First Baptist Church where Lackey was minister.

I recall how each Sunday Lackey would begin his sermon, then, regardless of the topic, he eventually came around to sin in Drumright and would point his finger at Dad. One day Dad observed that Lackey was wearing a gun in his belt, so he decided that as a matter of precaution, maybe he should do the same. So for awhile, the preacher and the mayor both wore guns to church. This reflected the tensions of the early days.

Dad solved the problem by transferring to the Presbyterian Church on South Penn across from the high school. The pastor, Robert Harkness, was also opposed to crime, but he worked with city leaders instead of with Lackey. He was a devout Christian, but he had one weakness: he loved to play poker. When city leaders met in Dad's office to discuss crime control, they usually drank and played poker. The preacher joined in the fun.

For 10 days in the bitterly cold winter of 1922, Drumright went without gas service as Shaffer Gas Co.'s supply ran low. Even the hospital had no heat. Mayor Nicodemus (r.) became a hero in state newspapers as he tapped a high pressure line of Oklahoma Natural Gas Co. *Photo courtesy Drumright Oil Field Museum.*

The Mysterious Stranger

In 1919, it was known for some time that the I.W.W. was agitating a strike of Drumright telephone operators, but the exact date of the strike was not known. Because Dad fought Lackey, the W.C.T.U., and the I.W.W., it was rumored that at a specific time, an attempt would be made to kill both Dad and Jack Ary and perhaps their families.

One morning my mother answered a knock on the door and a stranger handed her a sealed envelope and told her to give it to my dad. When Dad came home and read the letter, he immediately picked up the phone and called Gov. J. B. A. Robertson. The letter was a warning that a strike called by the I.W.W. would begin the next day. It told of a plan to kill both Dad and Jack Ary and warned their families might be killed if they did not leave town. The letter told of violence planned for Drumright during the strike.

Dad asked Governor Robertson to send national guard troops to Drumright. Robertson was a good friend of Dad's and he assured him troops would be in town the next evening. Dad called Jack Ary and a plan was set up to weather the strike until the troops arrived. Neither could figure the identity of the man who brought the letter, but Jack said, "What the hell, Nick. He's the best friend we ever had." Dad always said the man may have saved many lives.

Stories have been told that Dad and Jack were overpowered, tarred, and placed in the city jail, but this was not true. The plan of defense was for both to direct attention away from their homes and families. They stayed downtown until the strike started. Both then left in a car and went to Second Ward school. They backtracked from there to the rear of the city hall.

Dick Burgess, the fire chief, had a fire truck waiting in the alley and a ladder to the second floor ready for them to climb into the city hall. They made their way from the second floor down to the city jail and locked themselves in. They released themselves when the national guard arrived.

Unknown to the rioters, armed deputies had been placed among them as they marched toward our home on Tiger Hill. They stayed close to the house in case the rioters attempted to remove Mother and the children. Luck was with us as Earl Foster, a close friend of the family, got us past the rioters and into a car.

Years later we in the family asked Dad why he stayed and fought so hard, facing all sorts of opposition, threats on his life and the family. I don't think he was ever afraid of anything alive and he said, "I saw a challenge. I wanted the people of Oklahoma to know a damn Easterner could come and straighten out a wild oil boom town and make it a decent little city in which to live." Asked if he would do it again, he laughed and replied, "No way. One round is enough." He was proud of the many

Drumright II, A Thousand Memories

wonderful friends he made in Drumright and the decent people who had the guts to fight for what they wanted.

He achieved a lot of things such as paving the Main Street, getting a water system, building a sewage plant and lines, and doing away with outhouses. Fighting the I.W.W. and closing The Hump helped rid the city of the worst element of people who would not fit into the environment as first class citizens.

The Tiger Hill Toughs

As a parent, Dad kept a fairly tight rein on us. When he told us to do something, he only said it once. Because I was the mayor's son, he reminded me regularly that I should be a good example, especially since nearly everybody in town called me "Little Nick." I did most of the time but sometimes our neighborhood gang got into mischief. It was made up of boys who lived on Tiger Hill or within a block or two of it. We called ourselves the "Tiger Hill Toughs." We started playing together when we were in junior high and stayed together all through high school. Some of the members were Ralph Shadid, Stanley Zumwalt, Bill Foley, Garland Saine, Glen Gant, Don Smith, Cleburne and Otis Brown, Bob Moore, and the Heffington boys, Howard and Hobart.

Drumright had no recreational facilities then, not even a baseball diamond, so we had to make our own fun. We once even had our own football team and played Oilton, Shamrock and Cushing. Most of the time we were good, but once in awhile we got into mischief.

Rev. Robert Harkness of the Presbyterian Church told us one day we ought to get out, earn some money, and use it to have a watermelon party. We decided the idea was good but we had a better idea for getting watermelons. A bunch of us sneaked into Dr. Starr's watermelon patch west of town and took enough melons to feed an army. When we had the party at our house, the preacher became suspicious when he saw all the melons. We finally confessed we had swiped them.

The Toughs Go On 'Trial'

Dad thought this was a good time to teach us all a lesson so he connived with Jack Ary to have us all arrested. We spent the night in jail and the next morning we were told we were going on trial for stealing watermelons. The next day Dad and Jack rigged a mock trial for us. They had a defense attorney and a prosecuting attorney and Judge C. O. Beaver presided. The courtroom was packed and everyone but us boys knew it was all a joke.

After testimony, Judge Beaver told us we were convicted and would have to be sent to the penitentiary at McAlester. He said we would be driven to Sapulpa and then shipped on to McAlester. We were scared

Drumright II, A Thousand Memories

to death. They loaded us into cars and when we got about halfway to Sapulpa, they told us they had thought it over, and if we would promise never to do this again, they would let us go. We of course all promised and I doubt if any of us ever swiped watermelons again.

We did, however, get into mischief one more time. We set up a pop stand on Tiger Hill to make money. When business wasn't so good, someone suggested that Drumright people probably would like home brew better than pop. We made a batch and it was actually pretty good. When we put it on sale, business boomed immediately, but Jack Ary got suspicious when he saw a long line at our pop stand. Someone told him what we were doing. He put us out of business right away.

In addition to witnessing most of my father's trials and tribulations and having fun with the Toughs, I was active in high school and earned a letter playing center on the Tornado football team. One can perhaps imagine all the memories I gathered. When I left Drumright in 1930 I thought my world would come to an end. We had so many friends there. I have always been proud of my achievements at Kerr-McGee and I attribute much of my success to what I learned growing up in the oil field at Drumright. I've been away from Drumright for more than 50 years, but it will always be home to me.

P. J. Stephenson

He Considered the KKK 'Lawless and Un-American'

By Charles E. Stephenson*

My father, P. J. Stephenson, was born and raised on a farm in southern Ohio. His father moved the family to the territory of Oklahoma arriving where Ponca later became a city. Dad graduated from Ponca City High School in 1907, the year Oklahoma became a state.

Francis Marion Stephenson, my grandfather, opened a family operated general mercantile store. The business eventually failed primarily because too much uncollectible credit had been extended to the Indians of the Ponca area. This store was, however, a good place for the five sons and three daughters to gain business experience which later led them into various enterprises.

When he left the family business, Dad became a traveling salesman for a meat packing company. During this brief period, he learned of the oil discovery in western Creek County and decided to go into this boom area and open a clothing store. He arrived in Cushing by train on November 18, 1912, and on the same day took a six-hour buckboard ride to the oil field camp which was later to become Drumright.

The Store Becomes the Bank

Dad and Arthur O'Dell, a distant relative and one of Drumright's leading founders, opened a men's clothing store on Broadway and called it O'Dell & Stephenson. It was in a small, quickly erected wood building. The store first specialized in heavy duty work clothes. It became the best known retail outlet in town primarily because it was the only bank.

In 1912, the nearest full-service bank was in Cushing. The horsedrawn type of transportation of that time coupled with bad roads and a great deal of "boom traffic" created by oil field equipment and building material haulers made a round trip to Cushing a full day of travel. This inconvenience and the opportunity to obtain more retail customers caused O'Dell & Stephenson to set up a quasi-banking operation

---

*Charles E. Stephenson is the son of P. J. Stephenson, Sr., Drumright's first town clerk in 1913. A 1939 graduate of Drumright High School, Charles earned a Bachelor of Laws degree from the University of Oklahoma in 1948. He was associated with General Motors Corp., and the All-State Insurance Co., and retired as vice-president of Tech-Cor, an All-State subsidiary. He and his wife, the former Betty Jeanne Clanton, have been leaders in the Drumright Historical Society and in re-organizing the Oil Field Museum.

The Founding Fathers — P. J. Stephenson

in their store. There were no charges for this service. Dad claimed they never received a bad check.

Since they had to stay close to their business in Drumright, they let friends and acquaintances make their store deposits and obtain cash in Cushing for the business and its limited banking operations. With this capital they cashed oil workers' checks. The workers brought the checks for their wages to the clothing store where Dad or Arthur would give them a portion of their money in cash and an O'Dell & Stephenson check for the rest.

The store in those lawless days never carried enough cash-on-hand to give each worker the full amount of his check in cash. If the worker also had presented personal bills for board and room and the like, Dad or Arthur assisted him further by writing O'Dell & Stephenson checks to his creditors. O'Dell & Stephenson checks were distributed all over town. This banking experience became very valuable when Dad along with other founders directed Drumright's first bank, the Drumright State Bank.

In addition to the clothing store my father formed partnerships with others to build and operate the Roberts Hotel, the Briggs Lumber Company of Drumright, Yale and Stroud; Stephenson & Berry, later Stephenson & Shidler Dodge Motor Car dealership; the Kelvinator Refrigerator franchise, an oil company, and a pig farm which became a very poor investment when all of the pigs were "wiped out" by a cholera epidemic.

Organizing the Town

Although my father belonged to numerous civic organizations and informal groups dedicated to building the city and establishing law and order, he took the greatest pride in his participation in organizing the camp into a town, the moving of the post office to Drumright and in getting the railroad to Drumright. In 1914, he worked hard to establish a new Shaffer County with Drumright as the county seat.

In those early days the camp was a rough-tough area where gamblers, hijackers, robbers, prostitutes, and bootleggers preyed on oil field workers. Many of those workers and townsmen carried guns to protect self and property.

The Drumright *Journal* reported on Friday, June 26, 1925, in relating early day history that a meeting of pioneers was held in June 1913 to plan "the best method to bring order out of chaos, as up until that time all the law and order put into effect was what the county authorities did and it was a little enough at that." At a follow-up meeting on June 24, 1913, the Incorporated Town of Drumright was born and a chief of police appointed. P. J. was one of the organizing founders and

Drumright II, A Thousand Memories

at the June 24 meeting he was appointed the first town clerk. Drumright did not become a "City of First Class" until May, 1916.

The young P. J. Stephenson, Sr., (r.) who became the first town clerk and the first retailer in Drumright. Below, in January 1974 with his wife, Anna. He loved Drumright so much he did not want to leave town even for vacations. *Photos courtesy Charles E. Stephenson.*

A Tiger Hill Post Office

The nearest post office to the Drumright camp was located in the Tiger camp a few miles from Drumright. Residents of Drumright traveled to this post office and brought the Drumright mail to a local pool hall where it was scattered over a pool table. Local residents then sorted through it and picked up mail for themselves and their friends.

The local founders convinced the U.S. Postal Service that Drumright, being more populated, was a better location for the post office. It was then moved from Tiger camp to the highest hill in the area which became known as Tiger Hill, thereby honoring its first location.

The railroad first set up its main terminal at Pemeta, a few miles north of Drumright. The railroad had erected a station, freight depot and had even plotted a city for Pemeta before the concerned business community leaders requested train service to Drumright. After many discussions and several concessions (Dad called this blackmail) such as free right-of-way, much of which was donated primarily by Harley Fulkerson and Aaron Drumright, Drumright was awarded its terminal.

Dad, along with his many Democratic friends such as Dr. O. W. Starr, Homer O'Dell and E. W. Holland, was very active in politics. He was a lifelong Democrat and always voted a straight Democratic ticket in national elections. His biggest disappointment in his three sons was on those rare occasions when one of the boys would make the mistake of indicating that he was going to split his votes in a national election.

During World War II he was appointed the Administrator of the Creek County Ration Board. He enjoyed this position very much though it was at first a non-paying type of employment. He was commended highly by state administrators for his attempts to assist those citizens with real and justifiable needs for additional allotments and for his diplomacy in denying numerous requests which were unfounded. He resigned from this position to accept an appointment as county treasurer of Creek County to fill the unexpired term of a deceased treasurer. He was then elected Creek County Treasurer in the next ten elections.

Never A Klansman

During his entire adult life many of my father's activities were initiated by a deep desire for the establishment and maintenance of quality law and order. This was also the primary reason that he did not join the Ku Klux Klan—even though it was the peer group "thing to do" in the early years of Drumright. He considered the Klan's activities as lawless and un-American. Had he not been of this opinion he still would not have joined as his membership would have been an affront to my mother, who was of the Catholic faith.

Drumright II, A Thousand Memories

One of my mother's stories about Dad's experiences during the Klan period involved a trip he made to Massad's Grocery Store to pick up her favorite Monarch brand of canned goods. While at the store my dad was informed by Mr. Massad that other klansmen desiring not to be seen trading in a Syrian-owned store, entered the store from the rear and that it would probably be to P. J.'s advantage to avoid any further entry from the front. Since many of my Dad's friends were klansmen he was considered by association to be one also. Dad became incensed by this erroneous assumption. Mr. Massad knew the true facts before the discussion was finalized.

My dad really enjoyed living in Drumright and Creek County. Although Mother would frequently take the rest of the family on vacations to Texas, Dad always preferred to stay in Drumright close to his business and his many friends. I can remember only one vacation that Dad took with the family. It was to Lake Taneycomo in Missouri for four days. We were accompanied by his close friends from Drumright, the Earl and Bart Foster families. It was only in his later years that he would occasionally leave the area to visit his sons in Texas and Illinois.

So far, I have written this from a very partial and personal viewpoint. It would seem most appropriate to use an excerpt from the Drumright *Journal* of June 26, 1925, to summarize what others thought of Dad's contributions to the settlement and growth of Drumright:

> Mr. (P. J.) Stephenson is an enthusiast when it comes to things civic and in all endeavors to build up a bigger and better place in which to live. It takes such men as Mr. Stephenson to build up a community, and Drumright has been especially lucky when Old Dame Fortune directed his steps into this community.

Memories —
When Talking Ended and Shooting Started

The Day Sam Cook Went Hunting, The Day Officer Bice Shot Jeff Curlee, & The Day Willie Glimp Was Kidnapped

From the time he joined the Drumright police force, life was mostly turmoil for Curtis Bice and his wife, Pansy, a granddaughter of J. W. Fulkerson.

Chapter VIII

The Day Sam Cook Went Hunting

Either He or Deputy Braught Would Die Before Sundown

In the turbulent years from 1916 to 1924, a Drumright policeman was as likely to be shot at as for him to shoot someone else. Five Drumright men who served during that period were shot and killed. Four others were wounded but survived. Three men claimed to be chief of police at the same time. Most of the others were suspected of taking bribes from bootleggers and at least one was indicted. A warrant was issued for the arrest of Drumright's second chief of police, W. E. Maxwell, after he left town late one night but it was never served.

During this time, citizens were often divided — some unwaveringly supported the police. Others consistently condemned them and blamed them for liquor dens and houses of prostitution that flourished along Broadway. Some protested that police used unnecessarily rough tactics in making arrests and intimidated citizens.

Newspapers had their problems with police, too. R. L. Moore, an early editor of the *Derrick* and later of the *Drumright Post*, was beaten for printing unfavorable material. Lou S. Allard, Sr., *Derrick* publisher, was often threatened with violence. His home was ransacked as officers sought to get notes and records he was using for articles about the city government. On October 21, 1916, the *Derrick* published a front page editorial entitled "Police Intimidate Drumright Citizens."

> The police department in this city is probably the worst in the United States . . . People of this city, good, peaceful, law-abiding citizens, have been threatened and ordered to leave the city. They have gone into places when the owners were not home and ransacked the house and then tacked a search warrant on the door. They have searched places where there was practically no evidence to warrant them in getting a warrant and searching the place. Two cases we know of this week . . . and absolutely nothing was found. It is little short of a reign of terror . . . What is this city coming to? A well-regulated police department is to give protection to the citizens of any city — not fill their hearts with terror and give them orders to leave the city.

All of these troubles were fomenting a year earlier when Sam Cook joined the Drumright police force as a patrolman in June, 1915. One might wonder why any man would become involved in such a precarious situation, but Sam Cook was no shrinking violet. In announcing Cook's appointment, the *Derrick* said that Cook had been an outlaw, a bandit, and a train robber. It said he had killed three United States marshals, had twice been sentenced to hang by Judge Isaac Parker, Fort Smith's famous hanging judge, and had served five years in a federal prison. Looking back, it could be that Chief of Police Charles E. Tomleson considered Cook's qualifications ideal for being a Drumright police officer.

Police Are Arrested

Tomleson needed help of almost any kind. Shortly after he appointed Cook, Tomleson, himself, was arrested for impersonating an officer. Charged along with him were Cook and two other Tomleson appointees, E. H. Keller and Bert Wheeler. All four were booked at the Creek County jail in Sapulpa. Drumright had incorporated in 1913 but still had no elected mayor or chief of police. The city council was running the town and was bitterly divided. Two council members supported Tomleson and declared him chief of police. Two others fired him and hired A. D. Jordan. In the meantime, Jim Rippey had been appointed temporary chief while the squabble was going on but he refused to give up the office. The town had three men claiming to be chief of police. One solution seemed to be to put one of them in jail.

Tomleson was also accused of consorting with bootleggers and gamblers and taking pay-offs. Jordan was hailed by the new council members and the administrator, O. C. Elliott, as the man who could clean up the town. In the end, Jordan prevailed, but his victory was short-lived. His efforts to clamp down on liquor dens caused so much opposition that he was ousted and took a job as an Oilton policeman. E. H. Keller was named Drumright chief to replace Jordan.

Sam Cook had weathered the strife and remained on the force with Keller. But he was becoming bitter. County deputies had arrested him along with the others even though he was new on the force. And strife was growing between city and county officers over which had jurisdiction over Drumright liquor and gambling dens. Rumors were rife that liquor dealers were paying off officers. County and city officers accused each other of infringing on their "territory." Lew Wilder was county sheriff and his Drumright deputies were T. R. Braught and M. H. Vansickle.

Breaking Point Nears

In the middle of the controversy was a gang which called itself the "Big Six," which operated The Hump, a notorious den of gambling, prostitution, and liquor, west of Drumright, the Oil Exchange in Oilton and a similar den in Shamrock. County officers were accused of protecting these establishments.

Drumright II, A Thousand Memories

Through most of the turmoil, Sam Cook remained quiet. He knew that because of his past record he was on trial and he sought to alleviate doubts about his character. For the most part, people were saying he was a good officer. His past was being forgotten. But Cook had also been loyal to Chief Tomleson, the man who hired him. Whether he was involved with Tomleson in dealings with liquor establishments is not known, but he stood by his boss during the controversy. From the day that Tomleson was fired and city police were arrested by county officers, Sam Cook's feelings for county officers, especially Braught and Vansickle, bordered on hatred. Sometimes words were exchanged as he met the deputies on Drumright's crowded dirt Main Street. At other times, the officers turned up in the same liquor establishment.

By early fall in 1916, tension had grown in Drumright and it became apparent that a breaking point was near. Rev. R. W. Lackey, the Baptist minister, created near hysteria with his stirring sermons and crusade against "booze, bawdy houses, and gambling" in Drumright. The circumstances indicated talking was about to end and shooting might well begin.

Shooting Begins

It was on November 13, 1916, that matters came to a head. Sam Cook had been out most of the morning and then went to lunch at his

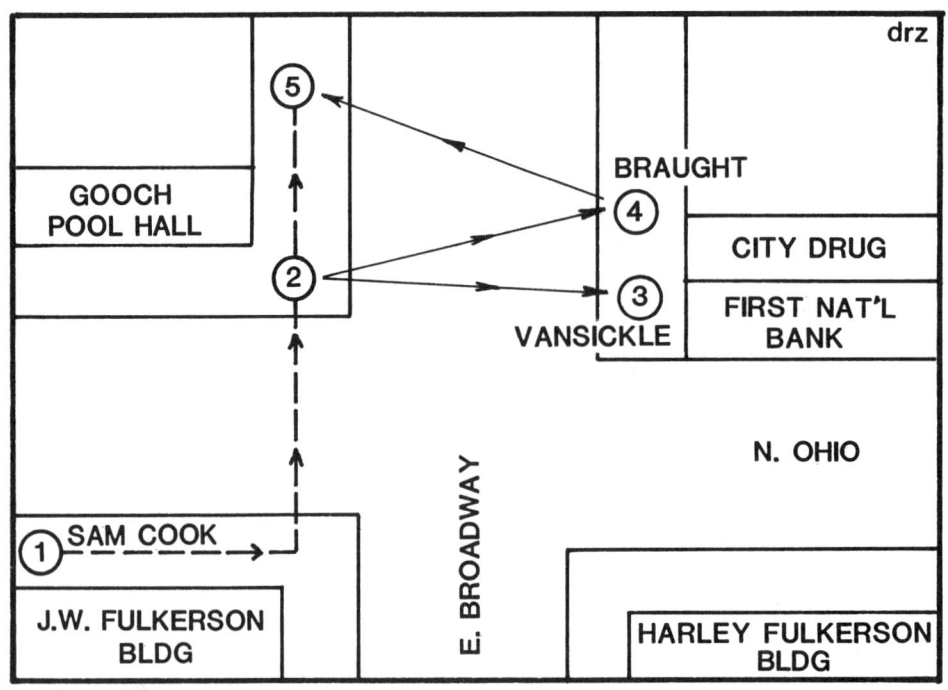

Sam Cook's death trail on November 16, 1916. (1) He sees his quarry. (2) He crosses Ohio Street and fires at Vansickle (3) and Braught (4). Braught returns fire as Cook moves up to Broadway to (5). *Drawing by Dwight Zimbelman.*

224

The Day Sam Cook Went Hunting

home on Drumright Street just a block from Broadway. When he entered the police staton at 1 p.m. he was upset and grim. Whether he had had an encounter with Deputies Braught and Vansickle that morning is not known. But he picked up a shotgun and several extra shells and walked out of the station. He intended to hunt down T. R. Braught. He vowed this would be the last day of life either for him or Braught.

It was about 3:30 that afternoon before he found his quarry. As he walked north on Ohio Street beside the J. W. Fulkerson building, he saw Braught and Vansickle standing in front of the City Drug Store. They had not seen him. As he reached Broadway, Cook moved quickly west across Ohio Street. He glanced quickly behind him into Gooch's Pool Hall and then looked straight at the deputies. They still had not seen him. Cook raised the shotgun and fired twice.

The first shot struck Braught in the arm and shoulder. The second hit Vansickle in the knees and legs. But Braught's wound had not disabled him completely. He lunged toward the door of the City Drug Store and crawled inside. Ed Thomas always kept a loaded gun in his drug store and someone quickly handed it to Braught. By the time Braught limped back outside, Cook had started up Broadway and had reached the site that later became Kraker Bros. Store. Braught aimed quickly and fired one shot. Evidently he was a better marksman than Cook. The bullet went through Cook's heart. Cook fell dead without a sound. His vow had been fulfilled but it was he, not Braught, who did not make it through the day.

The Sapulpa *Herald* called the shooting a murder and said it caused excitement even in Drumright where people were accustomed to such things. Said the *Herald*:

> Creek County is disgraced by another murder committed by officers and as a result there is a widow and orphaned children sitting today musing on conditions as they have been allowed to become in this fair land and finding what little consolation they can in the fact that January First and a new order of things in Creek County is almost here.

What the *Herald* meant was that if Cook had only been patient, Sheriff Wilder and his deputies would be out of office soon and his problem might have worked itself out.

Braught was held briefly and charged with murder, but the charges were dismissed after a preliminary hearing. Vansickle's wounds were found not serious and he was released from the hospital after a short stay. Funeral services were held 9 a.m. November 15, 1916, for Sam Cook at his home on East Drumright Street. His body was shipped to Henryetta for burial. He was 52 at the time of his death. His struggle for rehabilitation had lasted one year. Several pellets from Sam Cook's shotgun struck the front of the City Drug Store and several others remained lodged above the soda fountain inside for many years.

The Day Officer Bice Shot Jeff Curlee

The *Derrick* Praised Him But His Enemies Never Forgot

If Drumright thought the shoot-out between police officers would bring peaceful times, it was sadly in error. Tensions and strife abated from mid-1917 until World War I ended in November 1918. Then the struggle against immorality was renewed more vigorously than ever.

Many citizens felt that moral values had declined after the war and that in 1919 sin was rampant in Drumright and the oil field. Reminding them daily of this was a row of houses of prostitution directly across the street from the city hall in full view of the mayor and chief of police. Rev. R. W. Lackey of the First Baptist Church rallied his forces again, this time with the support of a vigilante group called the Overall and Hickory Shirt Brigade and a new crusading newspaper called the Drumright *Post*.

Soon the town was bitterly divided between the "ins" and the and the "outs." The ins were Mayor W. E. Nicodemus, Drumright's first elected mayor, the city council, Chief of Police Jack Ary, and other key members of the city administration. The outs were Reverend Lackey, R. L. Moore, publisher of the *Post*, the Overall and Hickory Shirt Brigade, and other citizens who had joined the cause. The outs believed the quickest way to stamp out sin was to oust the city administration. Nicodemus and Ary held to the belief that it was better to control dens of gambling and prostitution than to close up all of them. Several thousand robust young men were working in the oil field. The mayor and chief of police believed it would be dangerous to cut off all the recreation and close their hangouts.

Into this situation in 1919 came young Milton C. (Curtis) Bice as a new member of the Drumright police force. It was easy to see why Chief Ary chose him. Bice was more than six feet tall, handsome, and muscular. He was just back from service in the war, where he had been in the thick of combat. Toward the end of the war he was awarded the Purple Heart medal and was treated for shell-shock. He seemed to have recovered and was enthusiastic about becoming a police officer. He knew that Drumright was a rough town and he had no qualms about being able to take care of the duties and himself.

Circumstances were similar in many ways to those when Sam Cook had joined the police force in 1915. Fate seemed to play strange

The Day Officer Bice Shot Jeff Curlee

tricks on Cook. What appeared to be an opportunity for a new life proved in a way to be his undoing. Bice's life changed drastically, too, after he joined the Drumright police in the midst of great turmoil. He was to become one of the most controversial members of the Drumright police force and the day he shot Jeff Curlee would be debated for many years.

Ary assigned Bice the job of motorcycle patrolman and the new officer was a dashing figure on Broadway. He also impressed the girls. He had been married and divorced once, which people frowned on in those days, but this did not bother the girls. His towering figure, soft southern accent, and smile captured their fancy. Sometimes he took them riding on his motorcycle.

One in particular, Pansy Matlock, a granddaughter of J. W. Fulkerson, became his steady, and on August 2, 1920, they slipped away to Jeffersonville, Ind., and were married. For a time, they went to West Virginia where Bice worked in the coal mines, but when they returned for a visit to Drumright one day, he decided to rejoin the police force. Pansy's sister had been run down by a truck on a Drumright street and the driver had been impolite. Bice rejoined the police force, hunted the driver down, and rather unceremoniously dragged him to the police station.

The Sapulpa Trials

After that, Bice became Ary's right-hand man. They were the men most responsible for keeping law and order in a very lively oil town. They were apparently successful in their efforts but complaints about their methods increased. Citizens said they were being treated roughly on arrests for minor charges. One reported he was shot at when he failed to stop promptly. Bice became the most feared man on the streets of Drumright since the days of "Hookie" Miller. Some citizens filed formal complaints. Others took their stories to Reverend Lackey and the Drumright *Post*.

This provided Lackey with the ammunition he needed. In the fall of 1921, he and a group of other citizens were able to obtain a grand jury investigation of the Drumright city administration and police force. During the probe and subsequent trials, Judge Gaylord Wilcox appointed A. N. (Jack) Boatman and W. D. (Buck) Tharel to serve temporarily as mayor and chief of police respectively. Tharel recruited 20 men to guard the city hall with shotguns during the trials.

The trials were a great emotional ordeal for Drumright, and carloads of friends and enemies of Nicodemus and Ary struggled over the dirt road to Sapulpa to testify. The outs were unable to substantiate corruption charges against the mayor. He was declared innocent and returned to office. Although more than 100 citizens testified in his behalf, Ary was found guilty of "laxity in enforcing laws on booze and bawdy

Drumright II, A Thousand Memories

M. C. (Curtis) Bice, Drumright's controversial motorcycle policeman. Citizens complained he and Jack Ary were overzealous in making arrests. Some called him "the most feared man on the streets of Drumright since the days of 'Hookie' Miller." *Photo courtesy Julia Bice Hoover.*

houses and of being a party to an assault on a man." Several men who had been arrested by Ary and Bice testified against them. Ary was not permitted to return to office and Kelly Myers was appointed to replace him. The decision had little effect on Ary's long-term career. He served as a deputy sheriff until 1923 when he was elected chief of police. He remained in office for 20 more years.

The jury did not include Bice in its verdict and he was permitted to continue as a motorcycle patrolman. This undoubtedly pleased Bice, but he might have been better off had he, too, been suspended. For several months he performed his duties without incident. Then, on the afternoon of May 1, 1922, Bice encountered a group of men shooting dice in the middle of the old Shamrock road. He was not wearing his gun and he decided to go home and get it before making an arrest.

By the time he returned, the men saw him coming and climbed into their car. Bice gave chase, but on the old Cushing road, the driver suddenly turned the car around and headed straight toward Bice. The car knocked the motorcycle off the road and ran over Bice. He was critically injured and remained in the hospital for more than a week. The Associated Press announced that he had been killed. But Bice returned to duty, and once again he might have been fortunate had he

The Day Officer Bice Shot Jeff Curlee

remained off the police force, for on the morning of July 31, 1922, the police station received word that Jeff Curlee was in town.

Jeff Curlee Returns

Curlee's name was familiar to Drumright police. In earlier days he had operated the Avalon Rooms. The *Derrick* said he had been arrested numerous times for possession of liquor and for gambling. It said Curlee had later served time in prison for grand larceny, but had been at first paroled and then pardoned. Curlee had made no secret of his bitter feelings toward Drumright police. Whether Bice had arrested Curlee previously is not known, but he knew about him, and Curlee knew Bice.

Curlee had moved to a small community called DeNoya, later named Whizbang, and this was believed to have been his first trip back to Drumright. He had been in town for two days. Chief Myers was concerned because the informant said Curlee was carrying a gun. Myers obtained two warrants for Curlee's arrest — one for vagrancy and one for carrying a concealed weapon. He ordered Curtis Bice to bring Curlee in.

The Bennett building shortly after it was built in 1916 by James G. Bennett. The Bice-Curlee struggle took place in the side door entrance. Curlee once operated the Avalon Hotel two doors west. Vehicles illustrate the variety of transportation available then. In front is Ford roadster and an early version of a pick-up. Next to horse and wagon on side is the sporty Model-T with rumble seat, a touring car, and a sedan. In center is a rare view of the flag pole where citizens gathered for band concerts and other activities. *Photo courtesy Drumright Oil Field Museum.*

Drumright II, A Thousand Memories

Bice mounted his motorcycle and searched Drumright streets for nearly an hour before he spotted Curlee about 11 a.m. beside the Bennett building in the 100 block of South Penn. An elderly man near the corner said Bice approached Curlee on foot and said "Put up your hands." The two men then grappled with hands above their heads. Each seemed to be trying to reach for his gun. The struggle carried them inside an entrance to a stairway and they disappeared from view. In a moment several shots were heard. Bice emerged and Curlee was found crumpled at the foot of the stairs, his gun beneath him.

Feelings against Bice were still strong after the Sapulpa trials and some of those he had previously arrested sought to use the incident to arouse public opinion. Word spread that Curlee was unarmed and that he had been shot in the back while running up the stairs. Sheriff D. B. Livingston received word in Sapulpa that a riot was imminent. He quickly deputized 19 men and brought them to Drumright. The alarm was false and no incidents occurred.

A technical charge of murder was filed against Bice, but these were dropped after witnesses testified that Bice had followed proper police procedures and that Curlee had drawn his gun first. Four shots had been fired during the scuffle, some from each gun. The only bullet that found a mark was the one that hit Curlee. It did not hit him in the back.

Although he was cleared in the shooting and praised by the *Derrick* for his handling of the Curlee incident, Bice was never able to erase the rumors. They were retold for years. Bice was disheartened by the situation and decided to quit the Drumright police force. He first went to Sapulpa where he became a deputy sheriff and then to Muskogee where he worked for a brief time as a special deputy for the U.S. government. Apparently tired of police work and homesick for Drumright, Bice returned and opened a grocery store on East Broadway near Virginia Street across from Miller Hardware.

A Store is Blown Up

When he arrived in Drumright, trouble was awaiting him again. Bice lived in a small house near his store and late on the night of June 17, 1928, he heard a loud explosion. Without taking time to dress, he dashed from the house into the store, which was already in flames. Bice had been storing his money in the back. He ran frantically to retrieve about $900 in cash. Shortly after he entered the building, another explosion blew out the west wall. The roof, already in flames, collapsed on him. There was no doubt the fire was arson. Bice's enemies had struck again. Bice was near death, his body covered with burns, but he finally survived the ordeal.

During this stay in the hospital, Bice left behind an unsolved mystery. Apparently feeling that he was about to die, he asked to see

The Day Officer Bice Shot Jeff Curlee

Fed up with problems of a peace officer, Curtis Bice (right) opened this neat grocery store across from Miller Hardware on East Broadway. But his enemies set fire to the store one night and he was almost killed trying to save a stash of money. *Photo courtesy Julia Bice Hoover.*

Mrs. Emmalee Gibson, the grandmother of Kenneth Garven Williams, a 9-year-old boy who was kidnapped and murdered on June 8, 1922. When she arrived at the hospital on the southeast corner of Virginia and Broadway, two men blocked the door and refused to let her enter. After he recovered, Bice left Drumright again, and one can only speculate what he had in mind, since he had been a member of the police force and also a member of the Ku Klux Klan at the time of the boy's disappearance. Mrs. Gibson said she observed a stake-out near her house for several days after that.

Bootleg Ring

Bice was again disheartened by the turn of events. Within a short time he drifted from law enforcement to a life as a law violator. This was to bring him even more grief. He became involved in liquor dealings in Davenport and Earlsboro and later in Roxana, a small oil field community near Guthrie that is now a ghost town. The *Guthrie Register-News* once described him as "alleged king of a bootleg ring in Roxana."

But beneath the surface were even more sinister circumstances. The U.S. government believed that a major bootleg ring was operating in central Oklahoma, possibly with underworld connections. The ring

Drumright II, A Thousand Memories

involved not only liquor distributors but also peace officers in Seminole, Pottawatomie, and Logan counties. Bice allegedly had ties to that ring.

Bice's wife, Pansy, had for some time encouraged him to get out of the liquor business and return to a normal life. She believed now might be the chance. After some deliberation, Bice volunteered to testify to the grand jury about liquor dealings, especially in the Shawnee area.

Roy S. Lewis, U.S. district attorney, was elated. He immediately notified local and county officers, especially in Logan County, to "leave Bice alone and do not have trouble with him. He may be our most important witness." He also warned Bice that his offer to testify might endanger his life. Another witness, Sadie Webster, of Hoover City, had been killed and her death was being investigated. Bice told his family and friends he had premonitions that he, too, might be murdered. He took his family on a 10-week vacation in western U.S.A.

The grand jury proceedings had already begun when Bice returned to Roxana in early September. A former chief of police at Earlsboro had been arrested and brought back for the hearings. Indictments had already been returned against the county attorney and the former sheriff of Pottawatomie County. The jury and the district attorney anxiously awaited Bice's testimony.

A Set-Up For Murder?

These were the circumstances at 3 p.m. Thursday, Sept. 19, 1929, when Bice parked his car in front of the Famous Store in Roxana. With him was Bill Murphy, owner of a Roxana cafe. This was the day before Bice was to testify before the grand jury.

As the car came to a stop, Murphy jumped from the car and ran. Surprised, Bice looked up and saw why. A few yards away was a black coupe. Behind the wheel was Milo Beck, deputy sheriff of Logan County. Beck and Bice were bitter enemies. On the previous Saturday night, Beck had arrested Bice and accused him of "shooting up Roxana." On that night Bice, feeling the pressure of the grand jury hearings and sure that an attempt would be made on his life, had walked up a hill at Roxana and fired several shots into the air. Beck had been a deputy sheriff in Oilton in the early 1920's but whether he and Bice were acquainted then is unknown.

Conflicting stories exist on what happened in the next few minutes. Beck got out of his car and took a few steps toward Bice. He was facing the passenger side of the Bice car. He later said he intended to ask Bice the whereabouts of C. E. Dixon, who was wanted in Seminole County. Murphy told police Beck said, "Bice, I want to see you," and that Bice replied, "Don't come any closer, Beck."

As Bice dropped his hand from the wheel and edged toward the door, Beck opened fire. He fired five times. Two bullets hit Bice near

The Day Officer Bice Shot Jeff Curlee

Curtis Bice's tempestuous life ended on the Main Street of Roxana near Guthrie when he was shot and killed by a deputy sheriff he intended to testify against the next morning before a grand jury investigating a liquor ring in central Oklahoma. His body is partially out of the car at left. *Photo courtesy Julia Bice Hoover.*

the heart and another pierced his leg. He died on the scene after getting partly out of the car. His gun was partially out of his pocket.

For a time there were outcries about the shooting — that Bice had been murdered to keep him from testifying at the liquor hearings. Mrs. Bice said her husband intended to testify against several police officers, including Beck. She believed Murphy had been used to lure Bice to the scene. Murder charges were filed against Beck, but there was little follow-up.

Beck said he shot in self defense — that Bice was reaching for his gun and he simply beat him to the draw. Murphy backed Beck in his testimony. Although the district attorney had emphatically warned Logan County officers to leave Bice alone, Beck claimed he never received the message. The U.S. district attorney's office promised an investigation but its interest waned quickly since Bice could not now testify. On Sept. 26, one week after the shooting, murder charges against Beck were dropped.

Mrs. Bice was angry. "They freed him," she wrote in a letter. "It was the dirtiest piece of work I ever saw put over. I think they were afraid of the judgment of 12 men . . . The county attorney didn't even get the witnesses I asked for nor ask a question I wanted asked." Mrs.

Bice prepared to pursue Beck's prosecution but when the 1929 market crash came in October, she suffered heavy financial losses and was forced to abandon the effort.

Julia Mae Bice Hoover, Bice's daughter, who was only a child then, has stark memories of the ordeal. "Law enforcement officers and so-called prominent citizens in the underworld of Drumright, Earlsboro, Roxana, Marshall, and Guthrie communities were involved in the liquor ring," she said. "It was a way of life with them. My father had also been a law enforcement officer. His only problem was that he was going to disclose all of the others' involvement. Fearing his testimony, they set him up for murder. With his death, they were all in the clear."

Thus ended the tempestuous, controversial life of Officer M. C. (Curtis) Bice. His relatives said he was a good family man, Jack Ary and Kelly Myers said he was a good policeman. He had shown courage on the battlefield during World War I.

Would Bice's life have been any different had he not joined the Drumright police force at a time of the town's greatest strife and cleavages and if he had not been sent to arrest Jeff Curlee? These questions cannot be answered but certainly that day seemed to remain forever among the memories of early-day Drumright.

The Day Willie Glimp Was Kidnapped

Ben Clark said, 'I Won't Die With My Boots On'

The day of Friday, August 9, 1940, began like any other for Willie (Bill) Glimp and his family. It was peach-canning time and the family was gathered on the back porch of the Glimp home southeast of Drumright peeling peaches. Canning fruits and vegetables was an economic necessity during the great depression, and it was actually a family project. Willie, his wife, Ella, and her father, Francis J. (Dutch) Wisely, were doing the peeling. Gerry and Darla, the Glimp's two young daughters, were watching and waiting expectantly for the adults to hand them slices of ripe peaches.

It was early afternoon on this quiet sunshiny day. The only hint of trouble in the area was that five automobiles had been stolen from the streets of Drumright on successive nights the past week. On the previous Friday, Bud Wilson's 1940 Model-A Ford had disappeared from in front of the Miller Rooms at Virginia and Broadway. The next day a 1940 Ford coupe had been taken from the Robert Conway home at 310 S. Penn. On Monday, Eddie Shadid awakened to find that his 1938 Chevrolet had disappeared from 117 South Cimarron. On the night of August 6, U.S. Pierce's 1936 Chevrolet was stolen from 404 South Penn, and on Thursday night, August 8, a 1935 Chevrolet belonging to Bob Barr at 121 East Maple disappeared.

Police officers in several counties and towns were much concerned and had some ideas about the identities of the thieves, but most residents of the area were unconcerned—that is, until Friday, August 9.

As the Glimps peeled peaches and chatted, they heard the sound of a car pulling into the driveway and the beep of a horn. Glimp and Wisely went to greet George Oldenstadt, a neighbor to the south, and his friend, John Leonard. The two wanted to see Willie Glimp about help in harvesting Leonard's peanut crop. Oldenstadt and Leonard had scarcely stepped out of the 1928 black Model-A Ford sedan when their conversation was interrupted.

Suddenly and seemingly out of nowhere appeared two men, one brandishing a revolver. Both seemed desperate and one was drenched with blood. The latter was spokesman for the two. Although he was jittery and nervous, he tried to calm the frightened group.

Drumright II, A Thousand Memories

"We have to get out of this country," he said to Willie Glimp. "We have shot someone and we don't want to shoot anyone else." He ordered Glimp to get in the Oldenstadt sedan. "You are taking us away from here," the blood drenched man said.

Glimp protested the car wasn't his and pointed to his own rather dilapidated coupe. Dutch Wisely offered to drive, but the man pressed the gun into Glimp's back. "I believe you're a man who can stay cool," he said. "If you do that, we won't have to hurt anyone."

Then the desperado decided to trade his bloody clothes for some of Glimp's clothing. The Glimp's two small daughters watched as their father came around the house. Behind him was a man with a gun. After he had switched clothing, the man paused by the kitchen door.

"I saw you were scared," he told the children. "This is for taking your daddy away from you." He handed each a nickel. After warning the family not to notify the police for at least an hour, the two men herded Glimp into the car. The family watched as the car disappeared in a cloud of dust.

The events of August 9 had their beginning a month previously. On July 7, 1940, word was sent to police officers in Oklahoma that Bill Hall, 26, had escaped from the state penitentiary at McAlester. Hall had been sentenced to 10 years on May 20, 1939, for burglary. He was made a trusty in 1940 and used his new status to walk away to freedom.

A special alert was sent to chiefs of police Jack Ary of Drumright and Ben Clark of Oilton. A stocky man of 160 pounds, Hall had once lived in the Olive area and was reported to have attended Tiger School. He had once been a truck driver in Creek County oil fields. He knew his way around the side roads and how to find a hideout.

On July 26, another alert went out to police. Joe Lovelace, 22, and Carl Dickinson, 24, had left an honor farm in Genoa, Nebraska. It said Lovelace was serving time for forgery and Dickinson had been convicted for burglary. Lovelace was described as weighing 127 pounds, slender, and having protruding blue eyes.

Police paid little attention to the alerts until the morning of August 2, 1940. At 1:30 a.m., three men ate hamburgers and drank coffee in Mac's Hamburger Hut in Yale, then held up two employees. The descriptions of the robbers fitted two of the escapees.

While identification remained uncertain, officers were confident the robbers were hiding somewhere in the area. Cars were stolen, not only at Drumright but at Hallet, Oilton, and Stroud. Usually they were abandoned nearby. Police concentrated their search on the area.

Then came the fateful August 9. About 10 a.m. Mrs. Mary Bell glanced out the window of the small cafe she operated at the intersection of what is now Highway 99 and the old Oilton-Drumright highway. This was about a mile south of Oilton. A black Chevrolet sedan moved slowly

The Day Willie Glimp Was Kidnapped

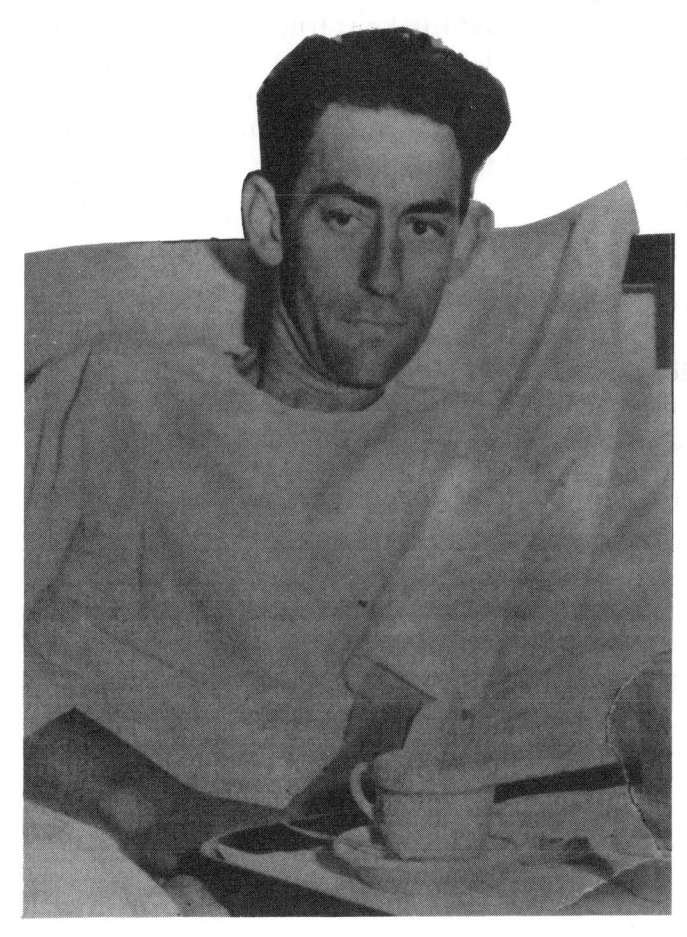

Willie (Bill) Glimp as he appeared in a Stillwater *Press* picture shortly after highway patrolmen trapped his kidnappers south of Perkins. In the same room with him was one of the kidnappers, Bill Hall.

off the pavement and stopped near the cafe door. The car motor was left running as two men stepped to the door.

Noting that she was alone, the stocky man pointed a pistol at Mrs. Bell. "This is a hold-up," he said, and watched as his slender accomplice stripped the cash register, then found another $50 in Mrs. Bell's purse. After warning her not to call police for 10 minutes, the men hurried back to the car and headed north. Mrs. Bell copied their tag number and immediately phoned Ben Clark. Within a few minutes he and Constable D. H. "Rabbit" Irwin were on the scene. A quick check revealed the car had been stolen from Bob Barr at Drumright.

Clark immediately sent an alert to all police agencies and a cordon was thrown around the area, but the robbers had disappeared. This meant one thing to Ben Clark: the robbers had found a hideout near Oilton. By telephone, word-of-mouth, and personal visits, Clark notified farmers and oil workers throughout the area to watch for strangers or suspicious characters.

Drumright II, A Thousand Memories

In less than an hour his efforts bore fruit. A farmer reported meeting a black man, Henry Washington, walking across the Seitsinger farm just northwest of town. He was carrying a sawed-off shotgun. Washington explained that he was hunting rabbits. This made the farmer suspicious and he followed Washington far enough to see him enter a shack about half-mile further west. Near the shack in some underbrush was a black Chevrolet.

"It's them," Clark said. Clark's wife, Myrtle, had driven their car to the beauty shop that morning, but Irwin had just driven up outside. Clark grabbed his .35 caliber automatic rifle and handed a revolver to Irwin. "Let's head for the Seitsinger place," Clark said, as he explained the situation to the constable. The tires on Irwin's new car screeched as he headed toward a road that ran just north of Oilton.

A Hail of Gunfire

As they drove down the road, a black Chevrolet suddenly appeared over a hill only 50 yards away. "There they are," Clark yelled, "block the road." The road was too narrow for two cars and Irwin tried to turn the car crossways. As it became stuck in the sand, Clark jumped from the car, rifle in hand. "Stop! Police!" he yelled at the oncoming car, but the driver increased the speed and headed straight toward Clark. Two men and a red-haired woman were in the front seat Henry Washington was in the back seat.

Clark put his rifle to his shoulder to fire, but before he could shoot, a shotgun blast came from the bandit's car. This was followed by pistol shots. The shotgun pellets hit Clark in the face, chest and arm. He was stunned but managed to get in sitting position and wipe the blood from his eyes.

Five times he fired the automatic rifle. Amid the curses and shouts in the car, he heard the woman scream, "No, Ben! Please don't shoot." She had learned Clark's identity on earlier trips to Oilton. Her pleas came too late. Clark's shots had sent a bullet through her leg and another into the driver, whom the police were fairly sure was Bill Hall.

As Clark fell to the ground, he heard Irwin fire four shots at the fleeing robbers. A few moments later, Clark and Irwin heard a shotgun explode in the robbers' car. They did not know at the time that this meant the end for the woman in the car. She had in the eyes of the robbers become a liability. Screaming in agony and unable to sit upright, she was making it difficult for Bill Hall to drive. She was bleeding profusely. Officers speculated it was Washington who fired the shotgun blast through the seat into the woman, but this was never definitely established. When they passed near the Oilton water tower, the men threw her body from the car. Hall had also been wounded and he turned driving chores over to his companion. At this point, Henry Washington decided that things

The Day Willie Glimp Was Kidnapped

were getting out of hand. He jumped from the car and disappeared in the brush.

He was captured a short time later by Deputy Sheriff Virgil Denny. He told Denny he fired the shotgun blast that hit Clark, but denied he shot the woman. He said he was not associated with the robbers but had sold them the shotgun for five dollars. They had given him one $2.50 payment and he was riding with them to town to collect the second payment. Hall later told police that Washington and the woman waited for them in a pasture on the Doolin farm while the Bell Cafe was being robbed.

Meanwhile, Mrs. Lela Seitsinger emerged from her home after hearing the shots. "Get an ambulance," Irwin shouted. "Ben Clark has been shot." In a few minutes, Paul Peck, operator of a funeral parlor in Oilton, arrived in an ambulance. He had stopped en route to pick up Mrs. Clark. Mrs. Seitsinger was bathing Ben Clark's face when they arrived. Mrs. Clark was relieved to find her husband alive, and even more so when he said, "Don't worry. I'm not going to die with my boots on."

Peck rushed Clark to the Cushing Hospital where Dr. D. W. Humphreys immediately began treatment. Eighty shotgun pellets and a bullet had hit him in the face. The bullet had taken a slanting route through his jaw and torn most of the flesh away. Dr. Humphreys was able to pull it together again. Clark remained in the hospital several days and underwent three transfusions, but he recovered and remained chief of police for many more years.

An Unhappy Life

The woman was identified as Jeanne Coffey of Asher, Okla., near Shawnee. She had dated Hall for several years before he was sent to the penitentiary. It was his overwhelming desire to see her, relatives said, that motivated him to escape. After his escape, she told relatives she was going on a trip to Kansas City, but Hall picked her up near Shawnee and she remained with him until her death.

Mrs. Coffey was the mother of two small daughters. Her suitcase contained a diary expressing her love for them and entries describing her unhappy life. Hall's relatives described her as a "good woman" who had not been in trouble previously. Her belongings included a short poem which was perhaps prophetic. Entitled "My Lurid Life," it read:

*For one abandoned hour
I cheated and I paid,
My unholy secret
In lavender is laid.*

*To the port of lonely hearts
For refuge I will fly
The public forgets,—but
Confidentially, not I.*

Drumright II, A Thousand Memories

Meanwhile Hall and his accomplice, as they drove a short distance from the scene of the shooting, observed a car coming toward them from a country road. It seemed a good time to dump the bullet-ridden blood drenched Barr car and get new wheels. Earl Williams, 17, was driving his father's new Chevrolet to town to get the mail. As he crossed a cattle guard, he observed the two men, one of them bloody, beside their car. Thinking they may have had an accident, he paused and asked, "Can I be of any help?"

"You sure can," replied Hall, pointing the shotgun at Williams. "Get out and give us your car." The youth complied and the two men took off hurriedly traveling south.

Hall knew the main highways would be watched closely so he headed for an area he thought he knew well enough to elude police — the oil fields southeast of Drumright. But as he came suddenly upon a dead-end in the country road, he overran it and the car bogged down in a corn field. As he pondered his dilemma, he saw a farm house about a quarter of a mile away with a car in the driveway. A few minutes later Bill Glimp, Frank Wisely, and George Oldenstadt found themselves looking into the barrel of a .38 revolver.

Hall herded Glimp into the living room and the rest of the family into the kitchen while he shed his bloody clothes and donned a shirt and trousers belonging to Glimp. Hall was almost obsequious as he apologized for what he was doing and promised no harm would come to Glimp. After handing the Glimp daughters each a nickel, he, his accomplice, and Glimp took off in Oldenstadt's 1928 Model-A. He warned the Glimps not to notify police for at least an hour.

At first Glimp drove around the area of Litchfield and the Tidal Refinery, then headed west over several country roads. As darkness came, neither Glimp nor his captors had any idea where they were.

The Glimps had no telephone, and Mrs. Glimp walked to Pleasant Hill school where she phoned her husband's brother Roy, and asked him what he thought they should do. Within a short time, he picked up Mrs. Glimp and drove her to the Drumright police station. Jack Ary immediately alerted police agencies throughout the area.

Among those who received the message were highway patrolmen J. R. Butler and John W. Boyd. They were assigned to patrol the area near the intersection of State Highways 33 and 40 about nine miles south of Stillwater. The patrolmen came east to reach the intersection, then turned south to Perkins a mile away.

The Chase Ends at Perkins

As they passed through Perkins and crossed the Cimarron River, they saw a car moving slowly west on a section line and entering Highway 40, which was still a gravel road. It was just before 9 p.m. Edging closer,

The Day Willie Glimp Was Kidnapped

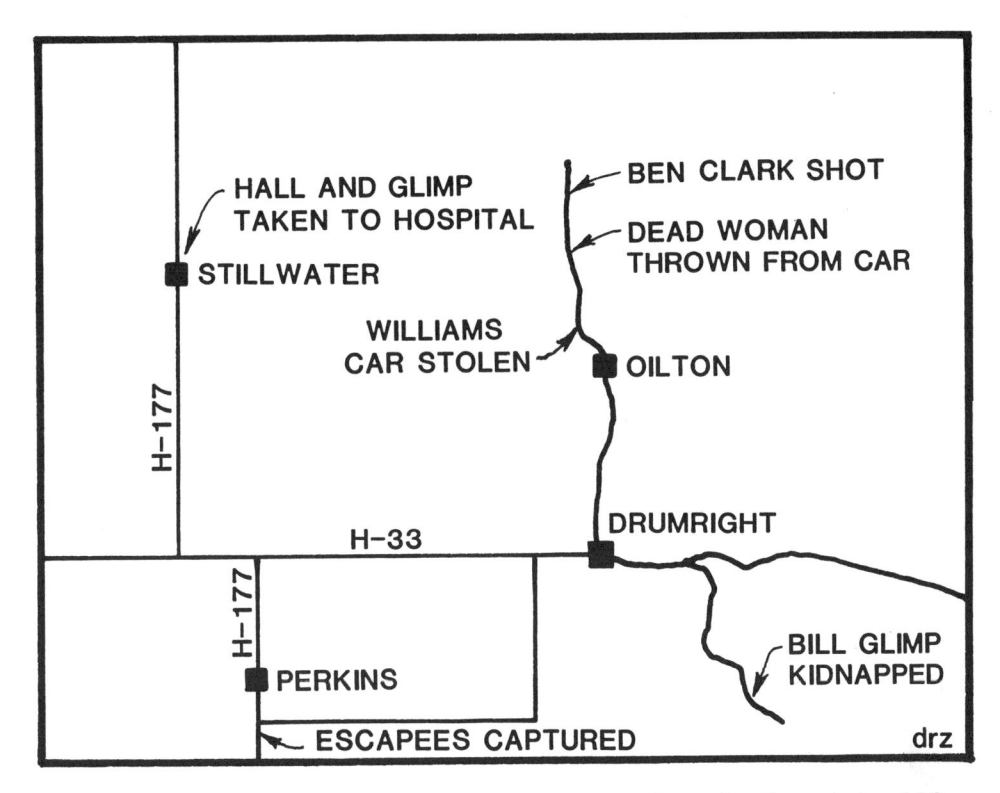

The shootings and kidnapping of August 9, 1940, started on a dirt road on the west edge of Oilton and ended with both the victim and a kidnapper in a Stillwater hospital. *Drawing by Dwight Zimbelman.*

the patrolmen recognized the Oldenstadt car. Boyd switched on the red lights, sounded the siren, and handed a shotgun to Butler. He already had his pistol in his lap ready for use.

Suddenly the black sedan stopped and one man leaped out with a shiny object in his hand. Boyd fired. On the other side of the car, another man jumped out with his hands up and tried to reach the weeds by the side of the road. Officers had been warned not to endanger the life of Bill Glimp, but it was dark and they were edgy. A pistol shot struck Glimp in the leg. A third man sat upright in the car with his hands up. During the gunfire, he had lain on the floor of the car.

Bill Hall and Bill Glimp were rushed to the Stillwater hospital, where, ironically, they were placed in the same room. Hall was chained to his bed. He was critically injured and at first was not expected to live. He said he didn't care—the one person in his life that he loved, Jeanne Coffey, was dead. Bill Glimp's wound was painful but not critical. His survival was assured, and after 11 days, he returned home.

Meantime, a fingerprint specialist at the Stillwater police department contacted the Oklahoma State Bureau of Investigation and established that the fingerprints of Hall's accomplice matched those of Joe Lovelace.

On August 15, 1940, the two men pleaded guilty to armed robbery before Judge C. O. Beaver. Hall was on a stretcher at the time. Both were sentenced to life imprisonment. Henry Washington received a 10-year sentence. Hall asked Mrs. Glimp to shake hands. He told her he was sorry her husband had been shot. "I shook his hand," she recalled 45 years later, "but I was shaking all over."

Thus, August 9, 1940, had started like any other day, but before it ended, the lives of more than a score of people changed. A woman was dead and two children motherless, two men serving relatively minor sentences were now sentenced to life, three men had been shot, a highway patrolman had in the dark shot an innocent man, and others had endured anxious moments.* Ben Clark recovered and served 42 more years as Oilton's chief of Police. Bill Glimp came home after 11 days in the hospital and recovered fully. His family eventually overcame the shock of the kidnapping. George Oldenstadt's car was returned to him. One bullet had gone through a door and the car's body had buckshot marks all over it. It was a day to remember in Oilton and Drumright history, and at least eight participants in the drama were still around in 1986 to tell about it.

*Records of the Oklahoma Department of Corrections show that Bill Hall died in 1973 and that Joe Lovelace was pardoned in August, 1974.

Memories —

Ben Russell
PHOTOGRAPHER
Drumright, Oklahoma

Photographer with the soul of an artist.

Chapter IX

Ben Russell — Oil Field Historian

He Recorded the Past With an Eye on the Future

Benjamin Franklin Russell could appropriately be called the resident historian of the Drumright oil field. He came to Drumright with a camera and tripod on his back in November 1912. Through the wildest years he took several hundred pictures of history as it unfolded. Had his collection remained intact, it would be a complete graphic account of the oil field. But many of his pictures have wound up in private collections and museums. Those in this chapter are from a special group that have remained in the family album and most have not been distributed previously.

Thirty-four years of age, Russell was six feet tall and strong physically and mentally when he came to Drumright from Fort Worth after reading about the oil strike in a newspaper. Like others who flocked into the new town, he hoped to make money—but from photography, not oil.

Russell walked everywhere carrying his camera and tripod, both of which were very heavy in those days. An artist and a freelancer, he kept a constant eye for people and things that would best record the oil field history. It was all in a day's work for him to walk seven miles south to Shamrock, then back and north six miles to Oilton, as he covered the territory.

Sometimes while walking over the dusty oil field roads, he met teamsters pulling heavily loaded wagons and they offered him a ride, but he always waved back and said, "I'll get there before you do." Many of the wagons bogged down in muddy ruts or slowed down while fording bridgeless streams, and Russell always arrived ahead of them.

His camera was a bellows-type. Although flash bulbs were available then, he photographed most of his subjects in daylight. He carried an opaque changing bag to change plates and film on the spot. He developed and finished the pictures in his tent at night after his long journey in the field.

Russell's picture composition (the way he arranged subjects and angles from which he photographed), and the choice of subjects show he had an intuition for what might be historically significant. Examples of this are in the pictures in this chapter. Many of the scenes are as strikingly clear as though they were photographed recently. He lettered small captions on most of his pictures to help explain the scenes and people. Much of this quality may be attributed to his early background.

Ben Russell was born at Golden, Mo., in Cass County, north of Eureka Springs, Arkansas, on October 28, 1878. He spent most of his youth in Texas, however and attended Weatherford College. After that he taught school for several years. While in Texas, he became interested in photography. "I wanted to do something I really liked," he told friends. "I began working with a photographer. This fascinated me and I decided to try it." He set up his first studio in Anadarko in 1902, even before statehood. He enjoyed photographing Indian scenes, but when Oklahoma became a state in 1907, he moved to Oklahoma City and operated a commercial studio until 1912.

One day shortly after his arrival in Drumright, Gladys Bethea brought film to his studio to be developed and printed. From this a courtship began. Russell often rented a buggy and they drove along the Cimarron River. In some of his pictures she is on a high bluff of the Cimarron or on a swinging bridge. They were married July 8, 1917.

The Russells spent the remainder of their lives in Drumright. In 1919, as the oil boom slowed, Ben took over a famous early-day business—the New Smoke House where he had earlier served as an apprentice to Bob Achterman and Billy Roberts. And in the 1930's, he was president of the Drumright State Bank. The Russells had four children, Eileene, Jayne, Elva Mae, and Jim, all of whom attended Second Ward School and later Drumright High School. Ben Russell died on Oct. 15, 1962, and Gladys died Dec. 25, 1980. They are buried at Fairlawn Cemetery in Cushing. His pictures that tell the oil field story are scattered far and wide, but a select group that most people have not seen are on the following pages.

Drumright II, A Thousand Memories

Ben Russell's combined tent and studio appear rather bleak in the winter of 1912-13 . . .

. . . but his surroundings take on a brighter hue and an oil derrick has sprouted up in the background as spring begins to break through. The tent was on the site of the present First Christian Church.

Ben Russell and His Camera

W. G. Bass had meager success with a grocery store and several other businesses and then decided to experiment with something new. In 1916, he opened Drumright's first swimming pool called the Bass Natatorium on North Penn, just north of the present First Christian Church parsonage. In 1923 it closed for several years. It was then operated several years by the Ray Gillette family. A part of one retaining wall still stands.

Bass Natatorium Drumright, Okla.

Drumright II, A Thousand Memories

George Sebastman's outdoor dance pavilion with piano in center was also on North Penn in 1916. The board walk on the east side of Penn extended from Broadway to the red high school.

The Electric Theatre operated as late as 1916. Newspapers in both Drumright and Shamrock mentioned it but never gave its location. The First Christian Church held some meetings there. Theatre admission was five cents for children and a dime for adults.

Ben Russell and His Camera

This scene from North Ohio looking south toward Broadway puports to show the "new post office," but it's really what most Drumrighters think of as the old post office that served from 1916 until 1940. It was next to Gourley's Cleaners in the picture on the west side of Ohio. Across the street is the Travelers Hotel, where a new post office was built in 1940. Straight ahead is the almost new J. W. Fulkerson Building.

Broadway began to convert from wooden to brick and stone buildings in 1914. Ben Russell snapped this picture on the north side of East Broadway even before the buildings were occupied. The Aaron Drumright stone building is second from right.

Drumright II, A Thousand Memories

The Harley Fulkerson building (right) was new when this picture was taken in late 1916 or early 1917. In the background is the Traveler's Hotel.

Ben Russell and His Camera

The ice wagon climbs the dirt street to Broadway and Penn in this 1916 picture. Dimly to the right is a stack of bricks soon to cover Broadway. A few doors down the hill is Pioneer Telephone Co., forerunner to Southwestern Bell.

Drumright II, A Thousand Memories

This may be the interior of the Strand Theatre, where wrestling matches were held frequently. Wrestlers performed on the stage rather than in a ring.

Automobiles line up on Broadway in 1914 in front of two leading dry good stores, K. Wasaf and Markey Fall. This is the north side of the 100 block. It's too early for brick, sidewalks or curbs, but a board walk stretches across Broadway. J. M. Haggar worked at Wasaf's until he and Rose Wasaf were married in 1915.

Ben Russell and His Camera

The Happy Dozen Card Club shows what the socially elite of Drumright wore during the boom days. Note the shirt waists with long sleeves, skirts that touch shoe tops, and laced high top shoes with spindle heels. The dog appears unimpressed, but Ben often included animals and children in his pictures to heighten interest.

If a Drumright woman wanted to be included among the socially prominent, she took care not to be too daring lest she be called a flapper. These sewing club women obviously were taking no chances, although most of them appear to have used a "kid curler" on their hair. The hair was rolled up on the curler. When it was taken down, it had a puffed-up look. Ben apparently felt he did not need a dog for this picture. First on left on bottom row is Mrs. Billy Roberts, whose husband once owned the Wheeler farm.

Drumright II, A Thousand Memories

The New Smoke House was almost an institution from Drumright's earliest days, owned first by Billy Roberts and Bob Achterman and later by Ben Russell (above). Taxis parked in front waiting for customers to The Hump. It had fountain in front (Bevo was the favorite soft drink), and pool tables in rear. Boys at the red high school made it their favorite hangout.

Ben Russell and His Camera

55,000 bbl Tank of oil boiling over.

Ben Russell captured this fire scene just as the oil was beginning to boil over the sides of the 55,000 barrel tank.

Big Drumright Oil Field Fire, Aug. 27, 1914

Ben went into the field to get a close-up of the August 1914 fire, the worst in the field's history.

Drumright II, A Thousand Memories

River Bed Oil Field — As I saw it — ~Ben~

Ben's oil field pictures reflect the soul of an artist. In this one is a view of the Cimarron River bed between the oil derrick on the left and the high bluff on the right. Atop the bluff is his wife, Gladys.

Ben Russell and His Camera

Here, Ben frames a burning gas well between two oil derricks. This apparently is taken from a bluff or another oil derrick.

Drumright II, A Thousand Memories

Sunset on the Cimarron

Amid the hustle and bustle of oil activity, Ben stopped to catch this quiet scene of sunset on the Cimarron.

In the first days of the oil boom in the north pool, there were no bridges across the Cimarron. Ben again applies an artistic touch as he captures a familiar scene of teamsters fording the river with a huge boiler.

The quest for oil wealth was sometimes hampered during the winter as derricks were covered with ice. Ben entitled this picture, probably taken in 1915, "A Mountain of Ice."

Drumright II, A Thousand Memories

A few remnants of this Prairie pump station still exist on the old Oilton highway about a mile and a half north of Drumright.

A vast supply of casing and boilers was unloaded in Drumright for distribution to the great oil field.

Ben Russell and His Camera

Tucker Sand Gusher

This gusher came from the deep Tucker sand east of Drumright. It bears some resemblance to a tornado. The sand got its name from the Fred Tucker farm.

Drumright II, A Thousand Memories

The McMan Oil Co., named for Robert M. McFarlin and James A. Chapman, became one of the major producers of the Drumright field. Most of its operations were in the north pool. In December 1916, McMan sold its holdings to Magnolia Petroleum Co. for an estimated $35 million.

McMan was one of the first to operate a ferry across the Cimarron. This scene appears almost as an artist's painting as Ben's camera catches the ferry in the center of the river framed between two trees.

Ben Russell and His Camera

The sign states that this foot bridge, one of the longest across the Cimarron, was owned by Samoset Petroleum Co. It was 600 feet across.

Chapter X

Epilogue

A Time to Harvest History's Golden Grain

The Old Testament says "to everything there is a season, and a time for every purpose under heaven." This includes "a time to be born, and a time to die, a time to plant, and a time to pluck up that which is planted . . . a time to cast away stones and a time to gather stones together." This reasoning may apply also to history. Perhaps there is a time when a story must be written, and a time when an individual must respond to such a need.

The author considered these factors in contemplating whether to devote the time, resources, and effort to compile the detailed history of what was once the world's greatest oil field, the unique towns that grew from this, and the people who endured incredible hardships during the historical drama.

Once, one could stand on the Cimarron River bridge en route to Markham and see hundreds of oil derricks in either direction standing tall like mountain pines on the bluffs and even in the river bed. The old bridge is still there but Markham is gone and so are the derricks. Gone also are the long footbridges that crossed the Cimarron and the ferries that carried oil field equipment from one bank to another.

Tiger Creek is silent, too, and only a trickle of water flows down the stream that was in the center of the oil field. Once, men made a living skimming oil from its surface. The oil field towns have faded and a few have disappeared. Weeds, brush, and high grass obscure any remnants of Frey and Pemeta. An old concrete storm shelter is the last landmark of Crow.

After Drumright was named, other oil field camps had fun mimicking the name. First came Dropright, then Damright, Alright, Justright, and Gasright. These have faded into oblivion along with Gano and Oil City. A row of old store buildings and the boom days jail-house are most of what is left of Shamrock. Drumright, once a thriving town of 18,000 with thousands more on the outskirts, now has a population of about 3,000. Once-tough Oilton is a community of 1,000 and is peaceful even on Saturday nights.

In spite of these facts, there was living testimony at this writing to the oil boom story. What a miracle it was 75 years later to find people in their 80s and 90s and some near 100 who were an important part of the scene that started in 1912, and whose memories were still vivid and accurate.

Perhaps the reader can imagine the fascination the author felt as Etta Feild Caves, niece of B. B. Jones, told of traveling around the Drumright field in 1912 and 1913 with "Uncle Bernard" and Tom Slick; Homer Wilson described early-day Pemeta and the famous Turkey Track ranch, Paul Peck and Olive Clark Whitehead recalled watching Oilton spring up from a cotton patch; Lillian Ferren Beavers described the bringing of the first Blarney Stone to Shamrock in 1916; Cecil Albert recalled his four years in the old red high school; Chester Ferguson told of the day he watched Babe Ruth strike out at the old Drumright ball park; and of Ethel Cook Campbell, the first valedictorian, Everett F. Drumright, Everett Whorton, Roy Townsley, and Alva Bartley and Hervey Foerster, and Gladis Dix described the first days of the first oil field schools.

Sometimes the author sat under a tree with the old timers poring over memories and pictures. Other visits were in a car winding through the old Markham area with Lewis Lindsay or having Ada Jackson point out historic sights in Oilton. A tour of old homes and historic sites in the Olive area with R. D. (Bucky) Carroll was the author's first visit to that community.

One especially interesting exploration was with Bill Bedingfield as he drove his pickup over pastures and gullies on his farm to remnants of Bill Dunn's cellar home, to the site where the Markham Ferry crossed the Cimarron River, and to the concrete slab in a pasture that once was the base for a pump in the Villa town square.

From 1983 to 1986, these and others have been available as resources for telling the eyewitness story of the oil field from its earliest days. The author concluded that now must be the time to preserve this historical treasure. Ten years from now, or maybe even one year, could be too late. Their accounts provided leads to research at the Oklahoma Historical Society and other sources to verify and complete the story. While this account has departed somewhat from traditional methodology and form, it has sought to tell the oil field story the way the oil field people and their descendants would want it told.

APPENDIX

Pupils at Outlying Schools

U. G. #5 (former pupils from 1985 reunion list): Gene Adams, Eula Thompson Brown, Lora McClain Brewster, Doris McLain Bucklew, Frank Butler, Lila Barnes Calvin, Curt Clemens, Fontelle Clemens, Vera Arnold Coker, Ruth Butler Cooper, Wanda Pixley Corbett, Pauline Phillips Dickerson, Mildred Renfrow Foster, Bill Frazier, Darrell Frazier, Donald Frazier, Jessie Frazier, Opal Whitehead Haggard, Elk Harrell, Dorothy Dickerson Haulcomb, Mary Jo Henderson, Nina Dickerson Hicks, Evelyn Matherly Hoover, Lorranine Clark Jensen, Frank Jester, George Jester, William Jester, Faye McLain Johnson, Lola Riley Johnson, Theresa Weaver Jordan, Truman Latting, Juanita Meskimen Lemons, Sherman and Berrill (Forbes) Ledgerwood, Clyde Matherly, Cleo Matherly, Ted McGee, Darlene Norton McGuire, James D. McLain, Willard McLain, Dennis and Cora (McGee) Meskimen, Walter and Pauline (Matherly) Morris, Delores (Matherly) Newport, Lawrence Norton, Remmel Norton, Sherman Norton, George Oldenstadt, Carlos Patton, Ray Pixley, Fern Williams Rice, Blanche Adams Rickner, Donna Lou Phillips Robinson, Wanda Renfrow Rousey, Elonna Dressler Shelton, Waneta Thompson Smith, S. A. Stafford, Belle Jester Taylor, Howard Touchatt, James O. Tucker, Wilma Tucker, Elwood Wasson, Arlie C. Weaver, Ben and Doris (Barnes) Weaver, Maxine Barnes Williams, LaDoris Phillips Wright, and superintendent L. D. (Demont) Townsend.

Vida Way (former pupils and patrons from 1967 reunion list provided by Frankie Jo Posey): Opal Tamage Alcorn, Ray Apple, Billy Joe Ausbrook, Dale Ausbrook, Virgil and Eula Ausbrook, George Bales, Dorothy Rogers Ballard, Ruby Tamage Barker, Jean Brown Berger, Donna Dean Scott Brown, Florence Hill Calvert, Clarence and Dorothy Carpenter, Floyd Carpenter, Carrie Clark, Ruby Hill Damon, Earl and Edith Nelson Davis, Juanita Mize Duncan, Vernell Lemons Endicott, Audrey Gardner Hensley, Clint and Lucille Shelly Hufford, Clint Hufford, Sr., Eldon James, Mr. and Mrs. Dutch Kilpatrick, Lou Etta Barnett Lane, Lorraine Tow Larson, Helen Barrier LeFever, Ruth Rogers Lemons, William Lemons, Mary Lookebill, Ruby Lookebill, Ruth Brown Mitchell, Maynard Mize, Carl Morgan, Mrs. Fred Morgan, Joanna Apple Newman, Martha Sieres Nichols, Maxine Lemons Nichols, Frank and Bonnie Palmer O'Brien, Mrs. J. R. Palmer, Nelson Pate, Mrs. John Peden, Boyd Peelman, Lema Pope, Walter and Frankie Jo Ryan Posey, Ruth Hays Prall, Mr. and Mrs. Chris Schuler, Sr., Mr. and Mrs. Chris Schuler, Jr., Gene Schuler, Amy Scott, George Scott, Julian R. Scott, Julian P. Scott, Mary Alice Scott, W. S. Scott, O. H. Shuey, Willa May Clark Spradlin, Joe Stanley, Art and Claudeen Lookebill Tamage, Flora Wise Tarpley, May Tow, Charles, Bessie, and Claude Wimsett, and Myrtle Youtsey.

SOURCES AND DOCUMENTATION

Sources for much of the material in this volume are included in the text and in some cases, the picture captions. The documentation below is for chapters with historical material not included in the first volume, *Drumright! Glory Days of a Boom Town*. Those interested in pursuing a deeper study of the Drumright oil field will find the Sources and Bibliography in that volume helpful.

Chapter I — In the Beginning

William E. Dunn: Drumright *News*, March 26, 1915; Drumright *Derrick*, May 5, 1913; Bristow *Record*, Nov. 24, 1911.

Charles J. Wrightsman: Drumright *Derrick*, March 21, 1913; Bristow *Record*, April 4, 1912; Lloyd, Heather McAlpine (herein after referred to as Lloyd,) "Oklahoma's Cushing Oil Field," M.A. thesis, Oklahoma State University, 1976, pp. 14.

McMan Oil Co.: Drumright *News*, March 26, 1915; Morris, Lerona Rosemond, (hereinafter referred to as Morris), *Oklahoma Yesterday, Today and Tomorrow*, Guthrie, 1930, pp. p. 801;

Glenn Pool: Snider, Luther C., *Oil and Gas in the Mid-Continent Fields*, Harlow Publishing Co., Oklahoma City, 1920, p. 189; Morris, P. 779.

Thomas B. Slick: "My Father's Story," Thomas B. Slick, Jr., comments at Cushing (Okla.) Petroleum Festival, Sept. 9, 1952; Morris, 797-799; Lloyd, pp. 14-17. Interview by author, Etta Feild Caves.

Charles B. Shaffer: "The Well That Led to Fame," Cushing *Daily Citizen*, March 19, 1952; Drumright *News*, March 26, 1915; Morris, p. Lloyd, 15-16; Interview by author, Phoebe Shaffer Hurst.

Montfort Jones Estate: Bristow *Record*, Oct. 11, 1927.

Eastern Prophets: F. S. Barde Collections, Oklahoma Historical Society, Oklahoma City.

Chapter II — Shamrock

General information: Shamrock *Brogue* , Jan. 1, 1916; *Shamrock Blarney*, March 30, July 13, and Oct. 12, 1916; Drumright *Derrick*, July 10, 1976; *Creek County Democrat* (Shamrock) Feb. 20, 1917. Interviews by author: Lillian Ferren Beavers, Ben Ferren, Alma P. Friend, Phoebe Shaffer Hurst, Mary Hubert Lesco, D. C. Sellers III, R. A. Sellers, Jr., Kenneth Sullivan, David White.

Roy Smith poem: Drumright *Derrick*, March 14, 1968.

Chapter III — Pemeta

General information: Memorabilia of James and Maude Salisbury, from Ruth Salisbury Ruyle, Rowlett, Texas; "Pemeta Community was founded in 1800's," Roy Keith Shoemaker, Drumright *Derrick*, Feb. 28, 1985; Interviews by author: Homer Wilson, Wesley Bingamon, Roy Keith Shoemaker, Maggie Jones McClary, and Abe Nasalroad.

Turkey Track Ranch: "Diary of L. F. Carroll," *Chronicles of Oklahoma*, Vol. 15, March 1937, p. 67; "Boss Neff, Panhandle Pioneer," *CO*, Vol. 26, Spring 1948, p. 165; "Guthrie From Public Land to Private Property," B. B. Chapman, *CO*, Vol. 33, Spring 1955, p. 71; "Memoirs of a Pioneer Teacher," Harriet Patrick Gilstrap, *CO*, Vol. 38, 1960, p. 21; Wells, Laura Lou, *Young Cushing in Oklahoma Territory*, Cushing, OK, p. 7; "Turkey Track Ranch," Laura Lou Wells, Cimarron Family Legends, Evans Publications, Inc., Perkins, 1980, pp. 408-410. Letter, James Salisbury, Jr. to friend, March 28, 1974.

Sources and Documentation

Chapter IV — Oilton

General information: "Oilton, Oklahoma — Boom Town," Marie Harris Howe, typewritten, January, 1986; "Oilton, Oklahoma — The First Ten Years," Lillian Harris Hix, typewritten January, 1986; "Oilton Memories," Fred Harris, handwritten, February, 1986, (all prepared especially for this book.) Tulsa *Tribune*, Feb. 15, 1974; Tulsa *World*, May 25, 1970; Drumright *Derrick,* July 17, 1962; *Oiltonian* yearbook, 1919, 1920, 1921, 1922; Oilton *Gusher*, 1915-1922; Letters to author: Lora Davis Dentler, Jan. 16 and Jan. 26, 1986; Ray Harris, Jan. 10 and Feb. 27, 1986; Marie Harris Howe, Jan. 17, Feb. 6, 1986; Fred Harris, Feb. 8, 1986.

Interviews by the author: Oscar Anderson, Jr., Virgil Anderson, Ada Jackson, Lewis Lindsay, Burnie Mann, Dr. Dan Parker, Mrs. Jewel Phillips, William M. Phillips, Frankie Jo Posey, Paul and Fern Doolin Peck; R. E. (Sonny) Pope, Mrs. Mary Ramsey, Tom Spradlin, Jr., June Taylor, Mr. and Mrs. James Todd, J. D. Tyree, and Olive Clark Whitehead.

Churches: Drumright *Derrick,* July 17, 1962.

L. L. (Scottie) Scott: Garber *Free-Press*, Feb. 9, 1978; McCourtney, Bertharee Scott, *Richer Than Oil*, Oklahoma City, 1956. Letter to the author: Molly June Taylor, Feb. 18, 1986. Interview: Tom Spradlin, Jr., March 1986.

Chapter V — Olive

General information: "A History of Olive School," W. R. Whitehead, typewritten, Oct. 18, 1968; "A History of Olive Community," W. R. Whitehead, typewritten, Oct. 18, 1968. Letter to author: Ethel Cook Campbell, Dec. 9, 1985.

Interviews by author: Susie Lacey, Tom King, R. D. (Bucky) Carroll, Mrs. Lonetta Whitehead, and Myra Whitehead.

Chapter VI — Lest You Forget

Jackson Barnett: Muskogee *Times-Democrat* Jan. 31, Feb. 23, Feb. 24, Feb. 26, 1920; May 5, 29, 30, 31, and June 6, 1934; Dec. 18, 1939; *The Daily Oklahoman*, Feb. 29, 1920, May 20, 1923; Debo, Angie, *And Still the Waters Run,* Princeton University Press, 1940, pp. 338-346.

1916 Fires: Drumright *Derrick,* Feb. 5, 1916 and Oct. 9, 1916; Shamrock *Blarney*, Oct. 12, 1916. Interviews: Hervey Foerster and Wilma Kincaid Allard.

J. M. Haggar: J. M. Haggar to author, Nov. 18, and Nov. 25, 1985.

Chapter VIII — When Talking Ended and Shooting Started

Sam Cook: Drumright *Derrick,* Oct. 21, 1916, Nov. 13 and Nov. 15, 1916; Sapulpa *Herald*, Nov. 14, 1916; Nicodemus File, Drumright Oil Field Museum, p. 153.

M. C. Bice at Drumright: Drumright *Derrick,* July 22, Aug. 7, Sept. 16, and Sept. 9, 1922; "Milton Curtis Bice — A Biography, "Hazel Matlock Moss, Drumright Oil Field Museum.

M. C. Bice at Roxana: Guthrie Daily *Leader*, Sept. 19, 20, 22, 23, 26, 1919; The *Daily Oklahoman*, Sept. 21, 1929; Tulsa *World*, Sept. 22, 1919; Letters, Mrs. Julia Bice Hoover to author, Jan. 1, 1986, Feb. 16, 1986, Feb. 18, 1986, Feb. 24, 1986. Interview by author: Mrs. Julia Bice Hoover, March 1986.

Ben Clark-Bill Glimp Story: "The Kidnapping," Darla J. Graves, paper for English 101, University of Hawaii, April 28, 1965; "Trapping Oklahoma's Lethal Gunmen," Louis Smith, *Crime Detective,* December, 1947, New York, pp. 32-35 and 90-94; "Don't Tip the Cops," Ben D. Clark, *Official Detective,* undated, R.G.H. Publishing Corp., New York, N.Y., p. 32; Drumright *Derrick*, Aug. 11, 1940; *Daily Oklahoman,* Aug. 10, 1940; Tulsa *World*, Aug. 11, 1940; Stillwater *News*, Aug. 11, 1940. Interviews by author: Mrs. Ella Glimp, November, 1985, and Darla J. Graves, October, 1985; Mrs. Myrtle Clark, December, 1985.

Drumright Historical Society
Officers and Directors-1986
President
Robert W. Smith
Vice President
Mrs. Louise Kane
Secretary
Mrs. Jonnie Facker
Treasurer
William E. Scribner
Directors
Tom J. Caldwell
Jeff Hunter
Howard Huff
Haskell King
Ralph Rawdon
Mrs. Alene Saulsbery
Ancil Settle
Robert W. Smith
Charles Stephenson
Arts and Crafts Booth Chairman
Betty Stephenson
Publicity Chairman
Eileene Russell Coffield

Index

Abshire, F. B., 72
Admire, Eli, 74
Akin, Emma, 179
Akin, Oliver, 176, 210
Albert, Cecil, 157, 158, 165-168, 180, 183, 266
Albert, Frank, 64, 165
Alexander, Bess, 19
Allshouse, Elsie Bartley, 161
Allard, Lou S. Jr., 131
Allard, Lou S. Sr., 222
Alworth, Ralph, 97
Anderson, Oscar, 68, 74
Armstrong, P. R., 113
Arnold, Grace, 204
Arnspiger, V. Clyde, 157
Ary, Jack, 209, 211, 213, 215, 226-228, 234, 236, 240

Badger, Pat, 113, 115, 177
Balch, Bert, 182
Baldwin, E. C., 42
Ballard's Grocery, 72, 99
Bankston, J. P., 176
Barnett, Jackson, 115-121
Barnes, Maxine, 186
Barr, Bob, 235
Barris, M. J. (Jim), 131
Bartley, Alva, 165, 266
Beaver, Judge C. O., 214
Beavers, Lillian Ferren, 44, 266
Bedingfield, W. C., 12, 266
Bell, Mrs. Mary, 236, 237
Berkey, Judge Ben, 26, 47
Berry, Roy, 155
Bice, M. C., 226-234
Bice, Pansy Matlock, 221, 227, 232, 233

Biggs, Robie, 97
Bingamon, John, 55
Blake, Marguerite, 96
Bland, Dr. J. C. W., 67
Blarney Stone, 23
Bodwell, Charley, 68
Bowers, Leo, 42
Bradford, Harry, 97
Braught, T. R., 223-225
Bray, E. C., 42
Breeding, Homer, 28
Brill, Gladis Dix, 170, 171, 266

Brill, James A., 171
Brown, Cleburn and Otis, 214
Brown, Edna Mae, 43
Brown, Maizelle, 190
Butler, M. D., 72

Cackler, Gary M., 43
Cacy, J. H., 64
Cadenhead, Jim Frank Grocery, 110
Campbell, Ethel Cook, 105, 167, 168, 173, 266
Campbell, Johnny E., 43
Capshaw, Clifford, 157
Cargill, Dr. John, 48
Carnahan, Jack, 162
Carroll, R. D. (Bucky), 266
Caves, Etta Feild, 266
Cawley, Denny & Pat, 23,
Cheadle, N. F., 74
Childers, Russell, 97
Chronister, John, 131
Church of Christ, Oilton, 88
Church of God, Oilton, 90
Clark, Ben, 77, 235-239, 242
Clark Brothers, Oilton, 64
Clifton, Opal, 43
Coffey, Jeanne, 239
Colvin, S. W., 74, 192
Cook, Sam, 222-225
Corbin, Ted, 97
Cosden, Joshua, 15
Costello, C. R., 190
Coyner, Ruth, 176
Crites, Johnny H., 67
Crow, 12, 18, 19, 95, 265
Cunningham, George, 190
Cunningham, W. K., 88
Curlee, Jeff, 229, 230, 234

Davis, Leo, 155, 157
Denny, Virgil, 239
Dentler, Lora Davis, 64, 69
Dickinson, Carl, 236
Didlake, Olive, 104
Dix, Tom and Katie, 170
Dix, W. L., 202
Dix, Zola, 171
Doolin, Wallace, 64, 71, 99
Dover, J. M., 176

Drumright II, A Thousand Memories

Drumright
  Special Moments, 112-138
  Historic Homes and Buildings, 139-152
  Sports Memories, 153-163
  School Memories, 164-194
Drumright, Aaron, 1, 9, 128, 144
  personality profile, 196-199
Drumright, Everett F., 165, 169, 196, 266
Drumright, Florence, 196, 197
Duke, Lovella Sue, 43
Dunn, William E., 1-4, 16, 131, 179

Eastham, George, 92
Ellis, Dr. George, 75
Endicott, Larry, 43
Exeter, 3, 4

Facker, Fay, 23, 42
Ferguson, Chester, 155, 165, 172, 266
Ferren, Eric E., 35, 39, 40
Fielding, R. A., 190
Flynn, Leroy, 97
Foerster, Hervey, 122, 157, 164, 169, 266
Foerster, William, 122
Fogle, Harry, 74
Foley, Bill, 214
Foster, Earl, 213, 220
Fourth Ward School, 173, 174
Frazier, Glenn, 161
French, W. C., 146, 167
Frey, 9, 12, 19, 52, 54, 265
Friend, Alma P., 43, 45
Frost, Jack, 157
Fulkerson, Clarence G., 205
Fulkerson, Harley, 128, 139, 146, 219
  personality profile, 205-208
Fulkerson, J. W., 1, 9, 16, 128
  personality profile, 201-204

Gant, Glen, 214
Geiser, Chris, 23
Geiser, Louie R., 23
George's Grocery, 72, 74, 76, 99
Gerard, Ronald E., 43
Gibson, Emmalee, 231
Gibson, J. D., 131
Gibson, Myrtle, 171
Glease, Frank, 123
Glimp, Willie (Bill), 235-242
Goggins, J. J., 31
Goins, J. W. (Bill), 74, 82
Gowland, L. P., 64, 71, 72
Griffith, John, 131
Grimes, C. C., 46

Grubbs, Harvey, 179
Grubbs, James D., 43
Guisinger, C. W., 42

Haggar, J. M., 131
Hall, Bill, 236, 238-242
Hall, Claude P., 23
Hall, Phil, 72, 99
Harkness, Rev. Robert, 212, 214
Harrah, Sam, 64, 72
Harris, Fred, 74, 80
Harris, M. L., 71
Harris, Ray B., 86
Hatch, William T., 179
Hayes, Charley, 104
Haynie, Mr. and Mrs. J. W., 88
Hayter, Daisy, 107
Head, Pearl, 176
Heffington, Howard and Hobart, 214
Henderson, Leroy, 97
Hicks, Cade family, 54
Hill Oil and Gas Co., 24, 25, 27, 30
Hix, Lillian Harris, 71
Hoggatt, Pete family, 183
Holcomb, Forest, 107
Holcomb, Granville Hardware, 110
Holcomb, Stanley, 107
Holland, E. W., 219
Hoover, Julia Mae Bice, 234
Horn, Joe, 161
Howe, Elbert D., 74
Howe, Marie Harris, 75, 93
Huff, Howard, 145
Hulsey brothers, O.H.S., 97
Hulsey, Roy, 113-115
Hump, The, 170, 214, 223
Humphreys, Dr. D. W., 75, 76, 239
Hunt, J. B., 72, 99
Hurd, Willis, 109
Hurst, Simpson, 72

Irwin, D. H. (Rabbit), 77, 237

Jackson, Ada, 266
James, Harry, 113
Johnson, Wayne, 160
Jolliff, Doc, 77
Jones, Bernard B., 3, 4, 6, 9, 12, 15, 24, 110, 129, 266
Jones, Maggie McClary, 54, 179
Jones, Montfort, 3, 15, 24, 129
Jordan, Paul, 188

Keeler, Robert, 64, 72
Keller, E. H., 223
Kelly, Dan, 182, 183
Kersey, Blanche Wheeler, 179

Index

Kile, Eugene, 97
Kime, Carl B., 190
Kimes, Matthew, 46
Kincaid, Wilma, 172
King, Tom, 110
Krlin, Gary, 90
Ku Klux Klan, 47, 80, 170, 210, 219, 231

Lacey, Susie, 103, 108
Lackey, Rev. R. W., 202, 210, 212, 213, 226, 227
Landingham, E., 74
Landingham, Robert, 74
Lawrence, Harding, 176
Lebrecht, Jack, 97
Ledo, 99
Leonard, John, 235
Lesco, Mary Hubert, 47
Liberty Ward School, 41, 42
Lindsay, Lewis, 193, 266
Livingston, D. B., 230
Long, Dr. G. L., 76
Lounsberry, E. L., 97
Love, Kaki, 155, 157
Lovelace, Joe, 236, 242
Lowe, Anna Laura, 117-121

Mahan, Furman Grocery, 110
Mann, Burnie, 95, 99
Markham, 10, 12, 19, 191, 265
 school, 191-194
 map, 191
Markham, John H. Jr., 10, 15, 194
Maroney, Hugh, 193
Marrs, Frank, 10, 17
Massad, R. J., 143
Matherly, Harve G., 104, 109, 110
McClain, Carrie Fulkerson, 201, 202
McCoy, Perry, 155
McGeath, Maude, 74
McMan Oil Co., 15, 24
McPherson, John (Hap), 176
Methodist Church, Oilton, 87
Miles, Mabel Grimes, 43, 46
Miller, "Hookie", 209, 211, 227
Mills, Gordon T., 42, 45
Moore, Bob, 214
Moore, C. F., 176
Moore, Marvin, 97
Moore, R. L., 222, 226
Morriset, N. Lloyd, 97
Morrow Hotel, 123-126, 167
Morrow, R. J. (Bob), 124, 130
Murdoch, Mrs. William, 80
Murphy, Hazel Bartley, 161
Myers, Kelly, 228, 229, 234

Neal, Dr. William J., 204, 210
Nicodemus, W. E., 139, 226
 personality profile, 209-215
Nicodemus, W. E. (Edgar), 209
North American Refinery, 52
Norwood, A. L., 171

O'Dell, Arthur, 216
O'Dell, Homer, 219
Oil Exchange, 67, 84, 223
Oilton
 townsite selected, 64
 early hardships, 65-71
 business development, 72-80
 Laurence L. Scott, 81-86
 church foundings, 86-91
 school history, 92-97
 Oilton today, 99, 102
Oklahoma Pipeline Co., 52, 53, 55
Oldenstadt, George, 188
Oldenstadt, George Jr., 235, 240, 242
Oliphant, W. L., 89
Olive
 history of, 104-110
 postmasters, 105
 schools, 105
 first pupils, 105
 churches, 108
Overall and Hickory Shirt Brigade, 226
Overdeer, James, 176
Ownesby, J. B., 24, 28

Parcher, J. A., 178
Parcher, Mildred, 166
Parker, Dr. Daniel, 98
Patton, E. E., 190
Paulding, Haskell, 45, 186
Peck, Albert E., 19, 64, 72, 74, 85, 93
Peck, Mrs. Dollie, 86
Peck, Lloyd, 97
Peck, Paul, 19, 67, 72, 97, 99, 239, 266
Pemeta
 beginning of oil boom, 52
 town description, 55, 56
 social life, 56
 early day map, 57
 Turkey Track Ranch, 59
Pemeta School, 55, 178, 179
Perswell, Paris, 97
Peters, Frank, 164
Phillips, Dr. J. W., 75, 84
Phillips, Jewel, 76
Pinkston, Lou Ann, 176

Pope, F. E., 89, 95
Pope, Willie, 99
Powers, Julia, 92
Prince, Flossie, 107

Queen Bee, 85, 86

Ralston, Andrew Knapp, 192
Reap, E. A., 72
Reid, A. J., 35, 139, 148
Reynolds, Dr. S. W., 124
Ridenour, Paul and Lavern, 176
Roberts, Dale, 175
Roberts, Ed L., 174
Roberts, Ed L., children, 175
Roberts, William F. (Billy), 4, 16, 168, 245
Robertson, Gov. J. B. A., 213
Rogers brothers, O.H.S., 98
Rogers, Otis, 97
Russell, Ben, 169, 210
  personality profile, 244-245
  family, 245
Ruth, Babe, 153-155
Ryan, Bill, 90
Ryan, Joe, 77, 82
Saffa, Bill, 155
Salisbury, James, Jr., 60
Salisbury, James, Sr., 60
Salisbury, Maude, 60
Scheer, Mrs. Arnold, 145
Scott, A. Dean, 189
Scott, Bertharee McCourtney, 85
Scott, Clell, 190
Scott, Laurence L., 81-87
Second Ward School, 170-173
Seitsinger, Lela, 239
Sellers Bros., D. C. & R. A., 23, 31, 32, 35, 55
Sellers, R. A. Jr., 99
Shadid, Eddie, 235
Shadid, Ralph, 214
Shaffer, Charles B., 3, 6, 9, 12, 15, 24, 47, 129
Shaffer, Dale, 129
Shaffer, Herbert, 157
Shafter, 12
Shamrock
  poem, "Shamrock", 22
  beginning, 23-26
  Irish names, 28, 29
  business development, 31-40
  schools and memories, 41-49
Shanks, L. E., 145
Shelton, Judy Kay, 43
Sherrill, Ellen, 43
Shoemaker, Roy Keith, 56, 61

Sinclair, Harry, 15
Slane, Larry D., 43
Slick, Thomas B., 3-6, 9, 12, 14, 24, 47, 110, 266
Smith, Don, 214
Smith, Everett C., 23
Smith, Roy, 22
Snell, Ruth, 96
Snyder, Mrs. Flora, 112
Soapsuds Susie, 48
Spencer, Frank, 104
Spradlin, Tom, 86
Starr, Dr. O. W., 158, 210, 219
Stayton, Winifred, 165, 174, 178
Steiner, Edward, 130
Stephenson, Charles E., 216
Stephenson, P. J. Sr., 139, 147, 210
  personality profile, 216-220
Stevens, Elbert J., 43
Stracener, Silas, 113
Sullivan, Kenneth, 46

Taylor, Arlin, 161
Taylor, L. W., 87, 97
Terrill brothers, O.H.S., 98
Terrill, Frank, 64
Tharel, W. D. (Buck), 227
Third Ward School, 175
Thomas, Ed, 122, 155, 156
Thomas, Eph, 155-157
Thomas, Jim, 97
Tiger Creek, 1, 3, 4, 6, 9, 52, 55, 178, 205, 265
Tiger Hill Toughs, 214
Tiger School, 179-183
Tiger Town, 171
Tippin, M. P., 70
Todd, Jim, 97
Tomleson, Charles E., 223
Touchatt, Howard, 185
Townsend, L. D., 185, 188
Townsley, Roy, 175, 266
Tribbey, C. W., 92
Troxel, Robert J., 97
Tucker, James, 176
Turkey Track Ranch, 9, 59-62
Turkey Track Trail, 2, 60
Tyree, J. D., 67

U. G. 5 School, 185-188
  first graduates, 185
  first teachers, 186
  last graduating class, 188

Van Sickle, M. H., 223, 225
Vida Way School, 189, 190
Villa, 12

Index

Vinson, Beulah, 156

Way, Fred, 23
Weaver, Ivan, 180, 181, 182
Wheeler, Frank M., 1, 4, 15, 110, 165
Wheeler No. 1 Well, 9
White, Dr. E. E., 75, 88
White, Lazelle, 155, 157
Whitehead, John, 110
Whitehead, Olive Clark, 19, 266
Whitehead, W. R. (Roy), 104
Whorton, Everett, 173, 266
Wilder, Lew, 223

Williams, Kenneth Garven, 231
Wilson, Homer, 60, 266
Winterringer, Jim, 23
Wisely, Francis J., 235, 240
Wiseman, Alba, 81
Wiseman, Ruby Pearl, 43
Witt, Pete, 97
Wood, T. J., 131, 209
Woodrow Wilson School, 92
Wrightsman, Charles, 3, 4, 9, 15

Zumwalt, Loyd, 210
Zumwalt, Stanley, 214